ARCHERY
Seventh Edition

Wayne C. McKinney
Professor, Southwest Missouri State

Mike W. McKinney
Professor, University of Arizona

WCB Brown &
Benchmark
P U B L I S H E R S

Madison,Wisconsin•Dubuque,Iowa•Indianapolis,Indiana
Melbourne, Australia•Oxford,England

Book Team

Editor *Chris Rogers*
Production Editor *Deborah J. Donner*
Visuals/Design Developmental Consultant *Marilyn A. Phelps*
Visuals/Design Freelance Specialist *Mary L. Christianson*
Publishing Services Specialist *Sherry Padden*
Marketing Manager *Pamela S. Cooper*
Advertising Manager *Jodi Rymer*

WCB Brown & Benchmark

A Division of Wm. C. Brown Communications, Inc.

Vice President and General Manager *Thomas E. Doran*
Editor in Chief *Edgar J. Laube*
Executive Editor *Ed Bartell*
Executive Editor *Stan Stoga*
National Sales Manager *Eric Ziegler*
Director of CourseResource *Kathy Law Laube*
Director of CourseSystems *Chris Rogers*
Director of Marketing *Sue Simon*
Director of Production *Vickie Putman Caughron*
Imaging Group Manager *Chuck Carpenter*
Manager of Visuals and Design *Faye M. Schilling*
Design Manager *Jac Tilton*
Art Manager *Janice Roerig*
Permissions/Records Manager *Connie Allendorf*

Wm. C. Brown Communications, Inc.

President and Chief Executive Officer *G. Franklin Lewis*
Corporate Vice President, President of WCB Manufacturing *Roger Meyer*
Vice President and Chief Financial Officer *Robert Chesterman*

Cover photo by Shelby Thorner 1990/David Madison

Copyedited by John Mulvihill

Consulting Editor Physical Educator Aileene Lockhart, Texas Women's University

Contents

The Language of Archery 207

10

Preface

This book provides the reader with a substantive introduction to target archery, related archery sports, and correlated academic subject matter. Archery is a skill to develop as well as a topic worthy of serious scholarly study. The reader is familiarized with the many ways in which archery can be enjoyed.

Participation in one or more archery activities can enhance the individual's leisure time throughout life. Instruction in target archery is the starting point in this process. Many people who receive target archery instruction eventually try one or more of the other archery sports. The National Field Archery Association has reported that seven million Americans own archery tackle, and there are over two million bow hunters and bow fishers in the United States.

The major objective of this book is to introduce the reader to target archery. Target archery is the most demanding of all competitive forms of archery. The precision shooting requirements of this sport present exceptional mental and physical demands on the archer. We recommend that a person with a strong interest in bow hunting, field archery, or bow fishing first acquire considerable skill in target archery shooting mechanics. Target archery may be enjoyed at competitive levels ranging from community archery clubs to the Olympic Games. Furthermore, developing target archery skills *first* will serve the potential field archer, bow hunter and/or bow fisher as his or her "foundation for success."

This book possesses four unique features compared to other introductory archery books.

ONE UNIQUE FEATURE of this book is guidelines for utilizing the video camcorder and videotape for analyses of the archer's shooting mechanics, for enhancement of learning efficiency, and for the reduction of shooting errors. This is best accomplished when the archer is analyzed cinematographically by a qualified archery instructor. By using these teaching/learning techniques, the target archer receives a better instructional basis for establishing his or her "foundation for success" in target archery and the other archery sports.

A SECOND UNIQUE FEATURE of this book is an introduction to the archery sports of bow hunting, bow fishing, field archery, crossbow archery, and flight shooting. Opportunities for participation in archery by handicapped individuals are also described. Regardless of age, sex, or physical status, a person who desires to participate in archery can find an appropriate activity. Archery can be a sport for anyone motivated to accept the challenge. First, however, the individual must know that the participation opportunities exist.

A THIRD UNIQUE FEATURE of this book is a comprehensive and specific physical conditioning program for archers. One reviewer wrote: "This chapter is one of the best presentations I've ever seen on the specificity of physical conditioning for a given sport." Anatomic detail is presented to explain the joint motions needed to properly execute the shooting fundamentals. That is followed by scientifically based fitness guidelines that establish the intensity, frequency, and duration criteria for developing flexibility, strength, muscular endurance, and cardiovascular endurance. Energy expenditure values for various conditioning activities and archery practice are also described. *The prescribed exercises apply scientifically-based theory to the practice of conditioning to enhance archery performance.*

The emphasis is placed on the specificity of conditioning so the archer can improve skill execution for better scores in target archery, more game while bow hunting or bow fishing, or greater distances while flight shooting. An archer with good shooting mechanics plus an excellent health-related fitness status is more likely to achieve success than an archer with comparable skill who has an average or low fitness level. Competitive target archery is an athletic activity that requires specific conditioning in order for the archer to attain his or her potential while on the shooting line in tournaments.

Archery has a solid academic foundation in such scholarly areas as anatomic kinesiology, archeology, art, biomechanics, exercise physiology, literature, mechanical engineering, mythology, philosophy, physics, and religion. Furthermore, archery is an integral part of the development and history of the human race. The participant who chooses to become intellectually involved with the academic side of archery will greatly enrich his or her use of leisure time for life. *An introduction to the academic areas within archery that can challenge the individual intellectually is the FOURTH UNIQUE FEATURE of this book.*

For readers interested in bow hunting and bow fishing, Appendix A contains the names, addresses, and phone numbers of the government wildlife agencies in the United States and Canada. This provides readers with a ready reference for obtaining the latest rules and regulations related to bow hunting and bow fishing anywhere in these two countries.

Appendix B provides the reader with the names, addresses, and phone numbers of archery organizations throughout the world. These are the controlling organizations for such things as target archery, field archery, bow hunting, crossbows, flight shooting, handicapped archers, and senior citizen archers. This gives the reader easy access to learning more about the programs and opportunities offered by the organization(s) in specific areas of archery.

Special acknowledgment is made to Doug Kittredge, an expert bow hunter and toxopholite from Auburn, California. Our informal discussions about archery in the early 1960s at the University of Southern California led indirectly to the writing of the first edition of *Archery*. Dr. Aileene Lockhart is also recognized for extending the invitation to write the book.

Many illustrations in this text are from *Anatomic Kinesiology,* third edition, by Gene A. Logan and Wayne C. McKinney. © 1970, 1977, 1982 Wm. C. Brown Company Publishers, Dubuque, Iowa and from *Adapted Physical Education* by Gene A. Logan. © 1972 Wm. C. Brown Company Publishers, Dubuque, Iowa. Reprinted by permission.

Special acknowledgment is made to E. G. Heath of England for granting permission to reproduce several illustrations from *The Gray Goose Wing,* his classic book on the subject of archery, published by Osprey Publishing Limited in Berkshire, England.

The contributions of the following people to the six earlier editions of this book are appreciated: Doug Allen, Allen Archery; the late H. W. Allen, inventor of the compound bow; William Bartlett, Precision Shooting Equipment; Ken Beck, Black Widow Bow Company; Dave Brilhart, expert bow hunter; Wilbur Corley, expert bow fisherman; J. Robert Davis, expert bow fisherman; Jerry Day, Arizona Game and Fish Department; Debbie Finch, Accra 300; Jack Frazier, expert bow hunter; G. C. "Butch" Herold, former Executive Secretary, NFAA; Loyd Howell, Indian artifact hunter; Dr. L. Dennis Humphrey for taking numerous photographs; Mac Johnson, *Missouri Conservationist;* Garry Koehlbe, Precision Shooting Equipment; Diane Logan and Dr. Gene A. Logan, artists; Christine P. McCartney, Executive Director, NAA; Shirley A. Randall for manuscript preparation; Arlyne Rhode, Editor, *The U.S. Archer;* Bob Rhode, Hoyt/Easton; Larry Rogge, expert bow hunter; Pete Shepley, Precision Shooting Equipment; Paul T. Shore, former Publisher, *Bowfishing Magazine;* Ron Skirvin, Shure Shot; and Jack, Bob, and the late Norman Wilson, the expert bowyers and brothers who made the quality Black Widow Bow for many years.

The contributions of the following people to the seventh edition of *Archery* are appreciated: William Bartlett, Precision Shooting Equipment; Lawrence A. Brady, target archer; Patrick S. Brunhoeber, target archer; Diane Carr, target archer; Kathy M. Greene, target archer; Laura Howard, Precision Shooting Equipment; and Justin List, Mr. Teenage Arizona.

Finally, recognition and thanks are given to Iva and Jenni McKinney for their compassion and understanding of the authors during the writing process and for their assistance with checking the manuscript as well as galley and page proofs.

The content and objectives of the book are the sole responsibilities of the authors.

Wayne C. McKinney, Ph.D.
Mike W. McKinney, M.S.

Introduction to Archery

1

Participation in archery has produced many great challenges for human beings throughout history. The archery skill of primitive people meant survival, by providing their food as well as the skins of animals to clothe and shelter them. Skilled archers in ancient times were able to win battles for their tribes or countries. The military use of archery changed governments, territorial boundaries, social orders, and the course of world history.

Archery in our contemporary world is viewed as a shooting sport with many fascinating variations. Target archery is considered an athletic activity for the competitor who appreciates the pursuit of excellence. Archery is valued by the individual who enjoys the test of using meticulously matched and tuned archery tackle with precision on a target range, field archery unit, crossbow range, or during a bowhunt. It is for the man or woman who savors the aesthetics of being in the out-of-doors enduring all types of weather conditions on a bow hunt, throughout an archery tournament, or while bow fishing for sharks on the ocean or for gar on rivers. Flight shooting appeals to archers who love the ballistics, aerodynamics, and challenges of projecting arrows over great distances.

Archery can be enjoyed within a wide spectrum of physical, intellectual, and academic pursuits. As a result, all archery sports and related activities have the potential to enhance the leisure time of participants throughout their lives.

The current popularity of archery is well documented. It is used as a sport in its various forms by millions of people throughout the world. Target archery was officially included as a gold medal sport in the Olympic Games in 1972. This added considerable impetus to archery participation in all of the competing nations. For example, a Nielsen Survey taken after archery became an Olympic event indicated that 2,634,000 Americans participate in at least one of the archery sports. American target archers have had considerable success in international competitions (fig. 1.1), and growth has been seen in the other archery sports as well.

The major emphasis within this book is placed on introducing the reader to target archery. Target archery is the most demanding of all forms of archery in terms of precision shooting. It is highly recommended, therefore, that a person with a strong interest in archery sports where accuracy is also paramount, such as field archery, bow hunting, and bow fishing, first acquire considerable knowledge and skill in executing the fundamentals of target archery. Target archery competition as an avocational pursuit can be enjoyed by the individual who accomplishes those goals. Furthermore, your target archery skills will serve as a solid "foundation for success" if you wish to pursue one or more of the other archery sports in the future.

Figure 1.1
Mastery of target archery fundamentals serves as "the foundation of success" for target archery and almost any other archery sport you wish to pursue. The shooting line and spectator's stadium at the 1984 Olympic Games. (Photo by *The U.S. Archer*)

As can be seen in figure 1.2, the challenges in archery sports other than target archery can take on huge and exciting dimensions! When bow fishing, for example, how do you accurately shoot through water and safely land a shark that outweighs you? You will be introduced to several archery sports in Chapters 5, 6, and 7. These sports appeal to both sexes, and competition categories are established for men, women, and children by age groups. Archery is an equal opportunity sport! It provides people of all ages and both sexes with many chances to succeed as well as fail. For success would not be valued as much without the potential of failure.

Bow hunting, especially for deer and elk, is increasing in popularity each year in North America. Many gun hunters are (1) expanding their hunting seasons by using both gun and bow seasons for game, (2) switching to bow hunting due to the fact that the hunter is less likely to be shot by an unskilled gun hunter during the hunting season, and/or (3) changing to bow hunting because it is a purer form of hunting wild game than hunting with a rifle or shotgun. There are approximately 2,100,400 bow hunters in North America.

Bow fishing is also increasing in popularity. One reason for this is that many bow hunters simply like to extend their game seasons by "hunting" fish with the bow and arrow. If a person likes angling, gigging, boating, and bow hunting, bow fishing is a natural combination of those activities. You are introduced to bow hunting in Chapter 6 and bow fishing in Chapter 7.

Most individuals become involved in archery initially out of an interest either in target archery, bow hunting, field archery, or bow fishing. Once involved in the sport, many people learn that archery is a subject with a rich heritage in

Figure 1.2
Knowledge of target archery shooting fundamentals also allows the archer to pursue such specialized areas as bow fishing. "Suzie" J. Davis with a 6'11½", 165-pound, brown shark she landed while bow fishing. (Courtesy J. Robert Davis, Route 4, Box 380, Spearin Road, Salisbury, Maryland 21801)

world history, literature, art, religion, archaeology, and philosophy. In this book an attempt is made to introduce you to some of these academic areas of interest. The serious student of the humanities, for example, can satisfy intellectual curiosity by studying archery as it is portrayed by authors and artists in literature, philosophy, and art throughout history. Mythological literature, as one example, abounds with tales of archers and their diverse use of archery skills. Archery feats have been romanticized many times in literature, music, and via modern entertainment media. Art museums throughout the world contain many famous works of art depicting archers in action. The scholarly student may want to pursue the sport beyond the demanding challenge of shooting. *The study of archery from a liberal arts perspective throughout the history of the world should not be overlooked as a fascinating intellectual and academic pursuit.*

There are numerous scientific dimensions to archery. The physics of the sport has been the subject of academic and scholarly pursuits by professionals and amateurs alike for years. (See the Bibliography.) The sophisticated mechanical engineering changes seen in archery tackle over the last forty years of the twentieth century are one result of these pursuits. *There have been more scientific advances in archery tackle during this time period than throughout the previous history of humankind!* Archery tackle manufacturers have improved bow and arrow construction based on better research, engineering, and utilization of new materials. Arrow velocities and ballistics are improving, and that leads to excellent accuracy when archery tackle is placed in the hands of an expert archer.

Figure 1.3
"The Toxophilites." A pen and ink sketch by W. Murray, 1840. (From E. G. Heath, *The Grey Goose Wing*)

The biomedical sciences concerned with the archer himself or herself are fascinating. The study of human anatomic motions and physiologic functions as they relate to the demands of performing archery skill techniques has kept pace with the tackle changes. As a result, archers are also improving. Physiologically, the archer is an athlete who needs to be physically and mentally conditioned in order to meet the demands of his or her specialty. From a scholarly perspective, the anatomic kinesiology, biomechanics, exercise physiology, sport psychology, and sport medicine related to archery are interesting areas for study in and of themselves. The reader is introduced to some aspects of these academic areas in Chapter 8.

Archery can be a very rewarding lifetime activity when one combines the intellectual and neuromuscular (skill) perspectives of the sport. A person who pursues archery as a scholarly participant has long been known as a *toxopholite* (fig. 1.3).

Benefits of Archery

Each sport has the potential to provide unique benefits to its participants. The benefits and values of an eclectic sport such as archery are not the same for all participants. The outcomes are dependent upon such factors as the facet of the sport pursued, the intensity and frequency of participation, the personal goals and expectations, and many other individual factors related to one's involvement in the sport. Archery brings satisfaction as one achieves periodic improvement in skill level. Another potential value of archery is that it is also capable of humbling an individual periodically due to its complexity. Both of those types of experiences can be of personal value to human beings throughout our lives. Mastery of archery and the pursuit of excellence are worthy goals with many conceivable benefits to the individual. Value lies in the pursuit even if the sport is never "mastered"!

Shooting the bow and arrow seems to be an extremely simple procedure to the naive individual: NEVER UNDERESTIMATE THE COMPLEXITY OF A SKILL THAT APPEARS TO BE THE EPITOME OF SIMPLICITY WHEN PERFORMED BY AN EXPERT! The meaning of that statement will become more apparent as you learn about the demands of target archery skill and increase your awareness of the breadth and scope of the various facets of archery.

Those not aware of its many uses and physical requirements may consider archery an "easy sport." (The anatomic and physiologic demands on archers and specific conditioning for the sport are discussed in detail in Chapter 8.) It is true that an hour of target archery practice in one's backyard or on the local archery range is not as physiologically demanding as comparable time spent playing singles tennis or running. As an example, an hour of anaerobic target archery practice would expend 269 kilocalories of energy for a 152-pound archer. Jogging an hour at a 9-minute-per-mile pace for the same archer is an aerobic activity that would produce an energy expenditure of 799 kilocalories, that is, 530 more kilocalories than target archery practice. But, there is more to archery than just the acts of nocking, drawing, and releasing the arrow.

The serious target archer as an athlete must prepare for competition by specifically developing his or her strength, muscle endurance, and flexibility to excellent levels. That has the potential to enhance accuracy when combined with regular target practice. It is also recommended (see Chapter 8) that the target archer's conditioning include work to develop above average cardiovascular endurance for his or her age as measured by maximal oxygen consumption. If that is accomplished, the archer's daily shooting and conditioning workouts will be just as demanding in terms of energy expenditure as comparable time spent in other sports that many people perceive to be more difficult physiologically than archery, for example, weight training, court sports, running, and swimming.

The serious, conditioned bow hunter also benefits by having a good level of health-related fitness. A total conditioning program in addition to target practice is also recommended for bow hunters. This enhances one's chances of stalking, shooting, field dressing, and packing a large game animal out of the wilderness area for human consumption. The *unconditioned bow hunter* may find him or herself in the embarrassing position of being the "animal" packed out! That would not endear you to your fellow hunters. Archery in its many forms can be as easy or difficult as the participant desires.

One major benefit of archery is that the participant can find an area within the sport and adjust it to meet his or her own interests, needs, and physical capabilities. In its many forms, archery can be enjoyed by men and women, old and young, wheelchair athletes, the blind, and superbly conditioned athletes of Olympic caliber. Its versatility as described in this book has the potential to provide numerous benefits for archers with diverse abilities and interests. This is one reason archery has fascinated humans in virtually all societies throughout history.

The practice of archery on a regular basis has the potential to counteract a specific problem exhibited by students and people who work in offices seated at desks. These folk tend to protract their shoulders—the shoulder blades or scapulae are pulled away from the spine and held in that position for prolonged periods of time. The head is thrust forward as the neck is flexed. To observe this, look at people as they read, write, or work at desks. These shoulder girdle and cervical spine motions abnormally lengthen muscles in the back and shorten muscles in your chest and shoulders. Holding the protracted position of the shoulders for several hours each day causes physical discomfort. Normal breathing is inhibited, which has a negative impact on respiratory function. Such a posture adds to the tired feeling one may have at the end of the work day, because energy metabolism is adversely affected.

Shooting a bow for a period of time daily helps to directly counteract the atypical muscular actions described above. To draw a bow, the archer must concentrically contract (shorten) back muscles that have been lengthened throughout the day. These muscles are attached to your scapulae or shoulder blades. During the bow drawing process against the resistance of the bow weight, your scapulae are being adducted or moved toward the spinal column. The neck is stabilized in the extended position during shooting. The muscles lengthened during the day are shortened or contracted in this process. Conversely, the chest and shoulder muscles shortened while sitting are lengthened when the bow is drawn. The greatest benefit of this for the desk worker or student who reads several hours per sitting is to offset the potential for chronic, adaptive shortening of the chest and shoulder muscles. Breathing mechanics and respiratory processes are improved. Energy metabolism becomes more efficient, and the individual feels better.

There is a myth that the practice of target archery contributes to the development of "good posture" at any age. There is no scientific evidence to support that hypothesis. What such practice does do for the adult is offset potential static or hypokinetic problems such as the one described above. Archery practice could have some positive effects on proper alignment of the spine, shoulder joints, and shoulder girdles of young children who have not reached anatomic maturation. Target archery practice with the proper workload (bow weight) for a child with musculoskeletal problems in these body segments could be utilized as an enjoyable rehabilitative exercise. It most certainly has intrinsic motivating qualities not seen in most of the other rehabilitative modalities.

One major criticism of our society made by sociologists and psychologists is the decline of family unity. To paraphrase a familiar theological statement: The family that plays together stays together. With the onset of a wide variety of avocational activities for children as well as *adult-centered activities for children* (examples are Little League Baseball and Pop Warner Football), the family in

Figure 1.4
Archery sports have been family activities for years for Robie Davis, his wife, "Suzie" Davis, and J. Robert Davis. (Courtesy J. Robert Davis, Route 4, Box 380, Spearin Road, Salisbury, Maryland 21801)

modern society often finds itself literally and figuratively going in different directions during leisure time. Archery is one sport that can be enjoyed by all members of the family at home, on a field archery unit, bow hunting, bow fishing, or on a target archery range. There are psychologic and sociologic benefits inherent to an activity such as archery, because it has the potential to develop family unity (fig. 1.4).

Many athletic activities learned early in life cannot be used throughout a lifetime. Age is not a limiting factor in any area of archery. It can be enjoyed as soon as the individual is old enough to learn how to handle the tackle safely. Target archery competition, as one example, is found for both sexes in local archery clubs, high schools, universities, the Olympic Games, and the U.S. National Senior Sports Classic. The latter competition usually includes people from 55 to 90-plus years of age in the sport of target archery.

If you played American football as a teenager or young adult, as an example, you will likely not continue to utilize your skills on a regular basis in that sport for the next sixty years! One does not see many "middle-age" people getting together, putting on the pads, blocking and tackling each other from August through December each year! American football, like most team sports, is not an activity adults choose to pursue as participants in their leisure time. In contrast to a team sport such as football, archery can be enjoyed on a regular basis as an individual or team activity twelve months per year throughout a lifetime. Furthermore, you do not have to assemble a group of people to practice archery on a daily basis.

That factor contributes to the continuity and frequency of archery participation by individuals over years. Scheduling and depending on adult friends for your regular recreational sport practices, games, and workouts can be a figurative pain in the gluteus maximus!

One major biophysical value of exercise, when used at proper intensity, frequency, and duration levels is its contribution in helping the individual cope with distress. Uncontrolled *prolonged distress* has been identified as one of the major risk factors contributing to the onset of coronary heart disease. (CORONARY HEART DISEASE IS THE MAJOR ILLNESS PROBLEM IN OUR MODERN, SEDENTARY WORLD!) Emotional stress of this type tends to be cumulative in humans, and this is devastating to the cardiorespiratory anatomy. Using a "short-term stressor," such as some form of physical exertion on a daily basis, helps counteract the negative biochemical, anatomic, and physiologic effects of long-term stress on the cardiovascular mechanisms. Exercise at the proper intensity, frequency, and duration levels is one positive way to help cope with stress.

Psychiatrists and other physicians recommend "blowing off steam" in a socially acceptable way when you find yourself in a prolonged stress situation. Exercise as a "short-term stressor" helps maintain homeostasis and contribute positively to one's mental health. Exercise in the form of daily target practice on an archery range or field archery unit *plus* associated conditioning as described in Chapter 8 is a great way to expend energy and release emotional tension when you have had a "bad day" or are caught up in a prolonged stress situation at work or home.

Shooting the bow and arrow for an hour or more after a "bad day" has the potential to relax the archer. Indeed, exercise or physical exertion of any type with good intensity and duration performed on a regular basis will serve as a relaxant. *The concept of intense physical exertion or exercise being a relaxant is so abstract that it is not well understood by most people.* Exercise is a much better relaxant than the drugs used by many individuals ostensibly for that purpose. That is, vigorous exercise will work to relax the participant, while alcohol, nonprescribed tranquilizers, and other indiscriminate use of drugs are medically contraindicated and counterproductive. From the standpoint of health-related fitness, an hour of target archery practice (exercise) works better as a relaxant for the archer than either being a "couch potato" or using drugs such as alcohol allegedly to relax.

The difficulty of mastering archery skill is cited by many participants as a part of the sport's mystique and value. The attempt to master archery skill is a major motivating factor, because it is one sport where pure excellence is very difficult to achieve. You may work at it for a lifetime and never master archery skill to your satisfaction! As one example, a perfect FITA Round score in target archery is 1440, but a score of 1300 would make most expert archers very happy! Archery does provide you with many opportunities for human error. This facet of the sport, believe it or not, has the greatest appeal to many individuals who place personal value on pursuing excellence in their lives. Shooting "tight groups" of arrows consistently into the center ring during a FITA Round at distances of 90 meters (98.46 yards) or 70 meters (76.58 yards) is extremely challenging and difficult to accomplish. But, when an archer makes continued progress toward realistic shooting goals through intensity of effort, he or she places value on the process and enjoys the outcome. The result may not be perfect, but there is healthy personal satisfaction.

Archery can be an enjoyable social activity. Most cities of any size have archery clubs that provide opportunities for archers to share interests with fellow archers. These clubs are usually affiliated with a state and/or national archery organization such as those listed in Appendix B. The clubs, however, are locally operated, and they are funded by modest dues. Archery clubs usually have outdoor and/or indoor practice ranges, and intraclub and interclub tournaments are held on a regular basis. Members also compete in large professional and amateur tournaments conducted within the state, region, and nation. Clubs in communities are usually organized to accommodate specific interests for target archers, bow hunters, bow fishers, and field archers. Also, most community-based archery clubs are family oriented. As a result, competitions and other activities are scheduled for both sexes by age groups.

Archery clubs are also found in secondary schools, junior colleges, colleges, and universities. Intramural athletic competition is held on a yearly basis in many secondary schools and universities. Archery as an intercollegiate sport is part of the athletic club programs of some community colleges, colleges, and universities throughout the United States. Intercollegiate competition starts at a local league level and concludes in a national championship. These activities receive considerable attention and support from the National Archery Association (NAA). Many collegiate target archers have progressed to compete at the international level.

While many people become involved in archery clubs and use archery as a social activity, an archer can also practice and compete without contact with other people if he or she so desires. No partner or team is necessary to enjoy archery in any of its forms. It has been said that the greatest form of competition is with one's self. Archery sports allow the archer to compete as an individual even in competitive tournaments when the archer is a member of an organized team. Individuality is a trait valued by archers, and archery can be individualized as much or as little as the participant desires.

Appendix A contains the names, addresses, and phone numbers of most of the official wildlife agencies in the United States and Canada. These are primarily for readers interested in bow hunting and bow fishing. Current rules, regulations, and information regarding seasons and limits can be obtained by contacting the agency of your choice. Archers and students interested in areas such as biology, zoology, ecology, botany, and conservation may also want to contact these agencies to determine whether or not the game laws related to archery are written based on sound natural science principles.

Appendix B lists the names and addresses of archery organizations throughout the world. These are the controlling organizations for target archery, field archery, bow hunting, bow fishing, flight shooting, clout shooting, crossbows, archery for senior citizens, and archery for the handicapped. The reader is encouraged to contact the organization(s) of interest to see what is offered in terms of programs, services, and competitions for the archer.

Review

1. Name the several archery sport forms. Which do you think will be of interest to you?
2. Discuss what you consider to be the unique aspects and benefits of archery as a sport.
3. Find out whether there is an organized target archery club in your community. Visit one of the meetings.
4. What are the areas of liberal arts related to archery?
5. What are the scientific dimensions to be found in the study of archery?
6. What is the technical name for a person who pursues the scholarly aspects of archery?
7. Discuss the apparent paradox that intense exercise is a relaxant for the human organism.
8. Archery has influenced the course of human history. Can this be said of other sports—which and why?
9. Why is it recommended that a person who is interested in fishing or hunting with archery tackle first become skillful at target archery?
10. Describe, using archery as your example, the meaning of the statement: "Never underestimate the complexity of a skill that appears to be the epitome of simplicity when performed by an expert."

The Evolution of Archery

2

The history of archery is directly related to the early development of humankind. A few selected events are outlined in this chapter to help place archery's historical importance in some perspective for the reader. The bibliography contains some excellent references on the history of archery.

Archery skill was of vital importance for the survival of humans for thousands of years. In this respect, archery played a prominent role in the growth and development of individuals, societies, and governments within nations. Archery as an invention was as important to early human development as the discovery of the wheel and control of fire. Ancient people learned how to use the bow and arrow effectively out of dire necessity. If today's archer had to depend upon archery skill for personal safety, food, and animal skins, the motivation to attain great skill with the bow and arrow would be dramatically accelerated!

Primitive artists drew bow hunters on cave walls in many locations throughout the world. Many caves in Spain and southern France in particular have excellent examples of cave art with archery themes. Ancient sculptors carved archer warriors in Egypt and other parts of the Middle East to honor them for their feats. The bow has been used by primitive tribes on all continents as a musical instrument. Many theologians, as an example, believe that David's biblical harp was also his bow. A bow can be plucked much like the bass fiddle, harp, and other string instruments. Bows and arrows became a part of the culture, religions, and rituals of various ethnic groups throughout the world in a variety of ways.

Archery feats have given rise to many myths throughout history. The mythologic literature of Greece, as one example, includes archery exploits by such famed characters as Apollo, Diana, Hercules, and Eros. The romance surrounding Wilhelm Tell and his crossbow skill is a part of both classic literature and music. The English had Robin Hood. Ancient cultures in the Far East also had their archer heroes in literature written centuries prior to the stories about Robin Hood. Modern novelists and script writers continue to rely upon and embellish these stories. A Robin Hood movie is usually produced about every decade either in Hollywood or England.

Archery has been used as an integral aspect of religious ceremonies by numerous religions and sects in the past. The Assyrians concluded a religious ritual by shooting an arrow toward the sun. This same type of liturgy, The Sun Vow, was practiced by various Indian tribes on the southwest plains of America many centuries later. The assumed mystical connection of the arrow with the sun, moon,

Figure 2.1
A rare photograph of the late Eugen
Herrigel, author of *Zen in the Art of Archery.*
(From E. G. Heath, *The Grey Goose Wing*)

stars, and planets figured prominently in many ancient religions and cultures. From the standpoint of ancient astronomy, the "archery connection" is seen in the naming of a few constellations (see Chapter 9).

The Zen Buddhists place great value on archery. The Zen sect does not recognize any dichotomy between "mind" and "body." The Zen philosophy includes the concept that various exercises of the body (including such things as archery and some forms of the martial arts) can bring the practitioner into a state of one complete being. There are times when Buddhists hold the bow at full draw for many hours until they feel the union of "mind" and "soul." At that time, *Satori* is reached. When the archer is no longer conscious of himself or the target, the arrow is released. (The modern target archer holds the bow at full draw about two to five seconds prior to release.) Figure 2.1 shows Eugen Herrigel, the German author of *Zen in the Art of Archery.* He was one of the few non-Orientals accepted to study the Way of Archery with Zen Buddhists. His book is considered a short classic regarding the practice of archery and its relation to Zen. After his oriental studies and writing the book, however, Herr Herrigel returned to Germany where he became an impassioned member of the Nazi Party. That behavior was in conspicuous contradiction to the philosophy he learned while studying The Way of Archery and Zen Buddhism. The reader should compare and contrast Herrigel's stance and nonexistent anchor point in figure 2.1 with the archer's technique in figure 4.17. The extended draw without an anchor point is typical of how Zen archers hold the bow for hours prior to releasing the arrow into flight.

The ability of individuals and armies to use the bow and arrow to advantage has changed the course of history on several occasions. Let us look at a few of these events chronologically.

Figure 2.2
Mesolithic hunting scene from a rock painting at Los Caballos, Valltorta, Spain. (From E. G. Heath, *The Grey Goose Wing*)

Upper Paleolithic Period

It is virtually impossible to document exactly that time in prehistory when humans started using bows and arrows. Ancient bows are very difficult to find, because the wood and animal products from which they were constructed tend to deteriorate. But modern radiocarbon testing techniques can be used to date artifacts such as arrow points and stone tools believed to have been used in making archery tackle. It is generally agreed by archaeologists and others that humans started using crude archery tackle at a time during the Upper Paleolithic period, or ten thousand to twenty thousand years ago.

Drawings in caves, believed to have been inhabited by Cro-Magnon people, depict archers hunting for wild game. Their bows and arrows appear to have been constructed with considerable engineering sophistication. Due to the time it takes for archery tackle to evolve in isolated cultures, it is logical to assume that archery tackle must have been in use many centuries prior to the time of Cro-Magnon people. The results of radiocarbon testing techniques applied to stone artifacts tend to support this assumption. Figure 2.2 shows a Mesolithic hunting scene from a rock painting at Los Caballos, Valltorta, Spain. Note the various types of bows carried by the archers, and that the artists depicted the archers as being very accurate. They had to be in order to survive!

The oldest extant bows in museums date back to about 6000 B.C. These are one-piece wooden bows made of yew or elm found by archaeologists in Scandinavia. More sophisticated bows were recovered from the Holmgaard bog on the island of Zealand in Denmark. These bows are estimated to be from the Mesolithic period. Some museums in America have bows made by Indians of the southwest or arid region of the United States. These American bows, however, date back no more than a few hundred years.

Holocene Period

5000 B.C.

The Egyptians were able to free themselves from the Persians during this age. They became superior archers through development of archery tackle and diligent practice. The ability to kill from a distance with arrows eventually proved to be the Egyptians' most important combat technique during this time. Spears, sling shot devices, thrown darts, and slings were the primary weapons of war carried by the foot soldiers in this and other areas prior to the refinement of the bow and arrow. Enemies simply could not get close enough with these crude weapons to have a significant impact upon the Egyptian archers. Archery skill development made such things as slings, rocks, and spears obsolete as weapons of war.

1350 B.C.

King Tutankhamen reigned over the Eighteenth Dynasty of Egypt during this period. The Egyptians were known to have used an angular composite bow at this time. Howard Clark, an archaeologist, entered the tomb of Tutankhamen in 1922 and recovered 32 angular composite bows, 14 wooden self bows, 430 arrows, and an array of quivers and bow cases. The mechanics of the angular composite bow were superior to other bows of this era.

1000 B.C.

The Persians moved to the area north and east of the Black Sea and Caspian Sea to battle the Scythians. The Persians had learned the value of archery skills from their earlier defeats. Each army had the usual trained archers as foot soldiers, but the Persians added mobility by training some of their archers to shoot from the back of horses. Shorter bows were designed for utilization by archers on horseback. This proved to be too much for the Scythians. Mounted archers added another military strategy, and were used time and again by military leaders for several centuries.

A.D. 850–950

There are records indicating that during this century the Vikings, who could be very obstreperous, helped design another military strategy for the use of the bow and arrow. It appears that prior to some amphibious assaults, the Viking archers launched great clouts, or volleys, of arrows from ships into their intended target area. This was an early form of naval bombardment. The English would later utilize clout bombardment on land as an effective killing and panic technique in many of their wars.

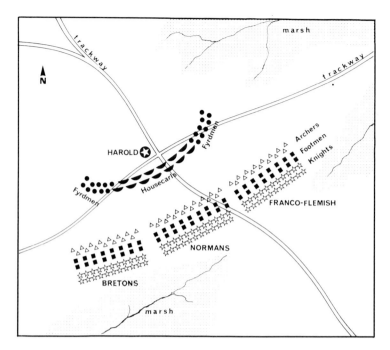

Figure 2.3
The Battle of Hastings, showing the positions of the Saxon and Norman armies at 9:00 A.M. on the 14th of October, 1066. (From E. G. Heath, *The Grey Goose Wing*)

A.D. 1066

The Norman archers taught the English a lasting lesson at the Battle of Hastings (fig. 2.3). The Normans planned and executed a false retreat maneuver designed to draw the English archers out of their hiding places to pursue what seemed to them to be fleeing Normans. When the English made their move into the open, they were attacked by the waiting Norman archers and slaughtered. In this particular situation, the English were superior in terms of their archery tackle and skill. They probably would have won the Battle of Hastings if the false retreat by the Normans had not been successful. This lesson was not wasted on the English military, because they used the same kind of tactics on the French some three hundred years later at the Battle of Poitiers.

A famous work of art, the Bayeux Tapestry, was embroidered by the women friends and relatives of the English archers who fought at the Battle of Hastings (fig. 2.4). This tapestry is a band of linen 20 inches wide and 231 feet long. Various aspects of the Battle of Hastings are portrayed on the tapestry. One segment shows clearly that King Harold was hacked to death by a Norman horseman instead of dying as a result of an arrow wound in the eye, as erroneously recorded by some historians. Figure 2.4 shows Norman archers carrying short bows and drawing them to their rib cage in order to obtain maximum range. The type of

Figure 2.4
A portion of the Bayeux Tapestry. (From E. G. Heath, *The Grey Goose Wing*)

Figure 2.5
Mounted Samurai warriors of Japan wore plated armor as protection, horned helmet, and a guard cover over the back. (Courtesy *Bow and Arrow Magazine*)

bow depicted on the Bayeux Tapestry is very inefficient from a physics standpoint, especially when compared to contemporary bows. Actually, the bows shown on the Bayeux Tapestry are believed to be closer to the Saxon pattern than to the longer Norman version. One explanation of this is that the people who embroidered this tapestry were not bow experts.

A.D. 1220

Like the Persians, Genghis Khan placed some of his archers on horseback with sophisticated short bows. His "Golden Horde" had great mobility as well as contempt for human life and values. These factors enabled Genghis Khan to capture territory, kill, rape, and plunder from the Pacific Ocean to the Volga River, and from the Caspian Sea to Northern Siberia.

The Japanese also used mounted samurai warriors effectively in combat situations (fig. 2.5). Their combat practice techniques and discipline are legend. They also held competitions among the samurai to determine who was the best archer on horseback. To understand the accuracy problems encountered by the mounted archer, the reader might try pulling an arrow from a quiver, nocking, drawing, and shooting at a moving target while mounted on a galloping horse. Keep in mind that the mounted archer was also under the stress of being a target of another archer's hostility! The idea that an arrow could be embedded in your body at any time is a stress factor that cannot be underestimated. Archery was really exciting in the old days under combat conditions!

A.D. 1252

It was during this period in English history that the longbow became the national weapon of England. This is a surprising historical fact, because recurve bow designs were well known to English bowyers and others. Various types of recurve

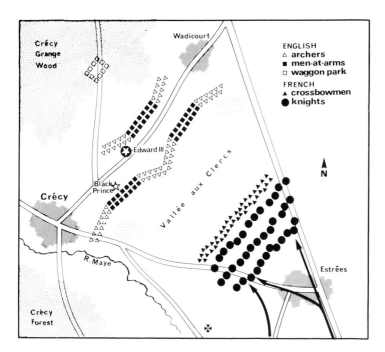

Figure 2.6
The Battle of Crécy, August 26, 1346. (From E. G. Heath, *The Grey Goose Wing*)

bows had been used for centuries and are portrayed in various works of art throughout the world. As one example, there is a series of statues dated 490–80 B.C., from the Temple of Aigina. These statues depict archers using highly sophisticated recurve bows.

Since the recurve design is superior from a physics standpoint in terms of arrow velocity and distance, why did the English choose the longbow as their national weapon? One possible explanation lies in the fact that the recurve bow must be made of a composite of laminated materials glued together. England is a damp country, and the crude glue used at that time was not durable like the epoxy resin glues of today. Consequently, a composite bow might fall apart when put to use by archers fighting in moist environments. Such a malfunction would have been fatal for the archer in the midst of battle. In these circumstances, the long bow, although not as efficient as the recurve bow, was more reliable for the highly-skilled English.

A.D. 1340–63

This period marked the start of the rise of English archery superiority. The Hundred Years' War with France was getting under way. The first of the large-scale encounters was the Battle of Crécy in A.D. 1346 (fig. 2.6). Edward III, King of England, had thirteen thousand archers at his disposal, plus three thousand knights and men-at-arms who were deployed in three divisions. It is interesting

Figure 2.7
The Battle of Poitiers, 1356. (From E. G. Heath, *The Grey Goose Wing*)

Figure 2.8
An archer of 1400 A.D. from a design, originally produced for a rifle shooting trophy, by Benjamin Wyon the medalist. This is now the emblem for the Grand National Archery Society of England. (From E. G. Heath, *The Grey Goose Wing*)

to note that a teenager, the 16-year-old Prince of Wales (the Black Prince), was the commander of one of these divisions. The English used their archers in wedge formations. This tactic, together with their superior skill with the bow and arrow, enabled them to slaughter the majority of the French archers. The French force, numbering approximately forty thousand, was soundly beaten. To recognize the efforts of some of his knights in this battle, King Edward III established the famous Most Noble Order of the Garter.

It was during this period that King Edward III declared mandatory archery practice for the English people. He also declared that all other sports would be illegal. This dictate by the king had a direct effect on the quality of archery skill for the entire population. This type of national legislative action would be analogous to President Franklin D. Roosevelt recommending legislation during World War II requiring every American to practice daily with the military rifle. Although the edict of King Edward III had positive ramifications for England, it is most likely that Americans would have frowned on that type of political legislation.

The Battle of Poitiers took place in A.D. 1356 (fig. 2.7). The English warriors were under the command of the Black Prince. They were outnumbered in this battle more than two to one, but were able to conquer the French. They did this by drawing the French into the open where they could be shot easily. This was accomplished by using false retreat tactics similar to that employed against them by the Normans three hundred years earlier. The French were killed by the thousands. The horses ridden by the French archers were special targets in this particular battle. The strategy was to wound the horses. The riders were unable to control the wounded horses, and that added to the chaos on the battlefield. It also made the individual French soldiers slower and easier targets for the English archers.

The Grand National Archery Society of England has a rich historical heritage. Its emblem is based on an archer circa A.D. 1400 (fig. 2.8).

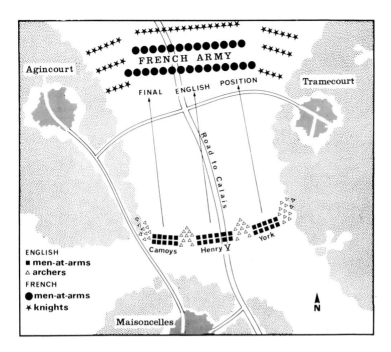

Figure 2.9
The Battle of Agincourt, October 25, 1415. Note how the space narrows between the two forests of Agincourt and Tramecourt, which hampered any forward action by the French. (From E. G. Heath, *The Grey Goose Wing*)

A.D. 1414

The Battle of Agincourt was the last great battle won by English archers. The English were outnumbered by the French four to one, but King Henry V was able to conquer the French chiefly because of superior military strategy and the archery ability of the English. In his *Henry V,* Shakespeare wrote that twenty-nine English were slain as opposed to ten thousand French archers. The critical day of the Battle of Agincourt is shown in figure 2.9.

A.D. 1453

This date marked the end of the Hundred Years' War. The fact that the English archers were superior to the French is historically significant both to those countries and to America as we know it. What if the French had won the Hundred Years' War? There would have been an entirely different series of events following the fifteenth century. The sixteenth century was marked by religious and social upheaval in England. Those events helped bring about the subsequent exploratory migrations to America by various English populations. It is doubtful whether the same volume of migration from England would have materialized had the French won that war. America would have been settled in due time, but

Figure 2.10
Archery of Edward IV (1442–1483). The archers in military costume are using the yew longbow and carry twenty-four arrows. (From E. G. Heath, *The Grey Goose Wing*)

the political, social, ethnic, and religious structures of the United States would have been entirely different. The edict of King Edward III requiring all Englishmen to practice archery helped shape English and American history!

A.D. **1455–71**

The Wars of the Roses resulted from the rebellious feudal power displayed by some English lords who had acquired power during the preceding years. Professional military archers returning from France were hired by these nobles for the purpose of solidifying their place in the political structure of the nation. Generally, the soldiers did a poor job simply because they lacked both the military leadership and discipline they had previously known. The last battle during the Wars of the Roses was at Tewkesbury. The significance of archery as a weapon of war was still evident, but firearms were beginning to be used. Just as slings and rocks are not effective against arrows in combat, arrows are no match for bullets. The use of archery as a weapon of war started to decline.

A.D. **1545**

In 1545 Roger Ascham published his book *The Schole of Shootynge*. This was the first book ever written in the English language about archery tackle and techniques. This classic archery textbook was also published later under the title of *Toxophilus*.

King Henry VIII's warship *Mary Rose* sank on July 19, 1545. Archaeologists recovered the longbows from that ship, and found that they were of superior design and better constructed than known earlier versions. One reason for this is that bowyers had started to use metal tools at this time to construct the longbows.

A.D. **1588**

The English and Spanish used gun powder and firearms extensively during the invasion of the Spanish Armada. Most historians use this battle to illustrate the decline of archery as a weapon of war. Nevertheless, archers were used on a smaller scale in battles and wars for the next four hundred years.

A.D. **1917–73**

The compound bow was invented in January 1966 by the late H. Wilbur Allen of Billings, Missouri. His main objective for inventing and subsequently manufacturing the compound bow was to make bow hunting easier and more efficient. It is now a very popular bow for hunting purposes, because it is easier to hold for longer times at full draw, produces greater arrow velocity than composite bows, and has better penetration capacity than recurve bows or longbows. These are important factors for the hunter. It is now legal to use the compound bow for hunting in all fifty states. The compound bow is also used extensively by field archers.

The basic concepts of bow design have undergone more changes since 1966 than in the preceding five thousand years! This technologic breakthrough was primarily due to the efforts and ingenuity of H. W. Allen. In recognition of his contributions to archery, the original Allen Compound Bow (fig. 2.11) is now in The National Museum of American History at The Smithsonian Institution in Washington, D.C. In addition, his contribution to archery is recognized by the Wilbur Allen Memorial Wildlife Area located in the Missouri Ozark Mountains. Deer may be hunted with bow only in this wildlife area.

During the Civil War, World War I, World War II, Korean War, and Vietnam War, bows and arrows were used for discrete military purposes. Their use seems incongruous in what is now known as the "atomic age," but it is a fact. Some military missions call for killing people very quietly. There are not too many ways for the military person to do this efficiently and live, especially from a distance. Expert archers have been trained in the military for sniper duties, reconnaissance work, and sabotage. Special arrows are made for demolition chores, and broadheads kill by penetration of vital organs and hemorrhage. Marines train men for this type of activity in their reconnaissance companies, and the U.S. Army trains special ranger groups and others in the relatively few martial arts that teach techniques for killing human beings silently. Archery is only one of these techniques.

Although outdated compared to more sophisticated killing techniques, an arrow with a broadhead is still a very effective killing instrument whether it be for a bear, shark, or human being. A razor sharp broadhead arrow shot from a

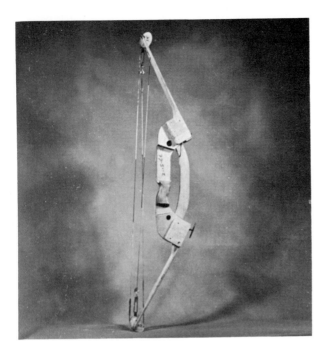

Figure 2.11
The original compound bow invented by H. Wilbur Allen of Billings, Missouri, in 1966 is now in The National Museum of American History at The Smithsonian Institution. (Courtesy Mrs. Elizabeth Allen and the *Missouri Conservationist*)

bow at short range has greater penetrating, killing, and/or trauma potential, for example, than a .45 caliber bullet shot from a pistol. Furthermore, a skilled military archer on a reconnaissance mission has a better chance of returning from that duty than a soldier or marine who kills with a noisy firearm. That is one of the main reasons archery has been used on a selective basis in modern warfare.

The Present Time

One hopes that archery will never again be utilized for killing human beings. During the last quarter of the twentieth century, archery has been used most extensively as a sport: target archery, field archery, bow hunting, bow fishing, flight shooting, clout shooting, and so on. SPORT IS THE SINGLE BEST USE OF ARCHERY!

Archery has evolved to the point that it is a diversified and significant recreational activity for millions of people all over the world. Target archery has been a part of the modern Olympic Games as an official gold medal sport since 1972, and that has not only focused attention on target archery but increased interest in the other archery sports. As we will learn in the next chapters, people keep finding and refining the ways in which archery may be used as an avocational activity during leisure time.

Review

1. No written documents tell us when archery was first developed, but it is believed to have been between ten and twenty thousand years ago. What evidence supports this belief?
2. What explanation has been proposed for the English military's adoption of the longbow rather than the more efficient recurve bow?
3. For what military purposes has archery proved useful in recent wars?
4. What information about the history of archery is depicted on the famous Bayeux Tapestry?
5. Why must documentation on bow designs be accomplished primarily through art rather than via archaeological artifacts?
6. Discuss the ramifications of the political mandate by King Edward III that required his subjects to practice archery.
7. What is the potential for damage by a sharp broadhead arrow shot at close range in comparison with a .45 caliber bullet shot from a pistol?
8. Why does the Zen Buddhist archer's stance and anchor point differ from customary practice?
9. Clout shooting is now one of the sport forms of archery. How did the Vikings employ clout shooting as a military strategy?
10. When and by whom was the compound bow invented, and how is this bow superior to the longbow and recurve bow?

Target Archery Tackle

3

In terms of precision shooting, target archery is the most demanding of all the competitive forms of archery. Furthermore, it serves as your "skill foundation" for most of the other archery sports if you ever wish to pursue one or more of them in the future. It is a serious oversight for an archer interested in bow hunting, as one example, not to attain a good level of competency in target archery shooting skills before learning to bow hunt.

The first step in learning target archery is to acquire an understanding of the equipment. *"Tackle" is the term used by archers for all of their equipment, such as bows, arrows, and related shooting gear.* There is an axiom in sport that a properly prepared athlete will be as good or poor as his or her equipment. The necessity for accuracy in target archery demands exactly matched, quality tackle for the archer to attain success.

The beginner should be provided with every opportunity to learn the sport efficiently. It is extremely important that the first set of archery tackle be matched properly. *Matched tackle means that arrows, exactly alike in every detail, should be chosen for use with a specific bow. The bow weight must be suitable for the individual archer and the arrows to be shot. Finally, the bowstring must match the bow and arrows.* Each archer differs in muscular strength, length of limbs, and aesthetic preferences. Therefore, great care must be taken to acquire archery tackle suitable for the unique anatomic attributes and other differences of each archer.

The "matched tackle principle" is just as appropriate for the issuing of archery tackle in class situations as it is for individuals who purchase their own tackle. Students, unknowingly, will take mismatched tackle issued to them and try to learn to shoot with it. Efficient learning becomes very improbable in that type of situation. Mismatched tackle is a major mistake that archery instructors should try to avoid if at all possible!

A beginner mismatched for archery tackle will experience considerable frustration. It is possible to perform all shooting fundamentals correctly with inferior (mismatched) tackle and have little success in accuracy. The beginning archer learns bad as well as good habits with mismatched tackle. The archer tends to make improper compensatory skill adjustments in shooting mechanics. These are most often related to the poor tackle instead of his or her skills. That type of adjustment during the learning process becomes a bad habit when the tackle problem is removed. *It is extremely difficult to unlearn bad habits.*

In target archery, it is a must that the archer obtain a consistent, tight grouping pattern on the target. With cheap or mismatched tackle each arrow shot will have a different flight pattern, resulting in very erratic arrow grouping. Overcoming the human factors that contribute to accuracy problems is enough to make archery a challenging sport for beginner and expert alike. The beginning archer should not be additionally burdened by learning target archery using inefficient tackle.

If possible, beginning archers should receive instruction from a qualified archery instructor prior to doing any shooting on their own. The reason is that bad habits can also be learned by the individual who teaches himself or herself by trial and error. As noted, poor shooting techniques become very difficult to unlearn, and this unlearning would have to be accomplished *before* the proper fundamentals could be mastered. As a result, the learning process becomes much more difficult. Would you try to teach yourself to play the piano or perform brain surgery? Not likely! Mistakes learned on your own make perfection of techniques under the guidance of a good instructor more time consuming. In archery, as in any other area where neuromotor skills are learned, good instruction along with quality equipment must come first if you are interested in becoming a highly skilled target archer.

Ideally, the first set of archery tackle, matched for the individual, should be issued by a knowledgeable archery instructor. Quality archery tackle is expensive to purchase. Because of this expense, most students will wish to learn and try the sport for a period of time with issued, matched tackle to determine whether or not archery appeals to his or her avocational interests.

If you become interested in archery as a lifetime sport after you have received instruction and gained a functional level of skill, that is the time to purchase your own matched archery tackle. *It is highly recommended that your tackle be purchased from a professional archery shop where the salespeople are aware of the complexities of matching the individual components of the tackle to one another and to the requirements of the archer.* Most of these pro shops have indoor and/or outdoor ranges where the tackle can be used. It is highly recommended that you shoot with the tackle you intend to purchase. Places such as sporting goods stores and franchise operations are usually poor places to purchase archery tackle. Salespeople in such stores or franchise operations, as a general rule, simply do not have the technical and scientific information required to match arrows to bows and all tackle to the unique features of the archer.

It is recommended that the archer who plans to use target archery as an avocational activity purchase the following minimum amount of matched tackle:

1. Twelve aluminum, aluminum-carbon, or carbon/graphite arrows matched exactly to each other in terms of straightness, weight, diameter, wall thickness, spine, color coding, fletching, nocks, and points; matched for use with the bow purchased and to the draw length of the archer; one arrow case.
2. One working recurve or take-down bow with center shot design, cushion plunger, arrow rest, clicker, stabilizer(s), and bowsight. The bow weight must be matched to the archer and to the arrows. It is essential that the bowstring be matched to the bow and arrows to be shot; one bow case.

3. One leather finger tab or glove.
4. One leather arm guard.
5. One arrow quiver (hip or ground).
6. One bowstringer.
7. One finger or bow sling.

This amount of matched tackle is enough to enable the beginning archer to learn the sport efficiently and utilize it avocationally for a long period of time.

The overall cost is related to the quality of tackle purchased. The initial expenditure for archery tackle, although costly, is not too expensive when you prorate it over the years of use. Quality target bows are expensive, but they are used by some archers for decades. Archery manufacturers will replace and/or straighten bow limbs if and when they become cracked or torqued. Bow limbs on take-down bows can be exchanged to increase bow weight or to lengthen or shorten your bow. Arrows can be a costly operational expense for the archer. *Cost for archery tackle should never be reduced by purchasing inexpensive arrows.* Keep arrows in good shape by checking them for damage and cleaning after each use. Develop accuracy to the point that you do not blemish or lose arrows too often. Parts of arrows such as points, nocks, and fletching can be replaced if broken, and aluminum arrows can be straightened if bent.

The Arrow

Although there are some good, inexpensive Port Orford Cedar and other wooden arrows on the market, *wooden arrows are not recommended for use in target archery.* They are not reliable, and it is very difficult to match them for use with various bows. Their use should be limited to bows designed for wooden arrows. The longbow, as an example, may be best suited for wooden arrows from the standpoint of the physics involved. Finally, it should be remembered that when a wooden arrow is broken it is difficult to replace in terms of an exact match for mass weight, straightness, shaft diameter, point, crest paint, and fletching.

A serious mistake made by many beginning archers is to be issued a bow for use in a class situation and then purchase cheap, wooden arrows in a place like the university book store. No thought is given to matching the arrows to the mechanical properties of the bow. As noted, that diminishes the probability of learning target archery effectively.

Fiberglass arrows are satisfactory for use by learners if they are matched to each other and to the bow that will be used. They cost less than aluminum arrows, but they are manufactured with precision. Research has led to the development of a light, durable, and hollow fiberglass shaft. It is possible for arrow manufacturers to maintain quality control to the point that there are only microscopic deviations in regard to shaft thickness, shaft diameter, and actual arrow weight. The fiberglass arrow shaft always remains straight. This is an advantage of the fiberglass arrow over the aluminum arrow shaft. The fiberglass, like the wooden arrow, will break if it strikes a target stand or other hard object at an odd angle.

The frequency with which this occurs is minimal. Fiberglass arrows are damaged beyond repair if stepped on, because of compression of the hollow shafts.

Aluminum and graphite arrows are recommended as the most desirable target archery arrows for beginners and experts alike. Aluminum alloys allow manufacturers to construct arrows that are nearly perfect. When shot by a machine during ballistic testing from 50 yards, it is not uncommon to see arrows grouped within a diameter of two inches. Aluminum arrows are among the most expensive on the market. If the beginner desires to purchase aluminum arrows initially, he or she should keep in mind that there will be times when these arrows will completely miss the target and become lost in the grass. Also, aluminum shafts, unlike fiberglass arrows, will bend when they strike the target stand or other hard objects instead of the target mat. (There are, however, procedures and machines for straightening a bent aluminum shaft.) If the beginner accepts these factors prior to purchasing, aluminum arrows are highly recommended over fiberglass arrows.

It must also be kept in mind that arrow velocities are now greater due to improved bow design. Aluminum alloy arrows are better designed to handle the greater force capacity of modern bows than wooden or fiberglass arrows. They are manufactured in a wide range of sizes and arrow weights to match a greater number of bows, draw weights, arrow lengths, and shaft spine or stiffness needs. It is also easier to purchase an exact replacement for one of your lost or damaged aluminum arrows. These factors are additional reasons for using aluminum arrows.

The reader should be aware of the fact that archery manufacturers are now using new materials and combinations of "old materials" in making arrows. This practice widens your choice. There are now tapered aerodynamic arrows on the market made of aluminum and carbon materials. These kinds of arrows with superior performance physics will enhance accuracy in years to come. They have lighter mass weight than traditional aluminum arrows even though the diameter of the arrow shaft is larger. The new alloys allow increased strength to reduce mass weight by keeping the wall of the arrow shaft thinner. These factors contribute to better aerodynamics and accuracy.

Carbon/graphite arrows are relatively new to the market, but they are being used extensively by expert archers. These arrows do not bend, and they are shatter resistant. These shafts are lighter than aluminum with a higher static spine. Those features translate into higher velocities and flatter trajectories for these arrows over some aluminum and the older fiberglass arrows. Carbon/graphite may be the arrow shaft material of the future. It is recommended that the archer go to an archery pro shop and shoot aluminum as well as carbon/graphite arrows properly matched for his or her bow. Compare and contrast the arrows for accuracy, velocity, and trajectory based on how you shoot them. Pragmatically, one should purchase the style of arrow that performs best for you when matched to your bow.

Figure 3.1
Arrow terminology.

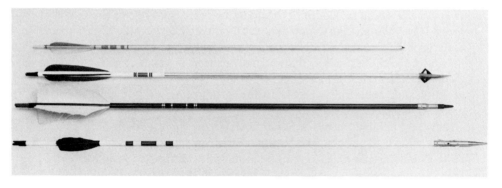

Figure 3.2
Arrow designs. From top to bottom: target arrow, bow hunting arrow with broadhead, field archery arrow with a field point, and bow fishing arrow with sting-a-ree point.

The term "end" applies to a set number of arrows shot on the range before archers go to the target to score and retrieve. The number of arrows in an end may be designated as three, five, or six in target archery. The most common number of arrows designated as an end in instructional situations is six. That is one reason for recommending that beginning archers purchase twelve arrows (two ends) initially. Extra arrows are needed in case of damage or lost arrows during classes or tournaments.

Terminology for the various parts of the target archery arrow is shown in figure 3.1. It should also be noted that manufacturers of arrows place informative numbers on the shafts. These numbers indicate the outside diameter of the arrow shaft in closest sixty–fourths of an inch and the wall thickness of the arrow in thousandths of an inch. This information is very important in the matching of ends of arrows when arrows are purchased initially and when an arrow has to be replaced.

For comparative purposes, figure 3.2 shows some common types of arrows used in the four most popular archery sports. Each arrow was designed for a unique purpose. The reader should visually compare and contrast these four arrows with that in mind. The arrow designs shown in figure 3.2 are for target archery (target pile or point), bow hunting (broadhead point), field archery (field point), and bow fishing (fishing point).

Spine

The spine of an arrow shaft is the deflection of the shaft, measured in inches, when depressed by a two-pound weight at its center. There are instruments that measure the degree of spine with minute precision. This measurement is important, inasmuch as the degree of spine deflection and uniformity are basic factors to consider when obtaining matched arrows. The spine deflection value must be compatible with the archer's bow weight.

One reason for matching bow weight and spine is a phenomenon known as the *Archer's Paradox*. Contrary to what the archer thinks he or she sees as the arrow leaves the bow, an arrow does not fly directly toward the target immediately upon being released. By means of cinematographic analysis, it has been demonstrated that the arrow shaft actually deflects or bends around the bow immediately after release. The reader can understand that an arrow shaft too stiff or too flexible could cause problems during this phase of its flight pattern. An arrow of sufficient spine, matched for the bow and released properly, tends to stabilize itself rapidly and follows an undeviating flight pattern during its trajectory toward the target. The fact that an arrow first deviates to the left for a right-handed archer when it leaves the bow, but ultimately stabilizes itself in flight to travel straight to the intended target, is the Archer's Paradox.

The combination of newer bow designs and materials, the use of cushion plungers and arrow rests, as well as the changes noted above in the materials used to construct arrow shafts, tend to minimize the Archer's Paradox. All of these types of engineering improvements ultimately have led to better accuracy in target archery tournaments.

What are some of the consequences of having improperly spined arrows for a bow? (It must be kept in mind that several factors other than spine determine accurate arrow flight. These will be discussed later.) Improper spine can cause the following arrow flight patterns: (1) an arrow naturally starts its flight by deviating a few degrees to the left for a right-handed archer. If the spine is too stiff, the shaft of the arrow or the fletching will actually brush the bow. This causes a reduction in arrow velocity. In addition, a flight pattern change occurs in the opposite direction. The archer's shot will be low and to the right of the intended target. (2) If the spine is too weak and flexible, the arrow may never stabilize and follow its intended trajectory. Instead, it will fly consistently to the left of the target. Improperly spined arrows are a definite causative factor for erratic arrow grouping.

What should be considered when selecting the proper spine for arrows? First, *the bow weight, that is, the pounds of pull exerted on the bowstring by the archer for his or her specific arrow length,* is very important. Second, the arrow length and weight to the grain must be known accurately. Third, the type and weight of the arrow point are also basic considerations. Target points are made very light. This places the quality target arrow's center of gravity close to its actual center. This makes the arrow aerodynamically sound, as compared to its heavier counterparts in bow hunting and field archery, as seen in figure 3.2.

By knowing these exact arrow measurements, the proper spine can be selected. There are charts for spine and weight specifications as well as shaft selection available from archery tackle manufacturers and in professional archery stores. One should be very careful and follow the guidelines set forth in these charts when matching and purchasing tackle. If you have a question regarding two spine classifications of arrows suitable for a bow, it is best to take the *stiffer* of the two arrows.

Correct arrow selection in terms of spine can mean the difference between tight groups and good scores versus erratic groups and poor scores during a target archery tournament. The stiffer, spined arrow that is light in weight will have a higher velocity. But, the increased spine must be compatible with your bow weight. The increased spine will provide fewer deviations in flight due to human errors at release or to wind conditions on the range. Finally, the technical matching of arrow spine to the proper bow weight that can be handled efficiently by the archer is a major reason archery tackle should be purchased in an archery pro shop. Archers who work there are usually much better informed about the sport than salespeople in your average sporting goods store or general merchandise franchise store.

Fletching

The feathers of an arrow are known collectively as fletching. Fletching is as important to an arrow as the tail assembly is to an airplane. The function of the two analogous parts is essentially the same. They both serve to stabilize airborne objects. Fletching stabilizes an arrow by channeling the wind currents encountered by the arrow during flight. Flight equilibrium is also maintained, in part, by high angular velocity (rotation) of the arrow around the longitudinal axis of its shaft.

The type of fletching one uses is largely a matter of personal preference. The trend seems to be away from the old, traditional turkey feather fletching to vinyl and plastic vanes. The latter vanes tend to be more durable than real feathers, and they do not become useless during inclement weather. On the other hand, feather fletching in good condition and shot in dry weather is more likely to exhibit better flight characteristics following a poor release. A poor release usually produces fletching contact with the bow. The relatively rigid plastic vanes striking the bow produce a yaw condition, or lack of stability, during arrow flight. This reduces the arrow's linear velocity and usually results in a low shot. While the same contact may occur between the bow and the feather fletched arrow upon a poor release, the adverse effects on arrow flight are minimized. The flexible feathers are less likely to rebound as much from the bow handle. As a result, the arrow flight is not as adversely affected. The better target archers are using firmer plastic vanes in competition. Plastic weighs more than turkey feathers, so your point weight must be adjusted accordingly for matching purposes when plastic vanes are used.

The length of the fletching is very important, because fletching helps stabilize the flight of the arrow after it bends around the bow upon release. Generally, longer and heavier arrows require longer and sturdier fletching. Shorter and lighter

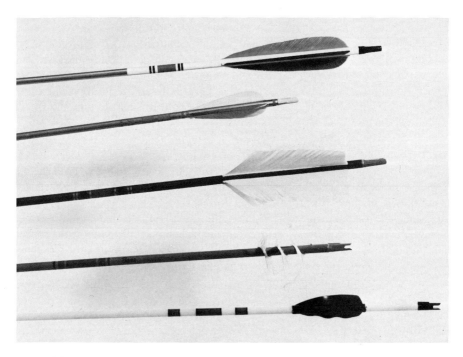

Figure 3.3

Fletching variations. From top to bottom: Hunting, target, flu-flu, spiraled flu-flu, and rubber fishing fletching.

target archery arrows require fletching only 3 to 3½ inches in length. Three-vane fletching of either plastic or feathers can be used effectively by target archers. Larger fletching is needed to add flight stability for heavier arrows as used in bow hunting and field archery.

Figure 3.3 shows fletching variations on hunting, target, field, and bow fishing arrows. The fletch on the top arrow, a hunting arrow, is 5 inches in length. The next arrow is a target arrow, and the fletch is 3 inches in length. The larger fletching on the middle arrow is 5½ inches in length. This type of fletch is designed to increase the drag resistance on a field or bow hunting arrow. Obviously, these arrows will not fly as far if a target is missed. Therefore, they are not lost as frequently by field archers or bow hunters. The next arrow shows a spiraled flu-flu fletch. This type of fletching is also designed to increase air resistance (drag) so arrows will not travel as far in flight. The bottom arrow is an example of rubber fletching on a bow fishing arrow. Fletching is not very important on bow fishing arrows, because the arrow simply does not have to fly very far to reach its intended target. Some bow fishers remove the fletching completely from their arrows.

Fletching is usually colored in a distinct and traditional manner. On a three-fletched arrow, two vanes will be drab in color and one vane will usually be rather flamboyant. The bright or odd-colored feather is known as the *index feather,* and is placed at a ninety-degree angle to the slit in the nock of the arrow. This can be seen in the upper two arrows in figure 3.3.

As a historical note, the two drab colored vanes were once known as *hen feathers,* and the brightly colored vane was called the *cock feather.* That terminology had an ornithological origin; that is, the feathers of male birds tend to be more colorful than the feathers of the female of the same species. Fletching terminology was changed to indicate arrow placement by using the term *index* for the vane that is usually pointed outward from the bow when it is nocked in the bowstring. It is recommended that experienced archers try shooting periodically, on an experimental basis, with the index feather downward or toward the bow. Flight patterns shot both ways should be evaluated. The best technique of fletching placement should be adopted permanently after a satisfactory evaluation period. Most archers prefer that the index feather be placed so it points outward from the bow.

Length

Length of the arrow varies for each individual. The length of your arms and the type of anchor point used are the determining factors. *The anchor point is the placement of the archer's bowstring hand on the chin or face with the bow at full draw.*

The beginner who has not determined his or her anchor point may want to purchase the first six arrows an additional inch longer than the measurement indicates. Anchor point adjustments are made as skill develops. It is much better to have arrows too long for the bow than too short. Accurate arrow lengths can be determined once all shooting fundamentals become learned properly.

There are several ways to establish an initial arrow length for yourself with and without the use of a bow. If you have a bow and an over-length arrow, mark the arrow in one-inch increments from the bottom of the arrow nock groove to the arrow point. After you have drawn the bow to your anchor point, note the inch mark nearest the back of the bow. That should be your arrow length if the anchor point is established. If not, add an inch as noted to the first arrows purchased.

Another commonly used method of determining arrow length is to have the archer hold both arms out to the sides at shoulder level (abduct both shoulder joints ninety degrees). Obtain the arm spread measurement in inches from the ends of the middle fingers:

Spread Measurement	Arrow Length
57–59 inches	22–23 inches
60–62 inches	23–24 inches
63–65 inches	24–25 inches
66–68 inches	25–26 inches
69–71 inches	26–27 inches
72–74 inches	27–28 inches
75–77 inches	28–29 inches
78+ inches	30 inches

Note: To change from inches to centimeters, multiply by 2.54.

Figure 3.4
The target archery arrow point should be matched in weight to be aerodynamically compatible with the total arrow configuration.

A yardstick may be used to determine arrow length if you do not have a bow and marked arrow. Two techniques may be used. First, stand at right angles to a wall. Place the clenched fist of your bow arm against the wall, simulating a bow hold. The elbow and wrist are extended, and your head is placed in the shooting position looking toward a target (the wall in this case). The distance along the bow arm from the wall to the corner of your mouth is your arrow length. The second technique is to hold, or have a person place, a yardstick on your sternum or breastbone. Hold both arms at shoulder level in front of you and move them to the yardstick. Your correct arrow length will be very close to the measurement at the end of your middle fingertips on the yardstick.

Points

Arrow points are manufactured in a wide variety of types and sizes. Target archery and field archery points are fairly standardized, but you will find a great array of bow hunting and bow fishing points. The beginning archer should start with light points for target archery (fig. 3.4). The various arrow points used in the other areas of archery will be discussed in Chapters 6 and 7.

Target archery points are designed to be ultralight to facilitate arrow aerodynamics. Proper point weight for each shaft size is just as essential in target archery as it is for the heavier broadhead points used in bow hunting. The nearly symmetrical equilibrium of the target archery arrow is very important for accuracy. Proper point weight, fletching size, and nocks are the critical components on the arrow.

Most of the more sophisticated target archery points on quality aluminum arrows are designed as nickel-plated steel points fitted to an aluminum sleeve. This unit is then placed solidly into the arrow shaft. Target archery points designed in this manner should not loosen and cause flight problems. They should be checked, however, after being shot. Arrows should be cleaned with a tassel after each end is shot. The added weight of even very small amounts of dirt causes erratic arrow flight. A *tassel* is a piece of cloth carried by the archer for the specific purpose of keeping arrows clean (see fig. 3.17).

The Bow

The bow has fascinated human beings throughout history. People have used it for hunting land animals and birds on the wing, fishing, killing their enemies, making music, drilling holes, and for a variety of other sporting activities.

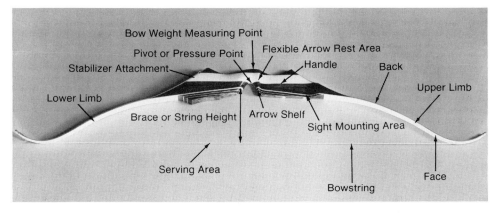

Figure 3.5
Target archery bow terminology. (Courtesy Black Widow Bow Company, H. C. R. #1, Box 357-1, Highlandville, Missouri 65669)

Bows have been built in all sizes and shapes (see Chapters 2 and 9). Some archers in the Far East used seven-foot bows with straight, uneven limbs; some African tribes use a three-foot bow with straight, even limbs; Englishmen of the eleventh century used a self bow made from one piece of wood five feet long with straight limbs; warriors at the Temple of Aigina used composite bows with duo-flexed limbs; the Navajo Indians of the southwestern United States used a short, composite bow for hunting purposes; most contemporary bow hunters use current versions of the compound bow invented by H.W. Allen in 1966; modern target archers prefer working recurve bows with center shot design and removable limbs.

Throughout history the diverse bow designs met their intended objectives in the hands of expert archers. That is an important fact to keep in mind in this age of very efficient archery tackle. *The skill and adaptability of the archer to his or her tackle remains the paramount factor for success.* Bow selection from a variety of quality bows is one of those "nice problems" that the contemporary target archer has, which never confronted his or her counterparts prior to the second half of the twentieth century.

The target archery bow has unique nomenclature that needs to be learned. This bow terminology is presented in figure 3.5. *The reader should also refer to Chapter 10 while reading text material for definitions of terms used in archery.* The bow shown in figure 3.5 is an older (c. A.D. 1960) one-piece recurve target archery bow.

Which type of target archery bow should be selected? A well-constructed working recurve bow will be more than adequate. A working recurve bow can be identified by observing the position of the bowstring on the face of the bow. The working recurve bow, as contrasted with the old longbow designs (see fig. 5.2), will have the string lying on the face of the bow for at least two inches at each end of the limbs. This feature greatly enhances the leverage potential of the bow, adds to better transfer of energy from the bow to the arrow, and increases the velocity of the arrow.

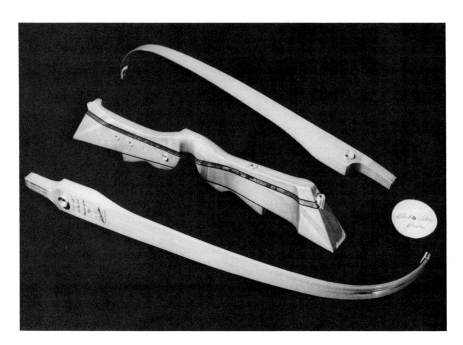

Figure 3.6
A take-down target archery bow showing the lower limb, handle, and upper limb. (Courtesy Black Widow Bow Company, H. C. R. #1, Box 357–1, Highlandville, Missouri 65669)

An example of an older model recurve is shown in figure 3.5. This excellent composite bow is of solid, one-piece construction. The limbs were made from laminated fiberglass and hard rock maple, with the handle section of Brazilian rosewood. A beginning archer may think about purchasing an older used bow of that type to learn the sport. They are extremely efficient, durable, and functional. In addition, they can be purchased from professional archery shops that trade and sell tackle at prices much below that of a new model take-down recurve bow. From the standpoints of cost and efficient skill development, the purchase of a used working recurve bow is a good way for some people to get started in target archery. You can always "trade up." You must keep in mind, however, that your arrows must match any bow purchased.

It should be noted that compound bows, bows with mechanical parts, and cam bows are not used in the sport of target archery as prescribed by National Archery Association rules. These bows will be discussed in Chapters 5, 6, and 7, because they are legal in the archery sports of bow hunting, bow fishing, flight shooting, and field archery.

If the target archer desires a state-of-the-art target bow, the finest tournament archery bows are three-piece, take-down bows. An example is shown in figures 3.6 and 3.7. Figure 3.6 illustrates a take-down target bow disassembled into the lower limb, handle, and upper limb sections. This bow is made of maple; other take-down models on the market have handles made of a magnesium alloy or carbon graphite. Take-down bows can be assembled quickly and easily. The

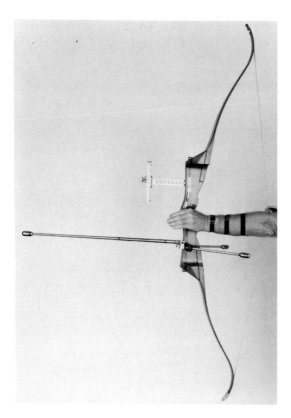

Figure 3.7
A competitive target archery bow equipped with arrow rest, stabilizers, clicker, and bowsight. This is the same bow as shown in figure 3.6. (Courtesy Black Widow Bow Company, H. C. R. #1, Box 357–1, Highlandville, Missouri 65669)

bow in figure 3.6 is reinforced and protected by a transparent glass covering over the laminated maple limb curves. This makes it very efficient in terms of leverage, durability, and arrow velocity. It also has aesthetic qualities, and that is important to many archers.

Draw weights for take-down bows usually range from 30 to 50 pounds. A distinct advantage of a take-down bow over the earlier one-piece recurve models is that the archer can change limb lengths and bow weights as desired. Limbs may be purchased in lengths ranging from 64 to 70 inches.

Figure 3.7 shows the equipped target archery bow. This is the same take-down working recurve bow shown in figure 3.6. It is equipped with stabilizers. The bow has three stabilizer inserts in the back of the handle riser plus one on the face of the bow. A clicker is mounted on the sight window. *A clicker is a shooting aid that ensures a consistent draw and helps the target archer concentrate on aiming and release of the arrow.* A bowsight is mounted on the bow. The bow is braced or strung, and the draw is being started in figure 3.7. This is the same type of target archery bow one would expect to see on the shooting lines of international archery tournaments, including the Olympic Games (see fig. 5.5).

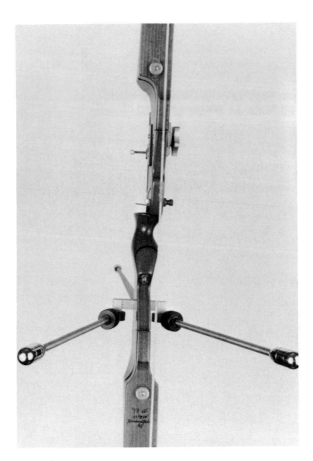

Figure 3.8
Sight window of a target archery bow looking at the bow face through the bowsight. (Courtesy Black Widow Bow Company, H. C. R. #1, Box 357–1, Highlandville, Missouri 65669)

Each archer equips his or her bow to meet individual requirements based on such factors as shooting idiosyncracies, target archery rules, and personal preferences. Each competitive target archer is unique.

A quality bow has a section cut away at the midline of its upper limb. This is called center shot design. The cutaway area is used as the sight window. This feature minimizes the components of the Archer's Paradox by aiding arrow clearance upon release. The arrow is able to move past the bow in a relatively close path to the bowstring alignment with the face of the bow. Another important feature of a bow with center shot design is the practical aspect of allowing the archer to see the intended target.

Figure 3.8 shows the center shot design of the same bow shown in figure 3.7. You are looking through the sight window toward the target in figure 3.8. Can you identify the: (1) bow face? (2) upper limb? (3) lower limb? (4) riser? (5) stabilizers? (6) pressure point? (7) arrow shelf? (8) arrow rest? (9) clicker?

(10) bowstring? (11) bowsight? and (12) bowsight adjustment knob? This sight window is 7½ inches, and it has been cut ⅕ inch past the center of the bow to facilitate arrow clearance. A take-down, working recurve target archery bow meeting the criteria outlined above is highly recommended.

Weight

The bow weight and literal mass weight of the bow are very important for entirely different reasons. *Bow weight is defined as the bow manufacturers' determination of the number of pounds required to draw the bowstring a given distance— usually 28 inches. Mass weight of the bow is the actual weight of the bow in pounds.* Mass weight of a bow should never be confused with bow weight. The mass weight of a good target archery bow with a stabilizer should be in the 3- to 6-pound range. This amount of mass weight helps the archer by adding to the bow's shooting stability.

Due to the efficiency with which good recurve target archery bows can convert potential energy into kinetic energy, considerable force can be transmitted to the arrow. That results in excellent arrow velocity. With the working recurves, this is accomplished at relatively low bow weights. How much bow weight is enough for each archer to attain good scores in target archery? Some guidelines can be supplied to partially answer that question, but the final answer lies in the muscular endurance and strength each individual has in the extensor muscles of the body, the shoulder joints, shoulder girdles, and upper limbs. (A muscle analysis of shooting and conditioning principles for the target archer are provided in anatomic detail in Chapter 8.)

Archery instructors generally agree that an archer should select a bow weight that he or she has strength enough to draw and hold without undue strain for multiple repetitions during class, practice sessions, or target archery tournaments. Generally, for most men, this means a bow weight should be found that is comfortable somewhere within a range of 30 to 50 pounds. Although the average adult woman has only 50 percent of the muscle mass seen in men, one should not deduce that a functional bow weight for all women is low. Observations by archery instructors verify that this is not the case. Strength in human beings is a product of genetics, central nervous system efficiency, and muscle mass. Therefore, many small people, male and female, are very strong and can handle higher bow weights. Generally, for most women, a target bow weight that is functional is in a range of 25 to 45 pounds. That range does not represent the upper range for all women, because some good, competitive women archers do shoot with higher bow weights. Bow weight is a highly individual matter, and the bow weight must be "matched" to meet the specific strength of the archer as well as the arrows to be shot from it.

As indicated, bow weights are determined according to the number of pounds required to pull the bowstring back to full draw for a given arrow length. Most bows are marked for bow weight at a 28-inch draw. As the draw diminishes in length when using a target archery bow, the bow weight also diminishes in pounds. Conversely, as the draw increases in length, the bow weight increases in pounds.

(Greater bow weights are required for bow hunting as compared to target archery. The bow hunter uses an overdraw device, *illegal in target archery,* to increase the bow weight.)

The archer needs to know the actual draw weight for the arrow length being pulled. The recommended method for doing this was established by the Archery Manufacturer's Organization (AMO). This procedure is accomplished as follows: Divide the draw weight marked on the bow by twenty, and determine how many inches, more or less, the actual draw length deviates from 28 inches. Multiply these two answers, and subtract (or add) the answer from the weight marked on the bow. The result of this calculation gives the archer the actual draw weight. As an example, assume that an archer has a 35-pound bow, but he or she is actually drawing 30 inches. Thirty-five divided by twenty equals 1.75. In this example, 1.75 would be multiplied by two, which is the extra number of inches being drawn above the 28-inch mark. The resultant answer of 3.50 would be added to the 35-pound bow weight. Therefore, an archer drawing a 30-inch arrow on a bow marked 35 pounds for a 28-inch draw would actually be drawing 38.5 pounds. One should use this process to determine your actual bow weight for the length of arrow used.

It is a good idea for some beginners to learn while using a bow weight lighter than they have strength to handle. It is easier to learn shooting fundamentals with a comfortable bow weight, because the archer's concentration is not distracted due to fatigue or other physical factors. As skill increases, bow weight can be increased to meet the individual's strength and muscle endurance capabilities. This teaching method is recommended in those learning situations where matched tackle is available and can be issued to the archers.

Some archers like to believe they need a very heavy bow weight. Let us consider what actually happens when the potential kinetic energy of a bow is doubled. What are the differences in terms of arrow velocity between 45- and 90-pound bows? Will arrow velocity be doubled? Tripled? Taking variable arrow weights into consideration, it has been established that an average 90-pound bow increases arrow velocity only 19 to 25 percent over a 45-pound bow. When an archer considers such factors as ease of handling, shooting over prolonged periods of time during tournaments, and accuracy difficulties, is a high bow weight really worth the extra effort needed to draw it? Most archers would answer "No." Contemporary target archery bows have excellent thrust force. This results in superior arrow velocities to handle the standard distances shot in tournaments. *An arrow velocity between 163 and 210 feet per second will be functional for target archery purposes.* Why stress yourself with a bow weight that is too high to handle easily?

The arrow velocity potential for today's bows and arrows is determined by calculating a ballistics coefficient based on the interrelationships of the (1) peak weight of the bow in pounds; (2) total weight of the arrow including point, nock, and fletching in grains; and (3) draw length of the bow. Bows with draw lengths over 30 inches—stable and efficient in terms of longer application of force on the arrow nock after bowstring release—have better ballistic coefficients than bows that do not meet these scientifically based criteria.

A working recurve bow with a ballistics coefficient of 0.140 would produce an arrow velocity of 210 feet per second. In terms of accuracy, flight efficiency, and trajectory, that velocity level could be better than an arrow projection of 240 feet per second. So, the choice of your ultimate bow weight should also be based on these types of technical and scientific factors. The greater bow weight may not be the most efficient. The efficiency of the bow ultimately boils down to three key factors: (1) design, (2) construction materials, and (3) the skill of the archer using it. The latter is the most important factor! Knowing the ballistic coefficient of your bow helps to match other tackle to the bow and determine its efficiency for the distances you shoot.

Let us consider some of the basic differences between the designs of the working recurve bow and the older longbow. This discussion is presented, because, unfortunately, longbows and recurve bows with longbow mechanics are still being issued for learning purposes in some archery classes. First, it should be noted that not all bows sold as recurve bows have recurve actions. In order to work efficiently, the bowstring of the recurve bow must actually touch the face of the bow for two to three inches at the end of both limbs. If the so-called recurve bow is not designed in this manner, it will respond essentially the same as the longbow. If you have been issued a bow in an instructional situation or for practice, check it out carefully. When the bowstring touches the recurve tips as shown in the bows in figures 3.5 and 3.7, this increases the leverage potential and adds to arrow velocity. There is an increase in the force-time relationship during energy transfer from the bow to the arrow. *The total effect of the force generated by the bow and applied to the arrow via the bowstring-nock arrangement is the product of the magnitude of force over the time during which it operates.*

The principle above is magnified, for example, within the design of compound bows and crossbows that utilize wheels, pulleys, and cams. These bows with leverage enhancement devices cannot be used in target archery competition. But, the modern design of recurve bows is very efficient. A recurve bow weight of 45 pounds will project an arrow at a rate of speed approximately 20 percent greater than a longbow of comparable weight. A working recurve bow tends to draw more smoothly than a longbow. This is particularly true of the modern takedown bow. These bows have less increase of weight during the last few inches of draw than bows with "longbow mechanics." *The phenomenon of ever increasing weight as one draws the bowstring hand toward the face is known as "stacking."*

Due to greater arrow velocity, which is derived through increased leverage, the working recurve bow tends to project the arrow on a flatter trajectory than a longbow. This aids accuracy considerably. Finally, the semicircular configuration of a longbow seen as it is being drawn tends to cause an uneven distribution of stress in the limbs. This factor also detracts from the overall efficiency and longevity of the longbow. This type of stress within the limbs does not occur within a good working recurve bow.

Can longbows be used in target archery? The answer is yes, but not by serious target archers in highly competitive tournaments against archers using recurve bows. The longbow is making a comeback of sorts as a result of its historical significance. Also, because of its inefficiency compared to contemporary recurve bows, the longbow presents a greater challenge to shoot excellent scores on a target archery range. Some target archers and bow hunters enjoy that type of test. Most longbows have been retired to museums, but some are alive and well in the hands of archers who want more sport and a greater degree of difficulty in shooting. More power to them! There are a few archery manufacturers who continue to make longbows. A beginning target archer, however, should learn to shoot while using a good, working recurve bow.

Length

Target archers are no longer using short bow lengths. They are simply too difficult to use. There is extreme pressure on the bowstring fingers at full draw, and this negates a smooth release of the arrow. Most target archers use bows ranging from 64 to 70 inches in length. The added bow length minimizes the pressure the fingers exert on the nock of the arrow during the draw and at release. A smoother release is provided by using a longer bow. In addition, the longer bows generally have greater mass weight. This factor helps the strong archer have better bow arm stability and a steadier bow hand while shooting.

The draw length or arrow length must be considered when selecting a bow for target archery:

Draw Length	Bow Length
1. 25 inches to 28 inches	64-inch limbs
2. 27 inches to 30 inches	66-inch limbs
3. 29 inches to 32 inches	68-inch limbs
4. 31 inches to 34 inches	70-inch limbs

Personal preference and kinesthetic feeling enter into bow length selection. As an example, a person with a 30-inch draw can use a 66- or 68-inch bow. Whichever length ultimately has the best kinesthetic feeling after shooting numerous ends of arrows is the bow that should be purchased. Most professional archery shops have indoor ranges where bows may be tried prior to purchase. Also, limb lengths can be changed as needed by using take-down bows.

Stabilizers

One or more stabilizers can be mounted on a target archery bow. The stabilizer can contribute to more efficient arrow flight by minimizing or negating some of the archer's fundamental shooting faults involving the bow arm. A stable bow means less vibration and torque of the bow from aiming through the release. A single stabilizer is shown mounted on a target bow in figure 3.9. The stabilizer is a metal rod screwed into the back of the bow on the bow handle, and it projects forward toward the intended target. The stabilizer can be adjusted for length to

Figure 3.9
Lawrence Brady shoots a bow equipped with one stabilizer. Can you locate the stabilizer?

fit the personal preference of the archer. (Hydraulic stabilizers for mounting on bows or v-bars are also now on the market.) The number, weight, length, and type of stabilizer is a matter of individual preference. Some archers prefer to use tapered stabilizers mounted on a rotor that pivots 360 degrees. This allows considerable adjustment flexibility for stabilizers. In contrast to figure 3.9, figures 3.7, 3.8, and 3.10 show different views of a v-bar stabilizer system mounted on the same bow.

A word of advice is in order regarding the use of stabilizers. *The beginner should learn basic fundamentals of shooting before mounting a stabilizer on the bow.* After the fundamentals have been learned to the extent that the archer is grouping arrows consistently, a stabilizer is then recommended for use. However, the archer should try to correct fundamental faults without using the stabilizer. If successfully done, this will mean higher scores when the stabilizer is used later in practice and competitive situations. A stabilizer should not be used as a "crutch" to compensate for fundamental faults of the archer.

Figure 3.10
A v-bar stabilizer system mounted on a target archery bow. (Courtesy Black Widow Bow Company, H. C. R. #1, Box 357–1, Highlandville, Missouri 65669)

Bowstrings

Like arrows, bowstrings must be matched to specific bows as well as the require-ments of the archer. This important fact is often overlooked by beginning archers who tend to settle for any old string that fits the bow being used. Big mistake! Archery manufacturers make recommendations regarding what type of bowstring and exactly how many strands should be used with specific bows. The number of strands in your bowstring can also have an effect on arrow spine. "Matched tackle" means that you are using the correct bowstring for the bow and arrows being shot.

Bowstrings come in varieties of Dacron, Kevlar, and Flemish. Dacron and Flemish tend to stretch too much with use, and that can have a negative effect on aerodynamics and accuracy. Kevlar string reduces the elastic component to a minimum, and it produces a good shot with an average weight bow when twelve to fifteen strands are used. Dacron strings will vary from eight strands for bows up to 30 pounds to twelve or more strands recommended for bows up to 45 pounds. Bowstrings can be adjusted by twisting, but utilization of this technique should be limited to a maximum of twelve twists to minimize friction and breakage.

Figure 3.11

The bowstring serving is equipped with two nock-locators. A kissing button is on the string above the serving. The bow is also equipped with a clicker, arrow rest, bowsight, and stabilizer. (Courtesy of Patrick Brunhoeber)

The middle portion of the bowstring is called the serving. The arrow is nocked or placed on the string at a specific point on the serving. As can be seen in figure 3.11, two nock-locators have been mounted on the serving. The nock-locators mark the exact nocking point for the arrow. The nock-locators shown in figure 3.11 are found on the serving immediately in back of the arrow rest. The added thread wrapping around the portion of the bowstring known as the *serving* is needed to protect the string from breakage, because this area of the bowstring receives the most wear and tear. The total diameter of the serving area is ultimately determined by the number of strands of your bowstring. This serving diameter should not be larger than you can accommodate easily based on your finger size. If it is too large, your release may not be as smooth as it should be.

Bowsights

The bowsight shown in figure 3.12 is the type used by members of the U.S. Olympic Archery Team. This target sight is equipped with a 10-inch dovetail extension. Sights of this caliber come equipped with operating features that make micrometer elevation and windage adjustments relatively easy and quick. The pointer can be moved easily and set as desired. Also, leveling the aperture with this sight can be accomplished by simply hanging the bow in a vertical position. You loosen the allen set screws at the top and bottom of the sight body. The aperture is leveled simply by turning the allen screw at the bottom left of the sight body with the key. The aperture does not move from its level position as you tighten down the screws at the top and bottom of the sight body. All of these features are important in a quality target archery bowsight, and there are several to choose from on the market today. *The beginning archer should learn target*

Figure 3.12
The Accra Combo 1103 target archery bowsight used by U.S. Olympic Archery Team Members. (Courtesy Accra 300)

archery by using a quality bowsight for aiming purposes versus shooting instinctively. Bowsights are mounted on the bow shown in figures 3.9, 3.10, and 3.11.

Accessories

The archer must have protection for the bow arm and bowstring fingers. The bow arm must be protected from possible contusions due to being slapped by the bowstring in the general region of your radioulnar and wrist joints (forearm). Bad shooting habits result when adequate forearm protection is not provided or when the arm is moved improperly. Without protection of the shooting hand, the bowstring fingers become severely irritated from the constant pressure and friction exerted by the bowstring. Two common leather accessories designed to protect the forearm and shooting hand, the finger tab and arm guard, are shown in figures 3.13 and 3.14. Both come in several sizes, shapes, and styles. These accessories are relatively inexpensive.

The finger tab is rather awkward to use at first, but it is absolutely essential for prolonged shooting during class, practice sessions, or tournaments while using the conventional three-finger release technique. If a finger tab is not used, tender skin may become blistered by the friction created when the bowstring rolls over

 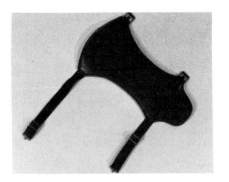

Figure 3.13
Finger tab. (Courtesy Wilson Brothers, Route 1, Elkland, Missouri 65644)

Figure 3.14
Arm guard.

the fingertips. This, of course, would have an adverse effect on your release and accuracy. If you shoot on a regular basis, the finger tab will become worn, rough, or less pliable. It is necessary to change tabs when that occurs, because a worn tab interferes with a proper release.

Some archers prefer shooting gloves instead of finger tabs. A shooting glove is shown in figure 4.13. The beginner may want to try shooting in practice with gloves and tabs prior to selecting one over the other for regular use.

The arm guard is placed on the bow arm between the elbow and wrist. The arm guard is shown in figures 3.14 and 3.16. The lower arm in the vicinity of the wrist is an area that can be "slapped" periodically by the bowstring when it is released. Shooting without an arm guard when that occurs can result in painful and serious contusions. Furthermore, following one severe blow by the bowstring on an unprotected arm, an archer has a tendency to flinch—flexion occurs in the elbow and/or wrist—when the arrow is released. These movements at the elbow and wrist are bad habits that the protection afforded by the arm guard tends to eliminate. Archery is fun, but no sport is a pleasure if you are injured frequently and do not experience some success. The arm guard and finger tab lend support to the archer.

A finger sling is another accessory that can help eliminate some problems during release and follow-through. The finger sling is shown in figures 3.15 and 3.16. The finger sling attaches to the index finger or middle finger and the thumb of the bow hand. It then extends across the back of the bow as shown in figure 3.16. It serves the purpose of keeping the bow from falling to the ground during release of the arrow and the subsequent follow-through. Therefore, the archer can concentrate more on the release and less on losing control of the bow. Target archery is a "mental game," and the more distractions you can eliminate while on the shooting line the better!

An arrow quiver is another accessory that the archer must obtain. *A quiver is a device designed to carry arrows.* There are shoulder, hip, ground, pocket, and bow quivers available. Those come in all sizes, shapes, prices, and materials. Most beginning target archers rely upon inexpensive, ground quivers. The hip

Figure 3.15
Finger sling.

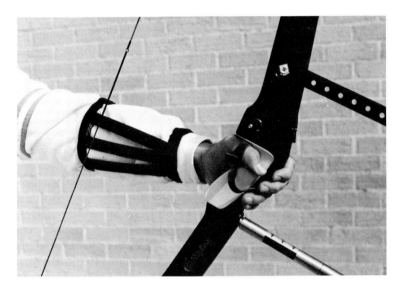

Figure 3.16
Arm guard and sling in use. (Courtesy of Lawrence Brady)

quiver, as shown in figures 3.9 and 3.17, is most commonly used by experienced target archers to carry arrows as well as other objects needed during practice or tournaments.

Another important accessory is the arrow rest. This small device is mounted just above the arrow shelf on the bow. The purposes of the arrow rest and cushion plunger are to maintain efficient arrow position, stability, and bow clearance. This device is important from the initial nocking of the arrow onto the bowstring past the time of arrow release and bow clearance. There are one- and two-piece metal and plastic arrow rests on the market. Cushion plungers and arrow rests are produced in a wide variety of choices. Arrow rests are shown in figures 3.8, 3.11, 3.16, 3.18, and 3.19. Some archers simply prefer to shoot from a modified arrow shelf on the bow without an arrow rest, but most serious target archers use cushion plungers and arrow rests.

Figure 3.17
A hip quiver is designed to carry arrows and other tackle items needed on the shooting line.
(Courtesy of Patrick Brunhoeber)

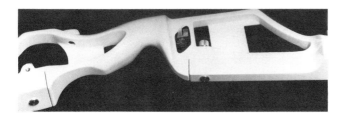

Figure 3.18
Arrow rest without an arrow.

Figure 3.19
Arrow rest holding the arrow at full draw.

A clicker is used extensively in target archery. A clicker is shown mounted on the sight window of the bow shown in figures 3.7, 3.8, 3.11, and 4.11. *A clicker is a shooting accessory that facilitates a consistent draw and helps the archer concentrate on aiming.* The arrow is ready to be released when the archer hears the "click" or sound as the fully drawn arrow point passes through the clicker.

Care of Archery Tackle

The Bow

The following care and treatment of a target bow will add to its longevity and effectiveness:

1. Always unstring the bow after use with a bowstringer. (It should be noted that some manufacturers prefer that the bow remain braced at all times, because improper bracing is a common cause of limb breakage and torque problems.)
2. Place the bow in a bow case for storage purposes. In the case of a take-down bow, remove the bow limbs prior to inserting them in the bow case.
3. Lay the bow in a flat place or hang it vertically if a bow case is not available.
4. To protect the outer surface of the bow, wax it periodically.
5. Use beeswax on the bowstring occasionally to minimize fraying.
6. Do not leave the bow lying on the ground when retrieving arrows from the target.
7. Do not drop the bow.
8. Draw the bow several times to your draw length prior to actually shooting an arrow, but do not release the string at full draw without an arrow in the bow.
9. Always use a bowstringer to brace the bow. Some manufacturers recommend that two feet be placed on the bowstringer for stability as the bow is braced.
10. A take-down bow can be stored while strung if desired. It should be hung horizontally.
11. Maintain proper limb and string alignments.

Arrows

The following care and treatment of arrows will add to their longevity and effectiveness:

1. Store arrows in an arrow case.
2. Wipe arrows clean after shooting.
3. Check fletching periodically and replace as needed. Fletching can be re- placed at a very low cost.
4. Do not carry arrows in a tightly clenched fist. This tends to damage fletching. Place the arrows between the fingers when carrying them back from the target to the shooting line.
5. Check nocks and points periodically and replace as needed.

6. If an arrow is embedded in a target up to the fletching or nock, remove the arrow by pulling it completely through the target. This protects fletching.
7. If an arrow is embedded or "snaked" into the grass on the target range, remove the arrow from the grass by pulling it in the direction of its flight. This protects fletching.
8. Always check aluminum arrows to determine that they are absolutely straight. Use a precision arrow straightener as needed.

Review

1. Why should the bow hunter, bow fisher, and field archer first become proficient in target archery?
2. Compare the efficiency and effectiveness of a working recurve bow with that of a longbow. Can a recurve bow have the mechanical characteristics of a longbow?
3. What do the following terms mean when used in connection with archery: (1) *cast,* (2) *stabilizer,* (3) *fletching size,* (4) *tackle,* (5) *Archer's Paradox,* (6) *point weight,* (7) *take-down bow,* and (8) *thrust force?*
4. Why should one spend considerable money on excellent instruction and matched tackle if one is a beginning archer?
5. What criteria are important in choosing a bowsight?
6. Distinguish between bow weight and mass weight of the bow. What should you consider when selecting your bow weight?
7. How do you determine your actual draw weight?
8. What arrow velocity do you need in target archery?
9. Describe the routine procedures for the care of archery tackle.
10. A stabilizer can contribute to efficient arrow flight by minimizing or negating some fundamental shooting faults. Why, then, is it undesirable for a beginner to use a stabilizer?
11. What is the purpose of a clicker mounted on a bow?
12. The time to seek expert instruction in any sport is after you have practiced on your own and thus have learned a little about the activity. Is this sound advice? Why or why not?
13. In what sense is it true that an athlete can be no better than his or her equipment? Turn this around: Will good equipment make someone a good athlete?

Fundamentals of Target Archery

4

The learning of target archery shooting skill not only serves as your foundation to participate in most of the other archery sports, but target archery in itself is a challenging "world class sport." Target archery during practice sessions and tournaments necessitates a merger of your physical skills and concentration capacities on every shot. Minute errors in executing the fundamental skills are frustrating for the target archer, because they lead to large accuracy problems, especially when shooting at distant targets. Exactness and consistency are attributes the target archer must possess. These learned habits are based on a thorough understanding of the shooting fundamentals presented in this chapter.

Target archery is a demanding sport to learn correctly, because there are numerous opportunities to err between the time the archer nocks the arrow, draws the bow, and releases the arrow on its flight toward the target. Those things most difficult to attain in life often are perceived to possess the greatest personal values. Therein lies some of the mystique and challenge of archery, as noted in Chapters 1 and 2.

Some basic techniques and fundamentals of target archery are modified by champions and other participants in the sport. Such changes in the execution of basic skills occur in all sports because of individual differences. Elite target archers, like other athletes, have numerous theories, preferences, idiosyncracies, and variations on their shooting styles. These skill modifications are developed over a period of years of shooting in practice and competition. Although not all target archers shoot exactly alike, when their fundamental shooting skills are analyzed, their performances have more similarities than differences. As a result, there is a stereotype of perfect shooting mechanics. *Those basic fundamentals of shooting, which are generally agreed upon as the stereotype of perfect skill or mechanics for target archery, are presented in this chapter.*

A few variations or modifications of the stereotype of perfect shooting mechanics are mentioned on occasion. The beginner may want to try these variations, but only *after* becoming very familiar with your tackle and basic shooting techniques.

NOTE: All discussions and illustrations in this textbook pertain to the right-handed archer.

Archery and Safety

The archer should keep the following concept in mind when archery tackle is in hand: *Archery is not a dangerous sport, but an arrow shot from a bow can kill or traumatize another human being on or near the target archery range.* As a consequence, respect should be shown for other human beings while on an archery range with tackle in hand.

Safety rules vary from range to range. All rules, however, incorporate the concept of always being aware of the whereabouts of your fellow archers and the trajectory limits of your arrows. When an arrow is placed in a bow it should be pointed *only* in the direction of the intended target. Furthermore, the bow should never be drawn at an angle greater than that necessary to hit the target. (Target archery is not clout or flight shooting!) That safety habit keeps an accidentally released arrow in the safety zone of the archery range. The archer must know beyond all doubt that no other human being is within arrow distance of the intended target plus the safety zone. This is easier to ascertain on target archery ranges than field archery units or in bow hunting situations.

Practice on a target archery range is performed on a common shooting line for all archers. Whistle signals are usually used to tell the archers when to shoot, stop shooting, and retrieve arrows. An archer should never move in front of the shooting line for any reason until he or she hears the whistle or signal authorizing retrieval of the arrows. Each archery instructor or Director of Shooting in a tournament will post or announce range safety rules. When these rules are followed in detail, and archers show courtesy and respect for one another on the range, target archery is one of the safest of all sports.

The archer should go to the range in comfortable clothing. Loose fitting golf sweaters, shirts, and blouses are not recommended clothing to be worn on the archery range. That type of clothing can become entangled with the bowstring after it has been released. It is also good practice to remove such things as watches, pens from pockets, and jewelry prior to shooting. These can become entangled in the bowstring. Also, footwear should be comfortable enough to enable you to stand for long periods of time and walk to retrieve arrows. Wearing shoes with heels is not recommended on a target archery range.

From the standpoints of personal safety and proper care of tackle, the bow and arrows to be shot should be given a visual inspection prior to shooting. The bow limbs and arrows should be checked for stress fractures. Bows with limbs cracked or permanently twisted should not be shot. Arrow nocks and fletching need to be checked to see if they are damaged in any way. The bowstring also needs to be examined periodically to determine that all strands are intact and the loops are properly notched on the bow following the bracing process. These simple observations can eliminate potential hazards.

Figure 4.1
Bowstringer. (Courtesy of Bow-Pal)

Bracing

Bracing the bow is the process of attaching the bowstring to the bow in preparation for shooting. Bracing the bow can create problems for some archers. As an example, bows are damaged more often while being braced than in any other situation. That is one reason some bowyers recommend that the bow be stored with it braced. *Working recurve bows should always be braced with a bowstringer.* If a bow is broken while using the older push-pull or step-through methods of bracing described below, some bow manufacturers will not replace the broken bows under their guarantees.

A bowstringer is shown in figure 4.1. Figures 4.2 and 4.3 show how to use the bowstringer. The bowstringer shown in figure 4.1 is equipped with two leather pockets, one longer than the other. Place the longer leather pocket on the lower tip of the bow, and place the shorter pocket on the upper tip of the bow. Turn the bow face downward, and place the feet shoulder width apart on the bowstringer (fig. 4.2). Grip the bow firmly and pull it straight upward. At the same time, slide the loose loop of the bowstring into its notch (fig. 4.3). Always check both bow notches to see that the bowstring is properly inserted prior to shooting. To unstring the bow, the above procedure is reversed. *The use of a bowstringer is simple, safe, and recommended at all times.*

If, however, a bowstringer is not available, there are two methods for bracing a bow manually: (1) the push-pull method and (2) the step-through method. The method used by the archer depends upon the weight of the bow, design of the bow, and strength of the individual.

For most lightweight bows and archers with average strength, the push-pull method of bracing is adequate. (This method works fine for bracing longbows.) The following is the procedure for using the push-pull method of bracing:

1. Place the lower limb of the bow against the instep of the right foot; be certain that the bowstring is placed in the notch on the lower limb of the bow.
2. Grasp the handle with the right hand.
3. Grasp the loop of the bowstring with the thumb and index finger of the left hand and slide it up the lower limb toward the notch of the bow.

Figure 4.2
Bracing with a bowstringer—Step One. (Courtesy of Patrick Brunhoeber)

Figure 4.3
Bracing with a bowstringer—Step Two. (Courtesy of Patrick Brunhoeber)

4. PULL with the right hand and PUSH down on the upper limb with the left hand while sliding the bowstring upward and into the bow notch. *For safety, keep your face out of alignment with the upper limb at all times!*
5. Check to see that both bowstring loops are properly inserted (fully) into each bow nock. This is a final safety precaution.

The step-through method of bracing is used more frequently than the push-pull method, especially with working recurve bows. Again, this bracing technique should be used only when a bowstringer is not available for the archer:

1. Assume an upright stance with the feet apart at shoulder width.
2. Step through or between the bowstring and face of the bow with the right leg.
3. See that the recurve of the lower bow limb encircles your left ankle.

4. Hold the handle of the bow on the upper thigh so both upper and lower bow limbs will bend.
5. Taking advantage of the leverage that this bow position allows, grasp the upper bow limb and bend it forward and downward with the right hand.
6. Move the bowstring upward, placing it in the bow notch with the left hand as the upper limb is being bent downward.
7. Check both bow notches to see that bowstring loops are properly inserted into each. Failure to insert them properly exposes the archer to danger during the shooting process.

If the bow should slip during this step-through procedure for bracing, clothing such as slacks, pantyhose, and trousers can be ripped. The archer can also receive contusions and abrasions in the process. Steady pressure should be exerted on the bow limb and proper placement of the recurve around the left ankle must be checked to prevent the bow from slipping. Also, if the bow is twisted during this bracing method, it may crack. As can be seen in figure 4.4, variations of this bracing method have been around for a long time. They did not have bow-stringers back in 490 B.C. If you have ever tried this bracing method while fully clothed, you might readily understand why the archer in figure 4.4 is bracing in the nude!

The actual distance from the bowstring to the handle or pivot point of the bow is very important. This is known as the brace, or string, height. Bowyers, individuals who make bows, indicate exactly what the brace height should be for each bow. Brace height is directly related to the length of the bow. As one example, the manufacturer's recommended string height for the bow in figure 3.19 is 9¾ to 10¾ inches for a 69-inch bow and 9½ to 10½ inches for a 67-inch bow. The archer should measure the brace height accurately after bracing the bow. A bowstring too close or too far away from the face of the bow will adversely affect arrow velocity and flight, because there is a direct relationship between brace height and spine of the arrows to match the bow.

At times the experienced target archer may adjust his or her brace height to compensate for individual shooting style. A higher brace height of an inch or less, as an example, may reduce bow shock at release and produce more stable arrow flight for some shooting styles. On the other hand, lowering the manufacturer's recommended brace height may compound shooting errors and problems. The amount of energy transferred to the arrow at the time of release will be affected if the brace height is inappropriate. A part of tuning your archery tackle is to make sure that your brace height is where it should be for the arrows being shot and for your particular shooting style.

A bowstring can be rotated or twisted in some cases to make minor adjustments for proper brace heights. The twists of the string should be limited to a range of three to ten for any single adjustment. The best situation is to have the proper size bowstring for the recommended brace height and bow weight of your bow. The bowstring must have the proper number of individual strands recommended for your bow weight to be compatible with the spine of your arrows, and the bowstring diameter should allow you to grasp it comfortably. Matching and tuning archery tackle are not easy tasks! There are many minute details to consider. Fortunately, archery manufacturers provide good guidelines for use of their equipment.

Stance

The right-handed archer stands with the left side of the body toward the intended target. The archer's stance must be consistent from shot to shot. The exact placement of the feet on the shooting line should be marked. Golf tees provide good markers for this purpose on grass ranges. They can be driven into the ground to indicate heel and toe placement for both feet. This procedure enables the archer to return to the exact stance on the shooting line after retrieving arrows. Stance deviations of even a few inches can cause sighting and aiming problems, which in turn lead to accuracy problems. *Consistency* is a key word in the sport of target archery.

Figures 4.5, 4.6, 4.7, and 4.8 show four different types of stance foot placement used by archers.

Many archers prefer the even stance shown in figure 4.5. In this stance, the shooting line is straddled and weight is evenly distributed over both feet. The heels and toes of the feet are aligned, and the middle of the instep of the foot is aligned with the center of the intended target. The beginning archer may want to try this stance and determine how it feels while shooting several practice rounds. Some archers use this stance, but it is not the stance of choice based on scientific criteria relating to static equilibrium and perception of the visual field. Based on those criteria, the open and oblique stances are better. But, individual choice is a pleasant fact of life in archery!

The open stance shown in figure 4.6 is recommended for the beginning archer during the initial learning period. The feet should be shoulder-width apart in the open stance. It is recommended that the body weight be distributed evenly on both feet. Initially, the archer should take an even stance with both feet in position so an imaginary line can be drawn through the insteps of your feet to the center of the gold on the target face. To "open the stance," the left foot is moved

Figure 4.5
Even stance.

Figure 4.6
Open stance.

Figure 4.7
Oblique stance.

Figure 4.8
Closed stance.

backwards approximately six inches as shown. The open stance allows the archer to see the target better than using the even stance. Many good baseball hitters use an open stance for the same reason, that is, they can see the ball better after it is pitched.

Once the placement of the feet has been determined for your open stance and you are comfortable on the line, foot placement should be marked. After shooting an end of arrows, you return to the *exact* foot placement each time. You may have to make body adjustments after gaining shooting experience. The way to make these adjustments is by rotating your trunk, or lumbar-thoracic spine. Keep the stance stable and rotate your lower spine as needed to align the bow with the target. This is important both for viewing the target better and for aiming purposes.

Some elite archers use what is called the oblique stance, as shown in figure 4.7. This stance is attained by placing the toe of the left foot nearest the target on a line with the target and pivoting the left foot so it is at a forty-five-degree angle to the target. The heel of the right foot is then placed in line with the toe

Figure 4.9
Body position for addressing the target in target archery—oblique stance. Shooting line is straddled. (Courtesy of Kathy Greene)

of the left foot. The oblique stance allows the bow arm to remain in a position where there will be optimum clearance of the bowstring when the arrow is released. Furthermore, with the weight distributed over the balls of the feet, total body equilibrium is enhanced. The target is also seen clearly while using the oblique stance.

A closed stance is shown in figure 4.8. The shooting line is straddled and the weight is evenly distributed over both feet. The left foot is simply moved forward a few inches so a heel-toe relationship exists between the left and right feet respectively. This type of stance is not very popular among archers, but it is an option.

It is recommended that the beginning archer learn while using the open stance. After you have learned archery shooting fundamentals to the point that you are comfortable on the range, try various stances during the shooting process. The final stance chosen should be the one allowing the greatest degree of comfort, stability, target visibility, and accuracy for the individual.

The phrase "addressing the target" simply means that the target archer assumes the stance of his or her choice and straddles the shooting line (figs. 4.5, 4.6, 4.7, and 4.8) prepared to shoot. The arrows in those figures show the direction to the target. The overall body position for addressing the target is shown in figure 4.9. The right-handed archer holds the bow in the left hand, and the left side of the body is nearest the intended target. If a ground quiver is used to hold arrows, it is placed in front of the archer in a convenient position so arrows can be easily reached without changing the stance.

Figure 4.10
Nocking the arrow. Note the traditional nocking angle. (Courtesy of Kathy Greene)

Nocking

Nocking the arrow is proper placement of the arrow in its shooting position on the bowstring. In target archery, this is started only when all archers have assumed their stances on the shooting line. The archer holds the bow next to the hip nearer the target, as shown in figure 4.10. The arrow shaft is laid on the arrow rest. The arrow nock is placed on the bowstring with the index feather upward at the serving. Bowstrings should be equipped with nocking points to define the area for arrow placement on the serving during nocking. Nocking points are placed slightly wider than the width of the arrow nock so adjustments can be made as needed.

The archer should place the arrow nock on the string one-eighth of an inch below the nocking point. A ninety-degree angle is formed between the arrow and bowstring. This "traditional nocking angle" can be seen in figure 4.10. The nocking position may be changed one-sixteenth of an inch or so in the bow tuning process if abnormal flight patterns such as fishtailing, porpoising, or minnowing are noted. (See Chapter 10 for definitions.) However, for the beginning archer, that type of problem in the flight stability of the arrow is more likely to be the result of poor release mechanics than of improper bow tuning. (See the bow tuning section in this chapter.) All skill fundamentals must be mastered in order for properly tuned tackle to be effective.

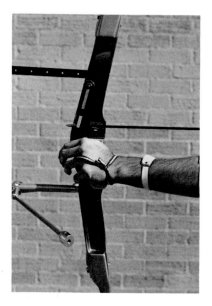 

Figure 4.11
Bow hold. The archer must keep the fingers relaxed. Note clicker, arrow rest, stabilizers, and finger sling.

Figure 4.12
Bow hold—hand pressure is exerted high, low, or on the bow's pivot point depending upon the type of bow used and the archer's preference.

Bow Hold

When discussing the bow hand, terms such as "holding" and "gripping" are misnomers. They tend to be misleading as far as archery skill is concerned. The archer does not hold or grip the bow as the draw is made. The bow is literally held only while nocking and after the arrow reaches the target. *During the process of shooting, however, the bow is actually kept in place by pressure on the bow hand at the pivot point of the bow.* This pivot point pressure you feel in your hand against the bow is the resultant counterforce of the force applied to move the bowstring in the opposite direction during the draw to the anchor point. *The bow should never be gripped firmly by the hand during the drawing, aiming, and release phases of shooting.* Avoiding a firmly held bow minimizes torque when the arrow is released. Torque of the bow prior to and at release causes erratic arrow flight.

As can be seen in figures 4.11 and 4.12, the bow is placed between the thumb and index finger. The bow arm-bow hold alignment technique should align the middle of the bow arm with the center of the bow. That will produce better balance between the pressures exerted on the bow handle and the line-of-pull of the bowstring. This balance of the two forces tends to reduce bow twist, or torque, as the shot is made, and that improves your accuracy because the bowstring travels in a straight line as the release is made. The arrow is not thrown off-line by lateral movement of the bowstring as it starts its flight.

The grip can either be high, medium, or low in regard to the position and pressure applied by the hand to the bow at the bow's pivot point. A high grip was the preference of archers who shot with bows made primarily of wood. The high grip was needed to minimize torques. Modern bow designs and materials have reduced (although not totally eliminated) torque problems, so more target archers now utilize medium and low grips effectively. Each archer should experiment with pressure placement of the bow hand high, on, or low in relation to the bow's pivot point. Pragmatically, the pressure placement that works and feels the best with your tackle is the one to use.

There is a tendency for the archer to let the bow pressure position slip slightly to the right or clockwise during the process of shooting. This is attributable to a lapse in concentration and/or the fatigue factor. This tendency can be counteracted, when noted, by a very slight counterclockwise rotation of the thumb against the bow handle while concurrently extending the thumb forward toward the target. The "rotation of the thumb" observed in this technique is actually due to a forearm motion known as supination.

There should be a relaxed feeling within the bow hand as much as possible. The palm of the hand should not apply pressure on the bow. The index finger may wrap around the bow, but it should not grip it. Some archers like to have the tip of the thumb and index finger relax and touch gently as a consistency checkpoint for the bow hold, but this is a matter of personal choice. Holding the fingers on the bow hand as relaxed as possible will also heighten accuracy. This is because the opportunity for muscle fatigue in the forearm musculature of the bow arm is lessened considerably by not gripping with the fingers. The large muscles that control finger motions (extrinsic hand muscles) are located in your forearm. If they are not being contracted to flex the fingers to grip the bow, the fatigue factor is minimized. This lessens muscle tremor due to tiredness and helps increase accuracy.

Even an undesired motion as small as one degree of the bow arm unit at the time of release has a negative effect on accurate arrow flight. Expert athletes in all sports know how to "relax under pressure" at critical times to ensure that they reach their potentials. Relaxing musculature consistently during the important bow hold is one of those times for the target archer.

Drawing

Drawing is the act of pulling the bowstring to the anchor point on the archer's face. This is analogous to cocking a pistol prior to firing a bullet. One major difference is that there are opportunities for human error while drawing a bowstring, while cocking a pistol is an error-free mechanical action. Drawing may start as soon as the arrow is nocked properly and the target archer is properly positioned on the shooting line.

Controlled breathing is very important during the drawing and subsequent aiming processes. A system should be found that is comfortable for the archer during the total drawing, aiming, and release time period. One procedure used commonly is to take a deep breath and exhale it just prior to starting the draw. Another deep inhalation is made promptly thereafter and the breath is held until the archer sees the arrow strike the target. The total elapsed time for breath-holding for most archers should be no more than ten seconds. That is the approximate time frame for drawing, aiming, releasing, and the follow-through.

Some archers use a variation on this breath-holding technique. When the sight pin is in place on the target during aiming, a small amount of breath is released or exhaled. The remaining breath is held as aiming is finalized. The release is made, and normal breathing resumes when the arrow hits the target. This breathing procedure tends to relieve some of the internal pressure in the thoracic region as well as muscle tension. Beginning archers should try different breathing mechanics until they find one that feels comfortable.

It should also be noted that breathing mechanics and subsequent respiratory functions are more efficient when the archer has a better than average cardio-vascular fitness status. The best measurement of this is your maximal oxygen consumption level. Maintaining an above average level of health-related fitness can prolong your career as a competitive target archer. (See Chapter 8 for fitness guidelines.)

The archer's head position remains fixed from the time the archer addresses the target (fig. 4.9) through the release and follow-through phases of shooting (fig. 4.21). This simple stable position of the neck tends to be a problem for beginning archers. It should not be if the following principle is observed: *The bowstring is drawn to your head (anchor point) instead of moving the head toward the bowstring during the draw.*

Figure 4.13 shows the commonly used three-finger bowstring grip. (It should be noted that some excellent target archers use a two-finger grip.) A shooting glove, such as that shown in figure 4.13, protects the fingers, but a finger tab (fig. 4.14) is recommended for use over a shooting glove in target archery. Proper placement of the fingers on the bowstring prior to drawing is very important to minimize release problems. The little finger and thumb do not touch the bowstring. The remaining three fingers are placed on the bowstring with them "hooked" on the string at or slightly past the first or distal interphalangeal joints of your fingers.

The large knuckle joints of the hand are not flexed at any time during the draw. These joints remain extended and stable at all times. The wrist is also kept straight or extended throughout the draw and release phases. The wrist should never move in any direction (flexed, hyperextended etc.) during the draw and subsequent release of the arrow.

Figure 4.14 shows the relationship between the index and middle fingers and the nock of the arrow while using a finger tab. Position of the fingers on the bowstring next to the arrow nock is difficult to maintain as the pressure increases during the draw. The essence of the problem lies in the nature of the musculature within the hand. As fingers are flexed, it is natural for them to be drawn tightly together into a fist. Such a mechanism is great for gripping objects. It is also highly functional in the sport of boxing. But it creates arrow flight problems for the archer!

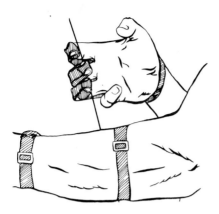

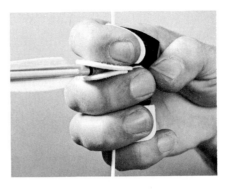

Figure 4.14
The three-finger grip while using a finger tab. Care must be taken not to exert undue or unequal pressure on the arrow nock. (Courtesy Wilson Brothers, Route 1, Elkland, Missouri 65644)

Figure 4.13
Traditional three-finger grip with shooting glove. (Logan)

Because the joints of the index and middle fingers are flexed and the pressure increases during the draw, the two fingers have a tendency to apply pressure on the arrow nock. Beginning archers find that the points of their arrows will wave around and fall completely off the arrow rest as the draw is made. This common problem is caused by excessive finger pressure on the arrow nock. The archer must compensate for the gripping effect of the hand musculature prior to the draw by placing the index finger one-eighth of an inch above the arrow nock. The middle finger can be placed the same distance below the arrow nock or just beneath the nock. It may seem that the arrow will become disengaged from the bowstring before the draw can be made, but this feeling will be eliminated by the use of properly placed nocking points and practice. The principle to bear in mind is: *Pressure exerted by fingers on the arrow nock should be kept at an absolute minimum prior to and during the draw and release.*

As the bowstring is being drawn, it will move from its position across the flexed distal joints of your three fingers involved in the grip to a position *diagonal* to that joint line. If you are performing correctly, the amount of pressure on each of the three fingers differs. The middle finger should have the greatest feeling of pressure, and the third finger will have control over a good percentage of the remaining force on the hand. The index or top finger has minimal pressure on it, because its role is one of control at the time of release.

The problem of pressure against the arrow nock exerted by fingers during the draw process is completely eliminated when using a release aid. As a result, release aids tend to take a considerable amount of "sport" out of archery. *That is one reason that target archery rules forbid the use of release aids.* One of the true challenges of target archery is the ability of the archer to control finger pressure on the nock during the draw and through release. Release aids are legal in other archery sports, and they are discussed Chapter 6.

As the draw is started, the bow is moved to a vertical position as shown in figure 4.15. The archer in figure 4.15 is midway through the drawing procedure. The bowstring hand is being pulled toward the anchor point on the face. During this pull or drawing action, it may be necessary for the archer to make a compensatory motion within the forearm (radioulnar joint) to maintain proper string alignment and pressure on the fingers as noted above.

There is a natural tendency to elevate the elbow slightly during the draw. The equal and opposite motion of the hand results in a slight diagonal change of the finger-string alignment noted above, because your hand moves downward as the elbow moves upward. If that string position were left unchecked, it would cause some unnecessary string torque and pressure on the arrow nock. Poor arrow flight would be the result at the time of release. That problem can be counteracted by rotating the forearm a few degrees clockwise (supinate the radioulnar joint) during the draw or upon reaching your anchor point. The result of that motion will move your little finger closer to your neck. The little finger should be close to the neck as seen in figure 4.19. The little finger at the end of your draw should not be in a position analogous to daintily holding a tea cup at a social event!

It is essential for the archer to understand that the force for drawing the bow is provided primarily by powerful muscles on the posterior aspect of the shoulder and within the shoulder girdle. (Specific muscular detail for drawing is presented in Chapter 8.)

Since musculature within the drawing arm does not provide the primary draw force, what is the role of this musculature during the draw? It is necessary that the archer keep the arm musculature as relaxed as possible during the draw. These muscles are handling external tension due to the bow weight; therefore, they are stabilizing the joints within the arm. There is no need to contract them further and create more internal tension. That would be counterproductive to good accuracy. The finger grip provides a "hook" on the bowstring. The shoulder and shoulder girdle muscles exert the internal, contractile force to move the string, while the bowstring arm is simply the lever through which the force is exerted. That is accomplished as much as possible without adding tension within the arm. This is another time when the skilled archer knows when and how to "relax under pressure." The potential for shot accuracy is enhanced, and that is the "name of the game" in target archery!

The completed draw is shown in figure 4.16. The bow arm and drawing arm should be studied carefully in this figure. The bow arm has been abducted or raised to shoulder height. The wrist and elbow are kept extended at all times, and they remain stable (nonmoving) throughout the drawing, aiming, and release phases. The bow arm will react by moving downward as the arrow is released. The drawing arm is in a straight line from the archer's elbow to the arrow point.

The bowstring should not slap the bow arm after it has been released if the bow arm position is correct. The arm guard may be brushed periodically. This can be caused by extraneous shoulder, elbow, or wrist movements. "String slaps" will diminish in frequency as the archer increases his or her skill level. Some

Figure 4.15
Start of the draw. (Courtesy of Kathy Greene)

Figure 4.16
Completed draw and anchor point. The bowstring is drawn to the stable head. (Courtesy of Kathy Greene)

archers, due to unusual bone anatomy of the elbow, require adjustments of their body segment positions to eliminate painful contusions caused by continued "string slaps" on the bow arm.

If the bowstring hits the bow arm above the arm guard, the archer's stance probably should be changed to the oblique stance described previously. For most individuals this should eliminate the problem. If such a stance adjustment does not work, a bow arm adjustment should be made. The arm should always remain abducted at the shoulder joint and extended at the elbow joint as shown in figure 4.16. To make the bow arm adjustment, the bow should be held in position horizontal to the ground initially. Slowly rotate the bow to the vertical position by laterally rotating the bow shoulder—move the bow counterclockwise—with the elbow extended. This may move the bow arm out of the path of the bowstring. This alignment should be checked visually by an instructor and the archer prior to releasing an arrow. If the above alignment adjustment does not appear to be satisfactory, the bow arm should be rotated clockwise by medially rotating the shoulder joint until the bowstring can be seen to clear the arm. This is called *canting* the bow. *The elbow should never be flexed to allow the string to clear the bow arm.* These bow adjustment procedures are recommended only for those people who have arm and elbow configurations that elicit continued "string slaps." The sport cannot be enjoyed if the bow arm is contused frequently. That trauma can be avoided.

The alignment of the drawing arm with the arrow and bow as shown in figure 4.16 is important. If the drawing form is perfect, there will be a straight line running from the tip of the elbow through the forearm, wrist, hand, arrow nock, and shaft to the arrow point. Due to anatomic differences, it is not possible for all archers to align the drawing limb perfectly with the arrow. However, all archers should attempt to come as close to this alignment as physically possible. If this is accomplished, there will be a smoother transfer of the potential energy within the drawn bow to kinetic energy into the arrow at release.

A straight drawing arm and arrow alignment facilitates a smooth release. If, as noted, the elbow is too high, it is inevitable that the index finger will exert pressure downward on the arrow nock at release. This produces porpoising and erratic arrow flight. The ACTION of releasing the bowstring should produce the desired REACTION of perfect forward or linear motion of the bowstring and arrow.

After you have read this chapter and shot a few ends on the range, it is highly recommended that you read the first section of Chapter 8, "Muscle Analysis of Shooting," to gain some understanding of the muscular control and forces needed as you establish a stance, nock, draw to your anchor point, and release. Finite control and accuracy in archery are reasons for keeping your tackle fine tuned. Just as important, the archer must be cognizant of "tuning" the muscles most involved in performing the sport of target archery.

Anchor Point

The term "anchor point" is defined as the place on an archer's face where the hand is placed consistently with the bowstring at full draw. Anchor points are usually described as being high or low on the face (figs. 4.17, 4.18, and 4.19). An anchor point on or under the mandible or jaw bone is termed *low.* An anchor point on or near the zygomatic arch or the bone inferior and lateral to the eye is considered to be *high.* Preference for a particular anchor point usually involves such factors as facial contour and type of shooting. Many field archers, bow hunters, and instinctive shooters use the high anchor point (fig. 4.19). These archers like to think they sight down the shaft of the arrow, but actually they tend to look over the arrow point. Variations on the low anchor point are used most often by target archers who rely on bowsights for aiming. Both types of anchor points can be used effectively for any kind of shooting. The archer ultimately should use the anchor point that feels most comfortable and is most consistent with good aiming for the type of archery sport of greatest interest.

It is recommended that the beginner utilize a low anchor point while learning target archery fundamentals. Figure 4.17 shows the traditional low anchor point. To learn and perform any athletic activity effectively, one must utilize as many senses as possible. The low anchor point involves the touch, pressure, sight, and kinesthetic senses. The index finger is placed under the chin, and moderate pressure is applied to the mandible or jawbone by the index finger. This low anchor position on the chin allows the bowstring to bisect and *gently touch* the chin, lips, and nose. The archer must not compress or apply heavy pressure on the tissue of these parts of the anatomy. For consistency, the upper and lower teeth must touch gently; that is, the mouth should be shut. The teeth should never be clenched.

Figure 4.17
The recommended low anchor point for beginning target archers.

Figure 4.18
The side of face anchor point. (Courtesy of Kathy Greene)

Figure 4.19
A high anchor point used most commonly for bow hunting. (Courtesy of Kathy Greene)

That type of tension is contraindicated in target archery. As noted, the more one can be "relaxed" during the process of shooting the better. Static contraction of the jaw muscles to clench your teeth has negative reactions in the degree of tension within the muscles of the neck and rib cage, and that interferes with breathing and respiration.

Some target archers use what is known as a "side of face" anchor point if the low anchor point described above seems awkward (fig. 4.18). The head is rotated toward the target as described previously. The bowstring is drawn to a point where it actually touches the side of the mouth, that is, the right side of the mouth for a right-handed archer. The chin is not moved to accommodate the string placement. The hand is anchored *under* the jaw, with the index finger in contact with the side of the mandible (jawbone), similar to the low anchor position. Some archers believe that one advantage of the "side of face" anchor is that alignment of the drawing arm and arrow is easier to attain.

Some beginning archers believe that they must change the anchor point and length of draw when shooting from varying distances. This is a disastrous mistake. The anchor point and draw remain constant for all distances. Adjustments for shooting varying distances are accomplished by changing angles of the bow arm at the shoulder joint. The extent of each adjustment is determined by the capacity of the bow to propel the arrow at velocities needed to cover the distance adequately.

Aiming

Bowsight and instinctive are the two aiming techniques used extensively by archers. Use of a bowsight for aiming is absolutely essential in target archery, and bowsights are also utilized by serious bow hunters who know how to gauge distances in hunting environments. (Exact distances are always known in target archery.) The most sporting technique for aiming in archery is called instinctive shooting. No aiming device is mounted on the bow, so this is often called "bare bow shooting." Learning how to shoot instinctively is interesting, because most archers describe this aiming technique with slight variations and fascinating embellishments.

The beginner should not be too concerned about any aiming procedure until he or she feels comfortable handling appropriate archery tackle and performing the basic fundamentals involving the stance, nocking, drawing, anchor point, release, and follow-through. To gain familiarity and confidence with the tackle and skill fundamentals, shooting should be performed initially over relatively short distances on the range. Shooting point blank eliminates the pressure to aim during the first few shooting sessions. Once a general understanding of fundamentals is acquired, the archer should turn attention toward bowsight aiming and grouping ends of arrows in small patterns on the target from various distances.

Bowsight Aiming

The use of the bowsight will greatly enhance one's ability to hit the intended target; consequently, the use of a bowsight is recommended in preference to any other target archery aiming technique. The archer must establish a bowsight setting on the bow for each shooting distance. This requires the archer to shoot a number of ends at each distance to experiment with bowsight settings. To use a bowsight, the archer places the sighting device in the middle of the intended target—gold on a regulation target archery face—and releases the arrow properly. This procedure is repeated until several ends have been shot. The archer must continually check the grouping patterns on the target face and note the direction of the hits from the gold. For example, if six ends of arrows are shot at a target without changing the bowsight setting and all arrows consistently group low and left on a regulation target face, *the archer must move the bowsight setting device down and left for the next series of shots in order to move the grouping into the center of the target.* If the adjustment of the bowsight is correct and shooting fundamentals are good, the next end should hit the gold. The principle to keep in mind for bowsight adjustments is as follows: THE BOWSIGHT SHOULD ALWAYS BE MOVED IN THE DIRECTION(S) OF THE ARROW GROUPING ERROR.

The bowsights shown in figures 3.10 and 3.12 can be adjusted to compensate for any directional error. They can be moved left, right, up, and down to assist the archer. As noted in the example above, if the bowsight were moved properly down and left (error directions), the next end of arrows shot should group in or near the gold on the target face. This will occur *if* the archer executes all of the other fundamental skills properly. A perfect bowsight setting cannot compensate for poor shooting mechanics, mismatched tackle, or improper tackle tuning!

Concentration and intelligent analyses of the situation play an important role in the process of aiming. Archery becomes a "mental game" once the shooting fundamentals have been learned properly. The total shot must be considered; that is, each step must be performed consistently and properly leading to aiming. Also, wind direction and velocity as well as other weather conditions (humidity etc.) are brought into the aiming decision. There is a subjective, kinesthetic feeling the experienced archer attains when the sight pin is being moved to and held on the gold during the aiming process prior to release. Progress is made only through intensifying your thought processes on the task at hand. Nothing must be allowed to interfere with one's concentration as the sight pin is being placed on the gold. When the fundamentals are under control, concentration regulates the aiming process and the degree of scoring success one has in target archery.

Does the sight pin always have to be absolutely fixed on the gold at the time of release? Each archer has adapted an aiming procedure based on his or her overall shooting style. Some do attempt perfection on every shot, and they strive for precise sight pin settings on the target at the instant the arrow is released. That can add stress and increase the frustration level for some archers, because it has the potential to deflate confidence when the arrow does not hit the gold. If the aiming procedure described above does not work for you, try moving the sight pin into a *target area* instead of a precise spot in the center of the target. (Keep in mind that you have a 4¼ inch "margin of error" on either side of the exact center of the target in target archery.) Release the arrow properly once the sight pin is in the boundary lines of your "target area" for aiming. Many excellent archers use this method with good results. It removes some of the stress concurrent with always fixating on a precise spot. Each person must define his or her target aiming areas for each specific shooting distance on the range.

One must be aware of what effect winds at different velocities and directions will have on the accuracy of arrows. Aiming rules for wind conditions differ with the archer and tackle being used. Aiming adjustments also have to be made for other weather factors such as wind, humidity, and rain. The experience of shooting in all kinds of weather conditions is the best teacher, so practice during winds, rain, extreme heat, humidity, as well as perfect weather.

Figure 4.20
Bowstring alignment used during aiming.
(Courtesy of Patrick Brunhoeber)

Sighting and aiming with the bow and arrow differ considerably from aiming a rifle. The rifleman tends to look down the top of the rifle barrel through a series of mounted sights. While using the low anchor point in particular, the archer does not and should not look down the shaft of the arrow. The line of sight should be through the aiming device on the bowsight toward the intended target. The bowsight is mounted above the arrow shaft to align with the archer's field of vision.

The target archery bow has an unofficial rear sighting device, the bowstring. When the archer's head is in the correct position, the archer tends to "look through" the bowstring. The string is set toward the right side of the bow as seen in figure 4.20. This avoids having the bowstring running through the sight window of the bow and spoiling your view. The bowsight is aligned with the center of the target. The checking of the bowstring alignment becomes automatic with experience, and most of your concentration for aiming purposes must be directed toward the bowsight pin. Using the bowstring alignment as a checkpoint does place the arrow in a definite direction relative to the target. The archer must be able to maintain control of the alignment between this "rear sight" and the centered front sight if accurate aiming is to remain consistent.

Peep sights are available for use as rear sights on bowstrings. These are designed to be used with front-mounted sights as shown in figure 3.12. However, National Archery Association rules stipulate that, "A bowstring must not in any way offer aid in aiming through peephole marking or any other means." *Peep sights on bowstrings are illegal for use in target archery.* They can be used in other archery sports.

There are archery authorities who contend that the eye nearest the target should always be closed during the act of shooting. This is a fallacy! What if the eye away from the target—the right eye for a right-handed archer—is the weak eye? Should the good left eye be closed and the weak eye remain open? Th could have a detrimental effect upon accuracy. Many superb right-handed archers shoot with both eyes open or with the left eye partially closed and the right eye open. Eye preference is a highly individualized matter. It is recommended that the beginner try shooting while using all combinations of eye openings and closures. Each archer should use the eye closure or opening that feels most comfortable and produces the best results. Some archers enjoy target archery without using either eye. They are blind! (See Chapter 5.) Archery is truly a sport that can be adapted for everyone.

Instinctive Aiming

Many people who hunt with rifles and bows use high anchor points. This allows them to partially sight down the arrow shaft and over the point if a bowsight is not used. Many bow hunters do not use a bowsight, but rely upon instinctive aiming techniques. Instinctive aiming is utilized by many field archers also. There are tournaments held in field archery for bare bow and instinctive shooters exclusively. Many excellent scores are recorded in these tournaments. The target archer can also use instinctive aiming techniques if desired. The lack of mechanical aiming devices adds to the spirit of true sport.

Each archer who uses instinctive aiming usually provides a slightly different version of how this task is accomplished. Basically, the instinctive archer must have excellent eyesight and depth perception. The term "instinct" for this style of shooting is grossly incorrect from a scientific standpoint. Through extensive practice over a long time, the archer increases skills related to kinesthetic awareness, conditioned responses to visual stimuli, correct reactions to wind velocities and directions, and judgment of the strengths and weaknesses of the tackle being used. These factors, and others, enable the skilled archer to adjust rapidly as he or she looks over the arrow point toward a point of aim and the intended target.

As noted, the instinctive shooter makes several cognitive judgments prior to releasing the arrow. The archer perceives a space or gap between the arrow point and intended target. The bow arm moves the arrow into position for the shot. Here is where individual differences abound. Instinctive shooters approach the shot by moving the bow downward, upward, left, or right toward the target. Most, however, choose to start with the bow arm held high and move the bow downward. (This is acceptable if the range safety zone is large enough to protect people should an arrow be accidentally released before the bow arm becomes parallel to the ground.) The release of the arrow is calculated to coincide with the visual perception of the gap being closed by the arrow point coming into view of the target. Most instinctive shooters will hold the bow motionless for a second when the gap has been closed in order to implement an efficient release. This is a "pure form of shooting," and there are many expert instinctive archers. This is particularly true in field archery and bow hunting. For target archery, the bowsight method of aiming is recommended unless you are competing in a bare bow tournament.

and Follow-Through

the arrow properly is the most important fundamental of shooting.
elements are: (1) relaxation and (2) concentration. The paradoxical
these two factors at this critical stage of shooting adds another dimension to the challenge of archery as a sport. As the reader realizes, it is extremely
difficult to relax during a time of intense concentration. Both of these elements
must be under complete control, however, to achieve any degree of success in
archery. That is another reason people regard target archery as a "mental game,"
especially among elite archers.

Releasing an arrow is not the result of forceful finger extension. It is an act
of relaxing or controlling muscular interaction within the bow hand, forearm,
and shoulder girdle (trapezius). When the muscles controlling flexion within the
three drawing fingers release some of their tension during contraction, the
bowstring will move forward as a result of the pressure brought about by the bow
weight at complete draw. If the release is good, the extending fingers will clear
the string as it moves forward. On the other hand, if the extending fingers are
not relaxed enough and touch the bowstring, that is a cause of erratic arrow
flight. The archer does very little muscular work at the time of release in terms
of consciously extending the finger joints.

As stated previously, the main problems are *relaxation* and concurrent control of hand, forearm, and shoulder girdle muscles in conjunction with maximum
concentration on aiming prior to and at the time of release. The archer starts
intense concentration prior to nocking and continues until the arrow is released.
It is too late to think about the shot when the arrow is in flight! That is the time
to either enjoy watching the arrow's perfect trajectory into the gold or analyze
the flight for problems.

How can the fingers be relaxed effectively under the tension of bow weight?
The key to this lies in understanding the location of the muscles and their tendons
that are under the greatest tension. Those muscles are within your forearm, but
the tendons are located on the back of the wrist and continue into the hand and
fingers. These are the finger joint extensor tendons, which are stretched as the
fingers flex to grip the bowstring. These extensor tendons can be palpated
(touched) on the back of your hand. As you make a fist, feel the tension increase
in the muscles in your forearm. This tension is increased considerably when the
bow weight is being held by the three flexed fingers. When you are ready to release an arrow, relax the gripping fingers by concentrating on releasing tension
within the finger extensor tendons on the posterior aspect (back) of your hand.
Concentration and release mechanics are aided by having a "thought focus point"
such as this.

A clicker is shown mounted on the sight window of the bow in figure 4.11.
A clicker is a shooting aid that has the potential to add consistency to form and
enhance scores. The arrow is placed under the clicker when nocked. If the draw
is made smoothly to the established anchor point, the arrow point will pass beyond
the clicker in about two seconds. The clicker will make a "click" sound against

the bow, informing the archer—who should be concentrating on drawing and aiming—that the release can be made. *The "click" should never be anticipated. A smooth release is executed shortly after the "click" has been heard.*

A clicker is not recommended as a shooting aid until the target archery fundamentals have been learned. The draw and anchor point must be established. Any change of anchor point would require a clicker change. When the shooting fundamentals are consistent, have the arrow point position marked on the bow when you are at your anchor point. The clicker is then placed on the bow so only one-eighth inch of your point lies under the clicker at full draw. The "click" of the clicker is made by continuing to move the draw arm elbow backward (horizontal abduction of your shoulder joint). It is very important for the archer to understand that the drawing arm moves through its range-of-motion without interruption. The drawing elbow is moved backward by large shoulder and shoulder girdle muscles (horizontal abductors) to the point that the clicker will be heard. The archer must never make extraneous motions with the bow arm to activate the clicker. If the clicker is mounted properly and the archer's shooting fundamentals are sound, it can be a beneficial shooting aid used to: (1) enhance shooting consistency, (2) facilitate aiming concentration, and (3) assist in the timing of the release.

A bow sling is recommended to help the archer during the release and follow-through phases of shooting. There are different types of bow slings available. Any one of these will help the archer keep the bow from falling to the ground after release. The type chosen is a matter of individual preference. In choosing a bow sling the basic thing to remember is that nothing should *prematurely interrupt* the bow's movement toward the target after the arrow has been released. The function of the bow sling is to hold the bow from falling to the ground *after* the arrow is in flight beyond the bow. If the bow sling or the archer's bow hand grasps the bow at or immediately prior to release, arrow flight will be erratic. The archer must work to ensure that this does not occur. The bow as well as the arrow should be free to move forward at release. The bow sling should ease one's mind about what happens to the bow once the arrow is in flight.

Figure 4.20 shows the use of a sling. The sling is a very valuable asset in shooting. The sling enables the archer to release the arrow without worrying about the bow falling to the ground. Extraneous motions of the wrist joint are thereby minimized. The sling supports the bow after the shot, and the archer can grasp the bow with the hand after he or she sees the arrow embedded in the target.

Figure 4.21 shows proper release form. The elbow of the bowstring arm should not extend appreciably after or during the release. The bowstring hand will usually move backward in a position relatively close to the chin or neck after release. This is a natural recoil action following release. The beginner must avoid the habit of trying to release the arrow by hyperextending the wrist—moving the back of the hand toward the forearm—or allowing the bowstring to roll off the fingertips under its own pressure. Release by "plucking" of the string is another cause of erratic arrow grouping. Also, the elbow of the bowstring arm should

Figure 4.21
Release and follow-through positions. Watch the arrow until it hits the target before moving the arms. (Courtesy of Kathy Greene)

never be extended and the arm waved around at or following the release. Arm actions like those of orchestra conductors and bull fighters should be avoided in the archery release! Upon release, the elbow remains flexed, and the bow will rotate clockwise from the pivot point during the follow-through phase (fig. 4.21).

To "follow-through" in archery means to hold the release position until the arrow is safely embedded in the target. The following are features of a good follow-through: (1) the fingers on the bowstring hand are relaxed, (2) head and eyes are turned toward the target following the flight of the arrow, (3) the bow arm is extended toward the target, and (4) the bow hand is gripping the bow with the help of the sling. Why is follow-through important? It is absolutely essential for consistent performance and minute accuracy. Any atypical motions observed in the follow-through phase of shooting were initiated a fraction of a second *prior to and continued through the release phase.* Motions of that type are contraindicated as far as archery accuracy is concerned.

Figure 4.22 and figure 8.1 show the important phases of target archery fundamentals from nocking to follow-through. *The appearance of simplicity is very deceptive!*

Scoring

Target archery competition is conducted in *rounds.* There are numerous championship and nonchampionship rounds, some of which are discussed in Chapter 5. Each round is different in terms of the number of arrows to be shot, and in the designated distances. A specific number of arrows are shot during each round before the archers are allowed to walk to the target, score, and retrieve arrows. The set number of arrows (usually three, five, or six) to be shot during a round is called an *end.*

A Nocking

B Drawing

C Anchor Point

D Release and Follow-through

Figure 4.22
Nocking through the follow-through in target archery. NEVER UNDERESTIMATE THE
COMPLEXITY OF SOMETHING THAT APPEARS TO BE THE EPITOME OF SIMPLICITY WHEN
PERFORMED BY AN EXPERT! (Courtesy of Kathy Greene)

There are two target faces used for scoring purposes in outdoor target archery rounds. The 122-centimeter (48-inch) target face is used at distances of 90 meters (98.46 yards), 70 meters (76.58 yards), and 60 meters (65.64 yards). An 80-centimeter target face is used in rounds when distances of 50 meters (54.70 yards) and 30 meters (32.82 yards) are used. The center of the target should be 51 inches above the ground, and the target face is inclined away from the shooting line twelve to eighteen degrees.

The official target archery faces are divided into five concentric color zones. These scoring rings are each colored differently. From the center or bull's eye outward they are gold, red, light blue, black, and white. Each of these concentric colored rings is divided into two equal halves for scoring purposes. (The exact center of the gold is marked, and it is known as the *pinhole*.) The ten concentric rings on the target face are used for scoring as follows: inner gold, ten points; outer gold, nine points; inner red, eight points; outer red, seven points; inner light blue, six points; outer light blue, five points; inner black, four points; outer black, three points; inner white, two points; outer white, one point. The outer or nonscoring area of the target is known as the *petticoat*.

Indoor rounds are shot at shorter distances. This requires the use of smaller target faces. Distances of 18 meters (19.69 yards) and 25 meters (27.35 yards) are common indoor distances. A 40-centimeter target face is used at 18 meters, and a 60-centimeter face is used at 25 meters.

Two archers on each target act as scorekeepers. Each archer tells the scorer the values of his or her arrows starting with the highest values first. Scores plus the number of hits per end are written on the score sheet, as shown in figure 4.23. High scores are recorded first for each end.

All arrows remain in their places embedded in the target mat until they have been scored and verified by the designated scorekeepers. Pulling arrows from a target mat mounted on a tripod stand should be done with caution. First, check to see that no one is standing behind you as arrows are pulled from the target. An arrow nock in the eye can be traumatic! The arrow should be grasped near the target face and pulled by the shaft with one hand. The other hand should provide a counterforce for the pull by being placed against the target mat (fig. 4.24). This simple procedure eliminates the embarrassing and costly experience of pulling a target full of arrows onto the ground. Fiberglass arrows can be broken and aluminum arrows may be bent when a target mat is pulled to the ground.

If an arrow is embedded in the target mat up to its fletching or nock area, it should be removed by pulling it completely through the mat in the direction of its flight. That practice keeps the fletching or vanes from being damaged or torn from the shaft. If an arrow "snakes in the grass" or lies horizontal to the earth and covered with grass, it should also be removed by pulling it forward through the grass.

There are several scoring variations to account for atypical arrow hits and other unusual situations. Arrows that *rebound from the target face* can be scored in several ways if they are witnessed. The most common procedure used for class situations and competitions other than international or national tournaments is

SCORECARD
SCHOLASTIC ROUND

Name Al Trombetta

Class Archery Techniques

40 yards						Hits	Score
9	9	9	9	9	9	6	54
9	9	7	5	3		5	33
7	7	7	5	3	1	6	30
9	9	9	7	7	7	6	48
Distance Score						23	165
30 yards							
9	9	9	9	9	9	6	54
9	9	9	9	7	7	6	50
9	9	7	7	5	5	6	42
9	9	7	5	3	1	6	34
Distance Score						24	180
Total Score						47	345

Figure 4.24
Arrow values are given to the scorer by the archer to whom the arrows belong. The scorer and other archers assigned to the target verify the scores. After all arrows have been scored, they are removed from the target. (Bud Clay and Linda Atwood)

Figure 4.23
A sample scorecard for the Scholastic Round.

to score these rebounds as seven points. An arrow that rebounds from the petticoat area of the target is scored zero, and it is not counted as a hit. A rebounding arrow can also be scored according to where it struck the target face, if it is witnessed.

In the classic situation whereby one arrow impales another arrow already embedded in a scoring arrow on the target face, the last arrow is awarded the same value as the struck arrow. The "fantasy tight group" for an end of six arrows would be to have the first three arrows hit the target around the "pinhole," and the final three arrows then impale the shafts of the first three arrows. The score for the end would be 60 points. This would be one definition of perfection in the sport of target archery! The mathematical probability of that occurring during a target archery round is about the same as a score of 18 being shot by a golfer for one complete round of golf.

Arrows that strike other arrows already on the target and deflect are scored in various ways. If an arrow deflects from an arrow on the target face but somehow attaches to the target, it is scored according to the target area where it is fastened. For example, an arrow that rebounds from an arrow shaft embedded in the outer gold or yellow and enters the target in the inner light blue is scored six instead of nine points. An arrow rebounding completely off the target after hitting an arrow on the target is scored the value of the arrow hit. However, it must be witnessed, and the damaged arrow has to be identified. If both criteria were met using the example above, the rebounding arrow would be given a score of nine after deflecting off an arrow already in the outer gold ring.

After scoring, holes are marked during competition. If an arrow is witnessed as passing completely through the target mat, it is given the value of the unmarked hole on the target. This happens often in school situations when mats become worn due to excessive use and target faces are overused. One option in these situations is to score the arrow as a seven if it passed through a scoring ring on the target face and the hole could not be identified. Overused target mats with their centers shot away can cause a problem with this scoring option.

A baseball thrown by a pitcher that hits the ground in front of the plate and bounces through the strike zone of the batter can be called a strike or be hit by the hitter. The analogous situation in archery whereby an arrow hits the ground, rebounds, and sticks in the target face does not score or even count as a hit for the archer.

If an archer becomes confused and shoots an end of arrows on other than his or her assigned target during a round, the score of those arrows does not count. Zeros are recorded on the score card. Hits are not recorded for the arrows, because they did not hit the correct target.

As noted on the example scorecard in figure 4.23, all legal hits are recorded. A hit is scored for any arrow receiving a score from one through ten. An arrow embedded in the skirt, or petticoat, of the target face or in the archery stand is not recorded as a hit. The recorded hits are important to break ties when they occur at the end of a round. Three criteria are used to break ties for individual competitors: (1) the archer with the greatest number of hits is the winner; (2) if hits are also tied along with the score, the archer with the most tens wins; or (3) if hits and tens are tied, the archer with the most nines wins. If they are still tied, the Director of Shooting will declare that they were truly equal in skill for the round shot.

Common Grouping Problems, with Coaching Suggestions

To shoot a tight group of arrows consistently in the ten ring of the target regardless of the distance being shot is the ultimate in target archery. The frustration of the sport is that arrows do not always group according to the desires of the archer. The main source of help for making adjustments to improve skill should come from the individual's archery instructor or coach. However, when such help is not available, the following teaching or coaching suggestions for self-help can be quite valuable. For the suggestions listed below, it is assumed that the archer is using matched tackle.

The Video Camcorder as a Coaching Aid

It is recommended that the archer employ a good video camcorder to videotape his or her shooting style. (This is also recommended for use by instructors in teaching and coaching situations.) The camcorder should be mounted on a tripod for most of the filming. Videotape your shooting technique with the camcorder placed at a *right angle* to you on the shooting line. Archery shots also should be videotaped from a rear view, where slow motion should pick up the first part of the arrow flight. If possible, videotape from a camera angle directly above the archer is advantageous for analysis. The camera can be rigged for the overhead angle in some indoor ranges. Views of the total body should be taken as well as close-up recordings of the fundamentals of nocking, bowstring finger placement, bow hold, drawing, anchor point, release, and follow-through. Close-up views of the release and follow-through are of particular importance.

You should make verbal comments on the videotape describing such things as your perception of breathing mechanics, weather and wind conditions on the range during the videotaped practice session, reaction to how you released the arrow, arrow flight observations and nature of flight deviations, and the exact location of the hit on the target (or miss) for each arrow released. The arrow grouping should also be videotaped after each end is shot. Shot location for each hit by number can be verified. Take videotape of several ends of arrows at various distances, and try to determine where your consistent shooting problem(s) lie. Make an attempt to rank your shooting problems from most to least serious. *You should work to eliminate only one shooting difficulty at a time, and that should be the most serious problem on your "shooting fault list."* When progress has been made, start working to eliminate the next shooting error on the list. You should retape periodically. By using two videotape recorders (VCR) simultaneously, you can compare and contrast your shooting mechanics frame-by-frame on the old and new videotapes.

For the best results in improving your skills, analyze the videotape with a qualified archery instructor and obtain his or her reactions and suggestions. If that is not possible, use the stop action and slow motion features on your VCR so you can later critique your shooting technique, determine and rank your consistent shooting errors, and try the appropriate change(s) for your primary shooting problem noted below.

Arrows Grouping Left

1. Check your stance. You may have inadvertently rotated your spinal column slightly to the left. Place your entire body in line with the target and maintain an even weight distribution over both feet.
2. Adjust your bowsight to the left.
3. Check your bow grip. Do not involve the fingers in the gripping process; push with the bow hand; use a finger or bow sling.
4. Your anchor point may have been moved to the right. Make certain the string placement is consistently touching the same facial areas and is aligned with the center of the bow.
5. Nock with the index feather skyward in the nocking position.
6. The bow may cant to the left during aiming and release; consequently, check to see that the bow is held perpendicular to the ground instead of being rotated counterclockwise from anchoring to release.

7. Check the position of the elbow on the bow arm; the elbow should be fully extended at all times from nocking through follow-through. You may be flinching or flexing the elbow at release.
8. Check to see that you are not applying too much pressure on the nock of the arrow during the draw and release with the index and middle fingers; allow an extra space between the gripping fingers and arrow nock; adjust nock-locators.

Arrows Grouping Right

1. Check your stance; align your body with the target instead of rotating the spinal column to the right.
2. Adjust the bowsight to the right.
3. Adjust your grip to eliminate any possibility of a clockwise torque of the bow during release.
4. Check to see that your string alignment has not moved to the left; align the string to touch the middle of the nose and lips.
5. Concentrate on extension only of the finger (interphalangeal) joints during release. Any extraneous actions such as plucking or pushing the string inward will cause a grouping error to the right.
6. Make certain that the bow is held perpendicular to the ground and not canted clockwise.

Arrows Grouping High

1. Check your stance for an even weight distribution, as opposed to placing too much weight on the foot away from the target.
2. Adjust your bowsight upward.
3. Make certain you are not pushing against the bow grip with the entire palm or heel of the hand.
4. Keep your mouth closed; upper and lower teeth should be touching—not clenched—from the time you reach your anchor point through release; check the anchor point to see that it has not moved to a lower position on your face. The hand must maintain contact with the jaw or side of the face.
5. Make certain that a ninety-degree string-arrow nock position is attained during nocking. A low nocking point causes the arrow to go high. Adjust your nocking points; place nocking points on your serving if you do not already have them.
6. Check your breathing mechanics; do not inhale during the drawing, aiming, or release phases; breathing should be done before nocking, and you should exhale after the arrow is in the target.
7. Push through the bow at all times from drawing to follow-through; do not raise (abduct) the bow arm at release.
8. Take time to aim so your release will coincide with the bowsight intersecting the desired target spot instead of releasing above the target. Are you completely still or stable at the time of release?

9. Check the bowstring fingers to make certain that the pressure is distributed with minimal pressure on the index finger.
10. Keep the wrist of the shooting arm stabilized and extended at release so no extraneous motion occurs in that joint.

Arrows Grouping Low

1. Check your stance and make certain that weight is not being distributed over the foot nearest the target.
2. Adjust your bowsight downward.
3. Rotate the head toward the target and draw the string to your face without flexing your neck and moving the head toward the string.
4. Draw to your regular anchor point, making certain that your usual facial points are contacted with the string hand; an incomplete draw will reduce arrow velocity and cause the arrows to go low on the target or into the ground.
5. Check to see that you have not nocked above the ninety-degree angle.
6. Hold your anchor point until the arrow is in the target. Allowing the string to move forward—"creeping"—prior to release reduces arrow velocity.
7. Check your grip to make certain that you are not applying pressure to rotate the whole bow toward the target.
8. Maintain the correct bow-arm position without lowering it (adducting the bow-arm shoulder) until the arrow is in the target.

Bow Tuning

If the archer understands and executes the shooting fundamentals properly and continues to have grouping problems, the bow may need to be tuned. Properly tuning a bow for an individual archer should result in appropriately spined arrows being shot accurately. Tuning is a very individualized process; that is, a bow properly tuned for one archer may not be satisfactory for another archer. The tuning process is another step in validating the reliability of your matched tackle. It may help to use a bow tuning method on several bows and ends of arrows on an archery pro shop range prior to purchase. This would help you determine the tackle quality and its relationship to your style of shooting.

There are several bow tuning methods, and you might want to try more than one. The Eliason Bow Tuning Method is described below. This procedure was developed by Edwin Eliason, the senior member (age 50-plus) of the 1992 United States Olympic Archery Team. Archery manufacturers, and others, also have very good bow tuning recommendations. Observations of arrow flight patterns must be made in the vertical and horizontal planes. The grouping patterns of arrows on the target must also be made. The bow tuning process determines what adjustments are needed to your tackle to cause the straightest flight patterns of arrows.

To determine vertical plane adjustments, the archer needs to shoot several ends of his or her fletched arrows while aiming at the same spot. The shooting should be at a distance of 10 or 20 meters, depending upon the skill level of the archer. Beginning archers should use the closer distance. Once a grouping pattern has been established, an *unfletched arrow* is shot, using the same aiming spot. The relative position of the hit of the unfletched arrow on the target to the fletched arrow group is very significant for making an accurate adjustment of your nocking point. If the unfletched arrow hits *above* the fletched arrow group, raise your nocking point until the grouping patterns coincide. Conversely, if the unfletched arrow hits below the fletched group, lower your nocking point.

To determine horizontal plane adjustments, follow the same shooting procedure; that is, use fletched arrows followed by unfletched arrows. You should determine the left or right deviations of the unfletched arrow hits in relation to the fletched arrow grouping. This is necessary to evaluate spine. If the unfletched arrow hits to the right of the fletched grouping pattern, the spine of the fletched arrows being shot is too weak. Conversely, if the unfletched arrow hits the target to the left of the fletched grouping pattern, the fletched arrow's spine is too stiff. The archer can make several adjustments to the tackle that will modify the spine of the arrows. If these adjustments, described below, do not work, new arrows may have to be purchased to match your bow.

The following are possible tuning adjustments when you have found that the *spine* of your arrows is *too stiff*. Arrows may need to be lengthened, and that would require a purchase. You may want to try the following adjustments first. Heavier points and/or insert weights may be placed on your arrows. A change of arrow nocks can also have an impact on spine. The arrow plate may need to be moved to the right; or try decreasing the spring tension on a compressible pressure point if you are using one. In regard to the bow itself, adding a stabilizer may help. Check your bowstring and decrease the number of strings to weaken spine. Decreasing the mass weight of the bow, increasing the bow weight, and/ or slightly increasing the brace height may also prove beneficial in alleviating horizontal fluctuations of arrows.

The following are possible bow tuning adjustments when you have found that the *spine* of your arrows is *too weak*. The arrows may need to be shortened, or lighter points need to be placed on the existing arrows. A change of arrow nocks may be advantageous. The arrow plate may need to be moved slightly to the left, or the spring tension on the cushion plunger being used could be increased. Try increasing the number of strands in your bowstring. If a stabilizer is on the bow, try shooting without it. Increasing the mass weight of the bow, decreasing the bow weight, and decreasing the brace height may prove beneficial.

Bow tuning helps to minimize or eliminate vertical and horizontal arrow flight deviations as well as clearance problems. It should be remembered, however, that the archer must have achieved good shooting mechanics in order for bow tuning adjustments to be effective. Bow tuning is ineffective when used in conjunction with or to help the archer rationalize poor shooting fundamentals.

Review

1. Make a list of important safety precautions to observe when on the range, or critique your target archery range rules. Beside each rule, indicate the chief reason for it.
2. What systems have been found effective in controlling breathing during the draw and aiming? Which one works best for you?
3. What is your score if your six arrows are located as follows in the target: one in the outer red, two in inner blue, two in outer blue, and one in inner white?
4. Name several common causes of arrows consistently grouped to each of the following, respectively: left, right, high, low.
5. If, after bracing, your string height is too low, what can you do to correct the height?
6. Which stance is recommended for beginners in archery? How can you ensure stance consistency?
7. Why is it a misnomer to describe the bow hand as "holding" or "gripping" the bow during the draw?
8. Although the archer's head position should remain fixed as soon as the target is addressed, some novices have difficulty holding this position until their follow-through. What can you do to solve this problem?
9. If your arrows are consistently grouped to the right in the blue ring with the bowsight placed on the gold at release, how should you adjust the bowsight? Can a bowsight adjustment help if your arrows are not grouped?
10. Describe the use of the clicker, your release, and follow-through.
11. When is it appropriate in target archery for you to nock your arrow? to shoot? to stop shooting? to retrieve your arrows? Why?
12. Why should all target hits be recorded (as well as the score)?

Target and Field Archery Sports

5

The purpose of this chapter is to provide an overview of the sports and activities archers pursue once they have a grasp of archery shooting mechanics. Archery consists not only of the traditional forms of target archery competition most people associate with the sport, but of such endeavors as crossbow competition, clout shooting, flight shooting, and tournaments for handicapped people. Field archery offers a variety of activities that relate target archery to bow hunting and bow fishing. You may want to learn more about one or more of the archery sports after being introduced to them in this chapter. (See Appendix B for names, addresses, and phone numbers where further information may be obtained about archery sport organizations and their functions for archers.)

There are three principal controlling organizations for archers: (1) National Archery Association, Incorporated, of the United States (NAA); (2) National Field Archery Association of the United States, Incorporated (NFAA); and (3) Fedération Internationale de Tir à l'Arc—International Archery Federation (FITA).

The oldest of these organizations is the NAA. It was founded in Chicago in 1879. According to the NAA Constitution last revised in 1990, "The corporation is organized and shall be operated exclusively for educational and charitable purposes and to perpetuate, foster, and direct the practice of the sport of archery in connection with the educational and charitable purposes of this corporation and to raise funds for carrying out these purposes." The NAA is recognized as the sport's governing body for archery in the United States. The NAA headquarters are located at the Olympic Center in Colorado Springs, Colorado. *The U.S. Archer* is the official publication of the NAA.

The NFAA was founded in 1939. According to the NFAA constitution, some of the organization's major purposes are, "To foster, expand, promote, and perpetuate the practice of field archery and any other archery games as the association may adopt and enforce uniform rules, regulations, procedures, conditions, and methods of playing such games. To encourage the use of the bow in the hunting of all legal game birds and animals, and to protect, improve, and increase the sport of hunting with a bow and arrow." This organization has a strong interest in conservation as it relates to bow hunting and bow fishing. *Archery* is the official publication of the NFAA.

The FITA was organized in 1931. This is the organization that promotes and encourages target archery throughout the world. The FITA organizes regional and world championships in target archery. Records are processed through this organization. Target archery organizations of the various countries are affiliated

Table 5.1 Competitive Age and Sex Classifications for Target Archery Tournament Rounds

Males		Females	
Men	18 years old or over	Women	18 years old or over
Boys		Girls	
Intermediate		Intermediate	
15 to 18 years old		15 to 18 years old	
Junior		Junior	
12 to 15 years old		12 to 15 years old	
Cadet		Cadet	
Less than 12 years old		Less than 12 years old	

with the FITA; this is necessary in order to coordinate national, regional, and international competitions. The FITA determines amateur eligibility for such tournaments. The NAA is affiliated with the FITA.

Target Archery

Target archery, like competitive road running, swimming, and cycling, is divided into functional competitive groups by sex and age. Virtually any individual, regardless of sex, age, or handicap, can find opportunities to compete in target archery tournaments somewhere. They are available at many levels for people with all degrees of skill. The competitive classifications are shown in table 5.1. An archer may elect to shoot in a higher age classification, but may not shoot in a lower classification.

To encourage proper archery instruction, competition, and motivation for boys and girls, the NAA has an active Junior Olympic Archery Development Program (JOAD). This program introduces archery to students in elementary and secondary schools and assists interested young archers in getting started correctly in the sport. The JOAD tournaments are very popular among young archers and their parents. Some of the world-class archers who represent the United States in national and international competitions started in this program.

The NAA also has a very active College Division. It promotes intercollegiate archery competition for men and women. The culmination of the college archery season is the U.S. Intercollegiate Archery Championships. College teams must be members of the NAA College Division in order to compete. Traditionally, there have been very strong intercollegiate archery programs in Arizona and California. (California has more college archery programs than any other state.) The annual NAA Intercollegiate Ranking Program for men and women indicates, however, that excellent individual archers and college archery teams are found in community colleges, colleges, and universities throughout the United States. If you are a college or university student, check to see whether or not your school

Table 5.2 Examples of World-Class Scores for the Single FITA Round

Distance	Total Arrows	Possible Score	Actual Score	Average Per Arrow
Ladies				
70 meters	36	360	336	9.33
60 meters	36	360	347	9.64
50 meters	36	360	337	9.36
30 meters	36	360	357	9.92
FITA Round	144	1440	1370	9.51
Gentlemen				
90 meters	36	360	322	8.94
70 meters	36	360	342	9.50
50 meters	36	360	345	9.58
30 meters	36	360	357	9.92
FITA Round	144	1440	1352	9.39

has an intercollegiate archery team and determine what it takes to become a member. Also, check with your intramural athletic director to see when archery competition is scheduled in the intramural athletic program.

Championship Rounds

The NAA has twelve approved championship rounds designated for competitions. The James D. Easton Round is recommended as the Team Round. An archery team consists of eight archers; however, only the combined score of the best four archers from a team is calculated as the team's total score for a competition. The archer with the best overall score for any round is the individual champion even if that person competes on a team.

The outdoor FITA Round is shot twice in individual and team competitions such as the World Championships. The FITA Round distances for men and women are very demanding—see table 5.2. For men, the longest distance is 90 meters (98.46 yards), while the longest distance shot by women is 70 meters (76.58 yards). If you have never shot those distances and want to gain some understanding of the challenges of target archery, it is recommended that you set up a 122-centimeter target at each of those distances, shoot, and score 36 arrows. At 90 meters, the best men in the world average approximately 8.90 for each arrow shot. The best world-class women average close to 9.00 for each of the 36 arrows shot at 70 meters! If you have shot from those distances, you should have gained some appreciation for that caliber of scoring.

A few elite men and women archers around the world shoot *above* 1300 for the single FITA Round—1440 is possible. A score of 1300 in an official FITA round is a noble goal for many very good archers. The FITA organization requires *minimum* qualifying scores for Olympic Tournaments of 1150 for women and 1200 for men in the FITA Round. As a result of these qualifying criteria, obtaining a position on a national team anywhere in the world is very competitive and challenging! (The world records for men and women for the FITA Round are considerably above 1300. See Table 5.2 for some examples of FITA Round world-class scores from the various distances.) If you shoot a score of 1200, as an example, that means the average value for each of the 144 arrows shot was 8.33! If you are an archer struggling to improve your shooting mechanics and scoring, keep in mind that one fantastic thing about archery is that you do not have to average 8.33 per arrow or better to enjoy the sport. That type of ability, of course, is great! But, in the pursuit of excellence there are many values within the quest itself. Therein lies part of the value and mystique of this multifaceted sport.

Table 5.2 is presented to show the reader who is learning target archery a few of the actual scores that have been attained in international competition. These scores represent: (1) what can be accomplished in the sport, (2) a challenge to beginning and intermediate archers, and (3) potential motivation for people who like to pursue excellence! If someone else in the world has shot these scores, why can't you? Can you be the first person ever to shoot a perfect score in a recognized tournament from 30 meters? 70 meters during a FITA Round?

Table 5.3 presents relevant information for the outdoor and indoor NAA Target Archery Championship Rounds.

A competitive round of target archery is controlled by a Director of Shooting. Judges are assigned targets and work under the supervision of the Director. The longest distances are shot first. In order to adjust to range and environmental conditions, there is a fifteen minute pre-tournament practice session. If this is not possible, archers are allowed to shoot a total of six sighter arrows prior to competition. No other trial shots in any direction are allowed on the range during the competition. The archer must be emotionally, physically, and psychologically ready when he or she steps onto the target archery range. *The mental aspects of this sport should never be minimized or underestimated!*

The Director of Shooting controls the contest by using a whistle to inform the archers when to start and stop shooting. A time limit of 2½ minutes is given to release an end of three arrows. Two blasts on the whistle is the signal for the archers to move from the waiting line to their positions on the shooting line. They address their targets. One blast of the whistle starts the 2½ minute shooting period for three arrows. Several short blasts indicate that all shooting must stop, because an emergency exists.

What type of tackle may the target archer use in competition? Compound bows may not be used. Bows must be of the classic designs such as the longbow (fig. 5.2) or recurve bow as seen in figure 3.7. The bowstring may have a serving and one or two nock-locators. However, neither the serving nor the nock-locators can be positioned to function as a rear sight device for the archer. An arrow rest is allowed for its specific purpose, but may not be positioned or used for aiming. One bowsight of the type shown in figures 3.7 and 3.12 is allowed. A bowsight may not include level devices, prisms, lens, or electronic gadgets. Stabilizers are

Table 5.3   NAA Target Archery Championship Rounds

Round		Distance	Arrows Per Distance	Total Arrows	Target Size	Total Points
Outdoor						
FITA	Men	90,70m	36	144	122cm	1440
		50,30m			80cm	
	Women	70,60m	36	144	122cm	1440
		50,30m			80cm	
Junior Metric		60,50m	36	144	122cm	1440
		40,30m			80cm	
Cadet Metric		45,35m	36	144	122cm	1440
		25,15m			80cm	
900 Metric		60,50,40m	30	90	122cm	900
Junior 900		50,40,30m	30	90	122cm	900
Cadet 900		40,30,20m	30	90	122cm	900
James D. Easton						
	(Team)	60,50,40m	20	60	122cm	600
Collegiate 600		50,40,30m	20	60	122cm	600
Collegiate 720		50,40,30m	24	72	80cm	720
Clout	Men	165m	36	36	15m	180
	Intermediate Boys	165m	36	36	15m	180
	Women	125m	36	36	15m	180
	Intermediate Girls	125m	36	36	15m	180
	Juniors	110m	36	36	15m	180
	Cadets	110m	36	36	15m	180
Indoor						
FITA Round I		18m	30	30	40cm	300
FITA Round II		25m	30	30	60cm	300

approved. Arrows must be marked with the archer's name, initials, or insignia, and all of the arrows must have the same colors of fletching, nock, and crests. No release devices may be used or built in to finger protection accessories. Other accessories such as clickers, bracers, bow slings, and quivers are allowed. If the archer wears glasses, the glasses may not be modified in any manner to assist in the aiming process. All of these items, and other tackle items, are checked by the Director of Shooting and the judges prior to the contest.

The NAA has a dress code during tournaments for archers, which must be followed. White clothing is *mandatory*. According to the NAA, ladies may wear, "Dresses, skirts, slacks, culottes or shorts with leg length not above crotch level. Suitable blouses or tops with color allowed on the upper 50 percent of exposed area. Tank tops may be worn providing the strap is at least three inches in width." Men may wear, "Full length trousers or shorts with leg length not above crotch level. Long or short-sleeved shirts with color allowed on the upper 50 percent of the exposed area." Guidelines also stipulate what can and cannot be worn in terms of the advertising of manufacturer's trademarks and logos.

Nonchampionship Rounds

Numerous nonchampionship rounds have been used for years. Some of these are excellent rounds to shoot in club, school, and class competitions (see figure 4.23). They are shot on the regulation 122-centimeter target face. A few of these rounds are listed below:

York Round

72 arrows at 100 yards
48 arrows at 80 yards
24 arrows at 60 yards

Columbia Round

24 arrows at 50 yards
24 arrows at 40 yards
24 arrows at 30 yards

Junior Columbia Round

24 arrows at 40 yards
24 arrows at 30 yards
24 arrows at 20 yards

Scholastic Round

24 arrows at 40 yards
24 arrows at 30 yards

Team Round

96 arrows at 60 yards—men
96 arrows at 50 yards—women

National Round

48 arrows at 60 yards
24 arrows at 50 yards

Junior American Round

30 arrows at 50 yards
30 arrows at 40 yards
30 arrows at 30 yards

Western Round

48 arrows at 60 yards
48 arrows at 50 yards

Hereford Round

72 arrows at 80 yards
48 arrows at 60 yards
24 arrows at 50 yards

Saint George Round

36 arrows at 100 yards
36 arrows at 80 yards
36 arrows at 60 yards

Windsor Round

36 arrows at 60 yards
36 arrows at 50 yards
36 arrows at 40 yards

Saint Nicholas Round

48 arrows at 40 yards
36 arrows at 30 yards

Albion Round

36 arrows at 80 yards
36 arrows at 60 yards
36 arrows at 50 yards

American Round

30 arrows at 60 yards
30 arrows at 50 yards
30 arrows at 40 yards

Note: To change from yards to meters, multiply by 0.9144.

The York Round was used in national championship competitions for years in Great Britain and America. The distances are demanding. This was especially true for the type of tackle (longbows and wooden arrows) used during the nineteenth century. The American Round was used to establish national men champions in the United States starting in 1911. A York Round champion was also named. For several years after 1914, the national championship was based on the combined scores of double American and York Rounds. Over the years from 1879 to 1985, the American women's championship was determined by using the

Figure 5.1
The Fourth Olympiad of 1908 held in Shepherd's Bush Stadium in London. The men shot the York Round. The central figure in the light suit is the British gold medalist, W. Dod. (From E. G. Heath, *The Grey Goose Wing*)

Columbia and National Rounds. The FITA Round for international competition came into vogue in 1956, and the Grand FITA Round was introduced in World and Olympic competitions in 1985. FITA Rounds are now used extensively to determine numerous outdoor and indoor championships; however, a new Olympic Round format was approved by the FITA in 1991 and initiated at the Olympic Games in 1992.

The Olympic Games

Target archery has been included in the agenda of several Olympiads during the twentieth century. Records indicate that medals were awarded in archery at the Olympic Games in 1900 at Paris, 1904 in St. Louis, 1908 in London, and 1920 in Antwerp. The sport was not revived for Olympic competition until the 1960s. Target archery was included in the 1968 Olympic Games as a demonstration sport, and it became an official gold medal sport starting with the 1972 Olympiad held in Munich. That event, highly significant to the sport of target archery, has resulted in an increased interest in target archery as an amateur sport throughout the world.

Figures 5.1 and 5.2 show some of the men and women competitors in the 1908 Olympic Games. These illustrations are interesting, because they give us a chance to compare and contrast the type of archery tackle used in competition in 1908 with tackle available to archers today. The longbow is predominant in both illustrations. The use of the longbow at this level of competition today would be most unusual! It is also instructive to compare and contrast the type of clothing worn by the competitors in 1908 with the type of clothing worn today. Also, the rather erratic arrow grouping shown in figure 5.2 would not place the archer very high in contemporary competition where tight groups are the rule rather than the exception.

Figure 5.2
The women competitors shooting the National Round at the 1908 Olympic Games. (From E. G. Heath, *The Grey Goose Wing*)

Archery competition at recent Olympiads has attracted the interest of spectators. As one example, there was tremendous interest in the sport of target archery at the Games of the XXIII Olympiad held in Los Angeles, California. (The actual competition site for archery was Long Beach, California.) This interest was demonstrated, in part, by the fact that the competition was observed daily by over 9000 spectators in a sold-out stadium (fig. 5.3). The reader should compare figures 5.1 and 5.3 to see the difference between spectator interest in archery for the 1908 Olympic Games and for the 1984 Games.

Interest in archery has also resulted in better shooting quality, as demonstrated by the excellent scores that have been shot during the past few Olympic Games (see fig. 5.4 for an example). The greater attention given to archery throughout the world has produced numerous elite archers.

Figure 5.5 is provided to allow the reader to compare and contrast the clothing, tackle, shooting stance, and equipment used by contemporary archers with that of archers at the beginning of the twentieth century (fig. 5.1). Take-down, recurve bows equipped with sights and stabilizers are used as compared with the longbows used in 1908. The reader should also compare the shooting stance of the archer on the line in figure 5.1 with the stance used by the archer in figure 5.5. The stereotype of stance mechanics has changed considerably over the decades.

Figure 5.3
The shooting line and spectator's stadium at the 1984 Olympic Games. (Photo by *The U.S. Archer*)

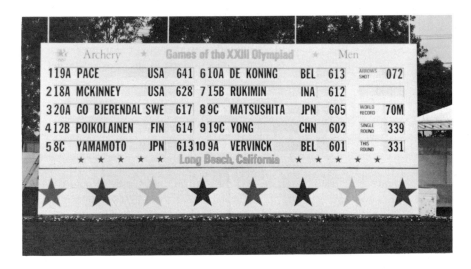

Figure 5.4
The men's scoreboard during the Games of the XXIII Olympiad showed the competitors' scores in progress. (Photo by *The U.S. Archer*)

Figure 5.5
Olympic archers on the shooting line. (Photo by *The U.S. Archer*)

The NAA conducts tryout tournaments to select the men's and women's teams that represent the United States in national, World, and Olympic competitions. Archers who shoot the best qualifying scores above the FITA minimal Olympic standards are provided coaching. Elite archers are receiving the benefits of having their shooting skills scientifically and technically analyzed by exercise scientists at the Olympic Center in Colorado Springs. Sophisticated analyses are made involving the archer, his or her tackle, and the interrelationships between the two while shooting.

Scientific studies of archers relate primarily to the anatomic kinesiology, biomechanics, and exercise physiology variables involved in shooting. High speed cinematography and videotape are utilized extensively. Physics instruments are used to measure and evaluate such elements as the forces and velocities contributing to or detracting from the archer's skill. This scientific information is communicated from the exercise scientists to the archers and their coaches with the intent of improving the technical or skill aspects of shooting. The merging of scientific theory with the technique or practice of archery has the potential to increase skill at all levels of competition. It is especially important at the Olympic level in order to provide a "competitive edge" to meet the excellent competition now seen throughout the world.

To determine amateur status and eligibility, the NAA is governed by the eligibility rules of the FITA and the International Olympic Committee. These rules are very specific, ranging from the allowable maximum value of trophies or prizes retained by the archer to the uses of prescribed and nonprescribed medicines as well as illegal drugs such as anabolic steroids. An archer desiring to be a member of an Olympic team must meet the amateur status criteria and be drug free.

Professional archers who do not meet the amateur status criteria for Olympic competition have their own organizations. The NAA and NFAA, as examples, provide Professional Divisions for shooting activities. The Professional Archery Association of the NAA was founded in 1961.

Individuals over the age of 55 still interested in top flight competition but who are not Olympic class archers or professionals may choose to participate in target archery each year during The U.S. National Senior Sports Classic. That event draws archers who are 90-plus! It should be noted that it is possible to be over the age of 50 and still shoot well enough to be a member of an Olympic team! That has never been the case, for example, for an athlete in the sport of basketball even if he or she is extremely tall.

The United States' archers have performed very well in Olympic competition. With good instruction and diligent practice, the individual reading this book (YOU!) could develop into an archery competitor or champion of national and international caliber within a period of one to two years. This is not impossible *if* the individual has excellent intrinsic motivation toward this type of goal. At any age (teenager, young adult, or individual 50-plus), with the proper attitude, interest, aptitude, and motivation you could possibly earn a position on the Olympic team in archery. It has been done! To represent one's country on an Olympic team is one of the highest honors an individual can achieve. It is both fitting and proper that archery, one of the oldest sports performed by humans, is now a part of the Olympic Gold Medal Sport's Agenda.

Crossbows

Crossbows have been a part of the history of humankind for over 2400 years. The Greeks developed a form of crossbow about 400 B.C., and the Chinese were using crossbows in battles as early as 341 B.C. The military use of these bows as weapons was very popular from the eleventh to the sixteenth century. They gradually declined as weapons of war with the onset of firearms. But, humans remain fascinated by the crossbow today. As a result, there is a growing interest in the use of the crossbow in sport. There are opportunities to use the crossbow (fig. 5.6) in such diverse activities as flight shooting, hunting, field shooting, and match competition. There are several state, national, and international championships organized to accommodate the interests of crossbow enthusiasts.

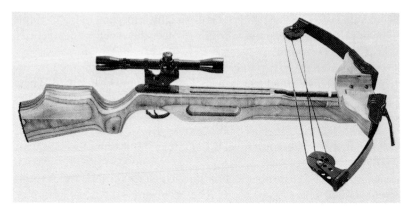

Figure 5.6
A modern compound crossbow; one of many designs used by archers for hunting, field, match, and flight competitions. (Courtesy Precision Shooting Equipment, Inc., 2727 N. Fairview Ave., Tucson, Arizona 85705)

The Internationale Armbrustschutzen Union (IAU) is the major international controlling organization for crossbow shooting. The IAU has nineteen affiliated members representing large and small countries throughout the world. Match crossbow competitions and field crossbow shooting are controlled by the IAU and its affiliates.

The main difference between match crossbow shooting and field crossbow shooting lies in the clothing allowed to be worn by the crossbow shooters. The match competitor can wear leather gloves, boots, and shooting jackets; whereas the field crossbow archer dresses like the target archer in NAA or international competition (fig. 5.3). All field shots must be made from the standing position, and all competition is on outdoor ranges. Match competition, on the other hand, may include indoor as well as outdoor targets. The indoor targets may be as close as 10 meters.

The International Field Crossbow Round requires a standard 80-centimeter FITA target face. Ninety arrows are shot; therefore, a perfect score would be 900. Thirty arrows are shot from 65 meters, 50 meters, and 35 meters respectively. *The better men and women shooters will have scores at or above 800 for this round.* As examples, the World Records through 1990 for the single International Field Crossbow Round were 856 for men (Pentti Hakkinen of Finland) and 832 for women (Sieglinde Wagner of Germany). That gives you some idea of what is being accomplished with crossbows.

The NAA conducts crossbow championships on an annual basis. Crossbow competition is usually in categories for men, women, juniors, and seniors. Most of the rules of target archery also apply to crossbow shooters, but the two always compete separately. Field shooting at outdoor targets is done with bows of 80 pounds or less. Fifty pounds is recommended for indoor competitions. No mechanical aids can be used to draw the bows unless the individual is handicapped physically. *The short arrows shot from crossbows are called bolts.* The crossbow shooter cannot use a magnifying sight, but prismatic sights and level bubble sights are allowed to be mounted on the bow. Binoculars and scopes may be used to locate hits on the target.

The reader interested in the crossbow is referred to the Bibliography for a few references on this fascinating part of archery. The National Crossbowmen of the U.S.A. is the United States affiliate of the International Armburst Union. *The Crossbow Chit Chat* is the official publication of The National Crossbowmen of the U.S.A. The U.S. Match–Crossbow Shooting Association is also affiliated with the IAU. Readers interested in learning more about crossbow activities are referred to Appendix B for the names and addresses of these, and other, crossbow organizations.

Clout Shooting

Historically, clout shooting as a sport can be traced at least as far back as the period of English archery prior to The Hundred Years' War. As noted in Chapter 2, clout shooting was used as a military strategy in many wars throughout history. The archers shot great volleys of arrows into the air in clout fashion toward their opponents. This was an early and effective form of aerial bombardment. The reader can readily understand the apprehension of a soldier as a volley of arrows numbering in the hundreds or thousands suddenly and silently descended into the area. In addition to being an effective killing technique, the arrival of arrows in this fashion often caused panic among the ranks. Retreat was common following a clout shooting bombardment in an area where soldiers were densely grouped along a combat line.

The fascinating sport of clout shooting evolved from that use of archery in war. As noted in table 5.3, the Clout Round is an official NAA Target Archery Championship Round. The circular target in clout shooting is laid out on the ground. Its outer circle measures 15 meters (49.20 feet) in diameter. It is divided into five concentric scoring zones that each measure 1.5 meters (4.92 feet) in width. The *Clout* is a brightly colored flag placed on a wooden pole 19.69 inches above the ground in the center of the target. The scoring values of each scoring zone starting from the center outward are five, four, three, two, and one. Arrows that stick in the clout flag are given the value of five.

Target archery tackle is used for the Clout Round. As you see in table 5.3, the Clout Round distances vary based on the sex and age of the archer. The longest distance is 165 meters (180.4 yards) for men and intermediate boys, and the shortest distance is 110 meters (120.34 yards) for junior and cadet boys and girls. Women and intermediate girls shoot from 125 meters (136.75 yards). All of these distances are challenging, and the distance adds "spice" to the clout shoot. You are given only six practice or sighter arrows prior to beginning the Clout Round.

The Clout Round consists of 36 arrows. All arrows are shot from the single distance specified for your age and sex. A perfect score would be 180, but that is easier said than done! Clout shooting is an intriguing part of the sport of archery. If space allows for range safety to be maintained, it is recommended that a few clout rounds be shot by students taking a course in target archery. It is fun!

Flight Archery

Most people think of archery in all of its forms as placing the emphasis on accuracy. Flight archery, or flight shooting, may be the lone exception to that "rule." *Flight shooting places the premium on how far an arrow or bolt can be projected from a bow or crossbow.* This sport has great appeal to individuals who are fascinated by the physics of the specialized bows constructed specifically for flight shooting. The biomechanical relationship that exists between the tackle and archer is also of prime interest to participants in flight shooting. The sport demands an understanding of trajectories and aerodynamic properties of arrows and bolts. The physics involving the interrelationships between the mechanical system of the bow, its kinetic and potential energy capabilities, and the forces acting efficiently on the arrow to put it into flight are all fascinating aspects of this sport. The strength of the archer to handle the forces required by his or her tackle is also of paramount importance in some aspects of flight shooting. Knowledge of the tackle of flight shooting must be integrated with the proper techniques of shooting in order to attain the desired maximum distances. Flight shooting is a unique archery sport!

What is the farthest an arrow has ever been shot by a human without benefit of fuel, explosive devices, or air currents in a recognized flight shooting event? As it should be, that record is held by "The Father of Flight Archery," Harry Drake (fig. 5.7). The record was set in 1988, and it would take a world-class mile runner about four minutes to run and retrieve the bolt! *Harry Drake's World Crossbow Flight Record shot on a salt flat in Utah is 2047 yards, 2 inches. That is 1.16 miles!* He has also shot an arrow from an unlimited footbow 2028 yards, that is, 1.15 miles! Those are amazing feats.

In competition, shooters are allowed a maximum of four rounds of flight consisting of six arrows each. They may use any type or weight of the bows sanctioned for flight shooting, or they can utilize a combination of types and weights of the several varieties of approved bows.

Competitions are held separately in flight archery involving "Regular Flight" and "Broadhead Flight." A regular flight bow may be designed with a special handle equipped with overdraw capabilities, but any recurve bow may also be used in "Regular Flight" events. The arrows are a minimum of 14 inches in length from the floor of the nock to the tip of the point. They are designed with a barrel shape, and the vanes are small. The "Broadhead Flight" competition involves the use of unaltered broadhead points as commonly used in bow hunting. There are established standards for men and women, and these specify the minimum weights of the broadheads.

Figure 5.7
Harry Drake, "The Father of Flight Shooting," using a 25 kg flight bow in an NAA Flight Championship. (Courtesy of *The U.S. Archer;* photo by Bob Rhode)

Figure 5.8
Flight shooting includes competitive categories for women and men. Sherrie Reynolds is shown using a compound flight bow in competition. (Courtesy of *The U.S. Archer;* photo by Bob Rhode)

Flight competition is divided according to age and sex. Men and women (fig. 5.8) categories are for people 18 years of age and older. Intermediate and Junior categories are for ages 12 through 17 years. The Cadet level of competition includes children 11 years of age and under. There are also divisions for "amateurs" and "nonamateurs" in this sport.

There are several bow classifications used in flight archery. Compound bows are divided into specific weight divisions plus an "unlimited" division for each age and sex group. In addition, there are competition classifications for crossbows and primitive bows. Broadhead flight shooting might also include recurve and longbow events.

Flight bows achieve high arrow velocities. Kevin Strother holds the World Speed Record of 588 feet per second with a bow of 180 pounds draw weight. "Fastest Bow" competitions are held periodically, and arrow velocities over 700 feet per second are expected in the future.

Table 5.4 provides the reader with a few examples of the distances achieved with specific bows in flight shooting. It is a very interesting and challenging archery sport that you may want to try.

Table 5.4 Examples of Flight Shooting Distances Attained with Different Types of Bows

Bow Category	Archer's Name	Distance Yards-Feet-Inches
Men		
Unlimited Footbow	Harry Drake	2028–0–0
Unlimited Longbow	Don Brown	356–1–2
50.0 lb. Primitive Bow	Daniel Perry	295–2–3
Unlimited Compound Bow	Bert McCune, Jr.	1159–2–6
Crossbow	Harry Drake	2047–0–2
Unlimited Primitive Bow	Daniel Perry	283–2–7
Women		
18 kg Flight Bow	Sherrie Reynolds	740–1–8
Unlimited Longbow	April Moon	217–2–3
Unlimited Compound Bow	April Moon	807–1–3
Unlimited Flight Bow	April Moon	1039–1–1
Footbow	Arlyne Rhode	1113–2–6

For further information on flight shooting, the reader may want to write to the NAA Flight Shooting Committee—see Appendix B.

Archery for the Handicapped

The people and organizations that govern archery have long recognized that archery is one sport that can involve virtually everyone as participants. The NAA rules specifically stipulate that no handicapped archer shall be barred from a tournament unless his or her mechanical aids provide an advantage over the other archers or the shots cannot be made within the time sequence. Archers in wheelchairs can shoot on the line from their chairs. There is also an organization for wheelchair archers, The National Wheelchair Athletic Association (see Appendix B for the address). This organization is involved with competitions in archery and other sports at state, regional, national, and international levels (fig. 5.9).

Archery as a sport can be adapted to meet the special needs of people with various types of disabilities. This is done in many school situations and can also be accomplished within the environment of a yard at home.

With some thought and ingenuity, archery tackle can be modified for use by people with all kinds of dysfunctions. As an example, blind people can now enjoy target archery thanks to eighteen years of effort and the creative genius of Al LeFebvre, a blind radio and sound repairman and target archer. He was blinded by diabetes mellitus. His "Sightless Sight System" for target archery was first used by blind archers in 1990 during a competition sponsored by The United States Association for Blind Athletes. The system allows the blind archer to zero in on the center of the target by listening through head phones for two audible signals transmitted from the target to horizontal and vertical bars on a specially built sighting stand for the bow. When both sounds are heard simultaneously, the blind archer releases the arrow. Upon learning the location of the hit, the blind

Figure 5.9
Former U.S. National Wheelchair Champion, Robert Norvelle, follows through after a shot. He has shot 2307 for the Double FITA Round. (Courtesy of *The U.S. Archer;* photo by Raenel Jones)

archer must attempt to make aiming adjustments just like any other archer. LeFebvre has further adapted his system to accommodate archers who are both blind and deaf. Two different levels of vibrations were substituted for the audible signals. As a result, archers who are both blind and deaf can literally feel when to release the arrows.

The National Wheelchair Athletic Association makes very few adaptations or special accommodations for the target archers in their competitions. Their events are not separated by classification of the disability except in the cases of some quadriplegics. If a quadriplegic can shoot without a mechanical release, he or she competes in regular archery rounds. If a mechanical release is needed due to upper limb weakness or some other abnormality, quadriplegics with common syndromes compete against one another in a separate division of each round. For shooting stability, novice quadriplegic archers who use mechanical release aids may be strapped into their wheelchairs during the first year of competition only. These archers may also receive help in nocking their arrows. All of the other challenging and difficult aspects of target archery must be met by the archer.

Jim Cowart, an adapted physical education specialist with the Alameda Schools in Hayward, California, is a professional who has modified archery tackle so his students can enjoy the sport. Figure 5.10 shows an adapted archery bow in use by a student with some neuromuscular limitations. The bow is mounted on a camera tripod, and a release aid (Stuart Hot Shot Release) was placed where

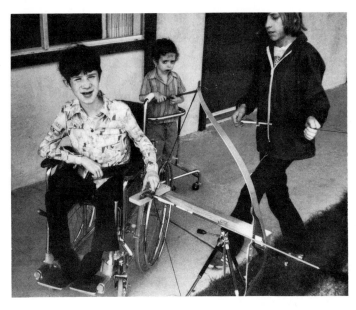

Figure 5.10
A student with muscular dystrophy enjoying the sport of archery by using an adapted bow with a mechanical release device. (Courtesy Jim Cowart, Schools of Alameda County, Hayward, California 94501)

the student could trigger it. The teacher or another student makes the draw and loads the string into the release aid, but the physically handicapped student must make the all-important vertical and horizontal aiming adjustments allowed by the camera tripod. When the student has the aiming alignment desired, the release aid is triggered by the finger motion. The arrow is on its way, and the student has the pleasure of knowing that he or she has plotted its trajectory. If the arrow does not go where it was intended, the handicapped archer must go through the same mental processes and make the necessary aiming adjustments in the same manner as any other archer.

Tackle modifications can be made to handle most problems the handicapped person would have in archery. If the student cannot keep or control the arrow on the bowstring, the serving can be increased in circumference or the plastic arrow nock may be narrowed. If the student cannot keep the arrow on the arrow rest while drawing, the Bear Arro-Guide arrow rest may be modified with a strip of plastic to contain the arrow without having a negative affect on its trajectory and velocity. Jim Cowart utilized these modifications with success for his adapted physical education students.

There are opportunities for handicapped archers to participate in virtually all aspects of archery. That includes not only target archery, but clout shooting, flight shooting, field archery, bow fishing, and bow hunting. *Archery can be a sport for everyone who enjoys it!*

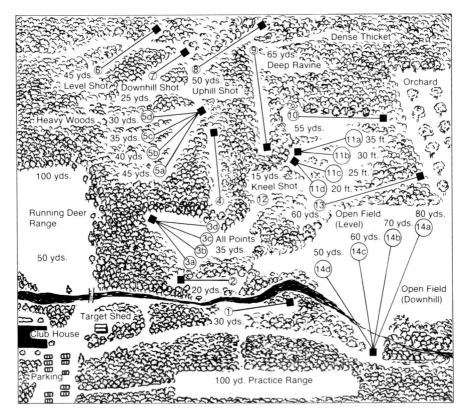

Figure 5.11
A field archery club with a 14-target basic unit.

Field Archery

Field archery is different from target archery primarily in that the target course is often laid out in wooded and hilly areas. Field archers walk the course. Twenty acres make an ideal field archery course, while shooting distances range from 15 feet to 80 yards. The size and type of target are determined by the distance and type of round being shot. *A field archery course consists of 14 targets; these are called a unit.* Two units or twice around one unit constitutes a round in field archery. Figure 5.11 is a diagram of a typical field archery club with a 14-target basic unit. These units are usually developed to simulate hunting conditions.

The NFAA has 50 chartered associations and more than 1200 affiliated clubs. These clubs have a membership representing over one hundred thousand archers. The clubs hold many local tournaments throughout the year for members. Each state holds a field archery championship, and these are well attended. The National Field Archery Championship Tournament draws from 500 to 1000 competitors annually.

Table 5.5 Field Archery Shooting Styles and Legal Equipment

Style	Sight(s)	Release Aid	Stabilizers	Nocking Point
Barebow	No	No	Yes	Yes
Freestyle	Yes	Yes	Yes	Yes
Freestyle Limited	Yes	No	Yes	Yes
Competitive Bowhunter	No	No	One	Yes
Freestyle Bowhunter (5 points & peep)	Yes	Yes	One	Yes
Freestyle Limited Bowhunter (5 points & peep)	Yes	No	One	Yes

The NFAA is dedicated to bow hunting, bow fishing, conservation, the preservation of large and small game animals, and to the promotion of a wide variety of competitions. The organization of the NFAA is structured to administer to the needs of the archers interested in these areas. (See Appendix B for the NFAA address.)

Shooting Equipment

The type of tackle that can or cannot be used by the field archer depends upon the style of shooting done. There are six styles in field archery: (1) freestyle, (2) freestyle limited, (3) barebow, (4) competitive bow hunter, (5) bow hunter freestyle, and (6) bow hunter freestyle limited. Compound, long, and recurve bows are all legal in field archery. Table 5.5 summarizes some of the major differences between shooting styles and the use of sights, release aids, stabilizers, and nocking points. Other equipment differences also exist regarding broadheads, arrow rest, clicker usage, and other equipment.

Since most field archers are interested in bow hunting and/or bow fishing, the total weight of the arrow needs to approximate the arrow weight when it is fitted with the broadhead point. Practice with broadheads or shooting with them at field archery targets can be impractical because of the damage they inflict. Field points are made to match the heavy weight of the hunting broadheads used by the archer. A threaded bushing can be fitted into the arrow shaft. Field points and broadheads can be used interchangeably. A single set of arrows can be used for field archery practice and hunting if the weights are matched perfectly. This setup is shown in figure 5.12. The field points are much easier to use for most regular practices. Broadheads should be used for practice before hunting season and to tune the hunting bow.

Figure 5.12
Interchangeable arrow for broadhead and field point use. A field archery point is being screwed into a threaded bushing at the end of the shaft.

Divisions of Competition

Age and sex divisions are established in field archery to provide equitable competition. In addition, the NFAA has a sophisticated handicapping system designed to be an equalizer for archers with different abilities. The divisions for competition plus the handicap system make competitions very interesting for all field archers.

The Adult Division is for men and women 18 years of age and older. Archers who are 16 and 17 years of age compete in the Young Adult Division, and the Youth Division is for archers ages 12 through 15. Cub archers are under 12 years of age. There is also a Professional Division for men and women 18 years of age and over. All of these divisions of competition and the styles of shooting noted previously provide opportunities for competition at the national and sectional tournaments. An additional division is added for archers 55 years of age and over at national tournaments. This is known as the Senior Division. It is optional at sectional and state levels.

In addition to these divisions of competition, the NFAA now has a program in place to accommodate the needs and interests of young people under the age of 18 who shoot with compound bows. This activity is known as the NFAA Junior Bowhunter Program. It provides a special award system plus competition for junior compound shooters. It is designed to help interested and motivated young archers into competitions at the state, sectional, and national levels. Guidance is also provided for young people who want to develop their hunting skills or who desire just to pursue the sport of field archery.

The Junior Bowhunter Program offers Indoor and Outdoor Field and Animal Rounds. These are the Freeman Bowhunter Round, Indoor Round, Animal Round, and Field Round. Achievement level scores for patches and awards are established for each of these rounds based on the shooting styles: (1) barebow, (2) freestyle limited, or (3) freestyle. What may or may not be used with these styles of shooting is outlined for you in table 5.5. The NFAA Junior Bowhunter Program helps the young archers get started in the sport correctly, and that is an important factor.

Official NFAA Rounds

The number of arrows shot, targets, shooting positions, rules, and scoring differ widely between field archery rounds. There are thirteen official NFAA Rounds. Eight of these are shot outdoors, while the remaining five are indoor rounds:

Outdoor

1. Field Round
2. NFAA Expert Field Round
3. Hunter Round
4. Animal Round
5. 15 Target "300" Field Round
6. 15 Target "300" Hunter Round
7. 15 Target "300" Animal Round
8. NFAA International Round

Indoor

1. NFAA Indoor Round
2. NFAA Indoor Championship Round
3. NFAA Freeman Round
4. Freeman Bowhunter Indoor Round
5. Flint Bowman Indoor Round

Generally, the target faces used for most of the outdoor rounds are 65, 50, 35, and 20 centimeters in diameter, based on the distances to be shot. Targets for the various rounds have different configurations, and the animal rounds use animal targets only. There are three-dimensional, life-size animal targets. These targets are placed in four diminishing size groups. Animals such as elk and moose are in the largest group, while ducks and jack rabbit targets are in the smallest group. The diversity of the outdoor rounds and their placement within the shooting unit help make field archery challenging.

The indoor rounds have targets of various sizes and designs. They are 40, 35, 20, and 16 centimeters in diameter, depending upon the round. Animal targets may be used instead of the 40-centimeter target face in the Freeman Bowhunter Indoor Round. Twenty yards is the greatest distance shot in the first four indoor rounds listed above. Thirty yards is the greatest distance shot in the Flint Bowman Indoor Round. These distances make indoor shooting popular.

Awards

Any effective organization has a system to recognize the efforts of its members. The NFAA has a good awards system ranging from NFAA Membership Pins to the Compton Medal of Honor. The latter award is the most highly esteemed honor in all archery. NFAA bow hunters gain recognition by qualifying for the following game awards: (1) Art Young Big Game Awards, (2) Art Young Small Game Awards, (3) Bow Hunter Pin, (4) Expert Bow Hunter Pin, (5) Master Bow Hunter Medal, and (6) the Diamond Buck Award for the largest deer based on antler measurements.

If a field archer telescopes an arrow during a round when the arrow is lodged in the highest scoring area of a target, he or she is eligible for entry into the Fellowship of Robin Hood. And, on a less prestigious note, a field archer who commits an unwitting error or "boner" while hunting is eligible to enter The Order of the Bone! Recognition is also given in the NFAA Bowfisher Program to those archers taking the largest rough fish during the year. The Bowfisher Program is discussed in Chapter 7.

Field archery, like other archery sports and activities, is a challenging and fulfilling endeavor. It can be enjoyed throughout a lifetime from "Cub" to "Senior" Division status.

Review

1. What are the main organizations for archers in the United States?
2. What equipment and tackle modifications are illegal in target archery competition?
3. How does the NAA contribute to the development of archers for the Olympic Games?
4. How does a field archer qualify for the Fellowship of Robin Hood and The Order of the Bone?
5. What is the NAA dress code for tournament competitors?
6. What would be a good, competitive score for the FITA Round?
7. During a round in target archery, what do several short blasts on the whistle by the Director of Shooting indicate?
8. Name the several types of competitive events for which the crossbow may be used.
9. Describe the differences between match and field shooting with crossbows.
10. How do the target scoring values for clout shooting differ from target archery? Are there also differences in the tackle?
11. What distances are attained in flight shooting with the various types of bows? What is the longest distance ever recorded for an arrow shot from any type of bow? How long would it take you to run that distance to retrieve the arrow?
12. Describe the ways in which archery may be used by handicapped archers and the levels of competition for handicapped archers.
13. The current World Speed Record for flight archery is 588 feet per second. What arrow velocities are anticipated in the future?
14. In what ways does flight archery differ markedly from other forms of archery competition?
15. What are the six shooting styles used for competition by the NFAA?

Bow Hunting

6

The sport of bow hunting has become increasingly popular in the last few years. Its gain in popularity is documented by the escalating numbers of archery hunters who register for licenses and permits with the official wildlife agencies (see Appendix A). As one example, in 1971, 6412 archery hunters went after deer in Arizona. By 1990, that number had increased to 19,325 archers who went into the field bow hunting for deer. During this same period in Arizona, archers seeking permits to hunt elk increased from 659 to 4800. A lottery system for permits had to be established. These same trends have been observed in other states: for example, 51,600 elk were harvested by bow hunters in Colorado during 1990.

There are numerous reasons given by hunters for using the bow and arrow as their primary hunting weapons. One of the most common is that the inherent challenge of bow hunting has rewards that cannot be met by any other hunting method. The bow hunter is limited to close shooting ranges and has to understand the animal's habits and the environment to be successful. Stalking becomes an integral part of the hunt. Seasons set by state game and fish departments are generally longer for archery than for firearms. This gives the archer a chance for more time in the field. Also, there is a wider variety of small and large game animals that can be bow hunted, and this makes the sport more attractive than gun hunting. Finally, many archers indicate that they prefer the relatively uncrowded conditions found in the field during the bow hunting seasons. Unfortunate hunting accidents are not likely to occur during bow hunting seasons; however, they are fairly common during firearm seasons.

With more people participating in bow hunting, there has been a corresponding increase in the refinements of archery tackle. Competition between the archery manufacturers has resulted in a wider selection of fine bow hunting equipment. With the large number of specialized hunting products on the market, the process of selecting equipment can become a confusing task. Because of this, it is necessary to have a basic understanding of what constitutes good bow hunting tackle. That will help you in making the correct purchasing decisions. It is recommended that hunting tackle be purchased from a professional archery tackle shop where people understand how to accurately match bows to arrows and archery tackle to the needs of the bow hunter.

With modifications, good bow hunting tackle can also be used for some other archery sports. Hunting tackle, for example, can be modified for use in field archery. The principles for purchasing hunting tackle are almost the same as those for buying target archery tackle discussed in Chapter 3. There are, however, major differences between target archery and bow hunting tackle. *The individual who wants to participate in bow hunting exclusively should purchase tackle designed specifically for bow hunting purposes.*

Hunting Bows

Modern hunting bows are different than bows wielded by the ancient people of Europe or the ones used by American Indians in the last century. Bows that have provided food and protected primitive people for centuries look like toys when compared to current bow hunting tackle. Though the primitive hunting bows were not as efficient, the individuals who used them possessed excellent hunting skills. Their very survival attests to that fact. Those people had a key motivational factor that most bow hunters today do not have—hunger!

Bows used commonly for modern hunting include the crossbow, straight bow (longbow), recurve, and compound. Each step in the progression from longbow to compound bow represents an improvement in the ability of a bow to transfer its potential energy into kinetic energy to project the arrow. While it is virtually impossible to make a bow that is 100 percent efficient, the best designs of today's bows are reaching an energy storage efficiency in the range of 80 to 84 percent.

Crossbows

The crossbow is one of the legendary weapons of archery. The saga of *Wilhelm Tell* helped romanticize the crossbow. Most people have read about crossbows, but they have never seen or held one. A quality crossbow camouflaged for bow hunting is shown in figure 6.1.

The use of the crossbow as a legal hunting weapon has gained momentum in the past several years. Some states now allow its use for a few of the larger game animals as well as for the "varmint calling" critters (coyote, bobcat, fox, etc.) and bird hunting. As with recurve and compound bows, specific criteria are established by state game and fish commissions specifying the poundage of the crossbow, length of the bolt, and size of the broadhead. In Arizona, for example, a hunting crossbow must have a minimum draw weight of 125 pounds and shoot at least a 16-inch bolt. The bolt must be tipped with a broadhead that has a metal cutting edge of at least ⅞ of an inch in length.

If you are interested in bow hunting with crossbow, keep in mind that state regulations vary regarding the legal use of this weapon. You must contact the appropriate wildlife agency in the state where you wish to hunt *prior* to going into the field. They will supply you with the latest rules and regulations pertaining to crossbow hunting. (See Appendix A.)

The crossbow has gone through several design changes in recent years. The newer generation of crossbows of the type shown in figure 6.1 use the same mechanical devices as the compound cam bows for increasing arrow velocity. They

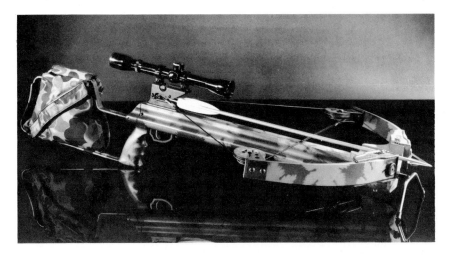

Figure 6.1
A hunting compound crossbow camouflaged and ready for use with a broadhead on the bolt.
(Courtesy Precision Shooting Equipment, 2727 N. Fairview Ave., Tucson, Arizona 85705)

also use modern construction materials that can withstand the added stresses on the bow limbs. These factors make the crossbow highly efficient for use in both target archery and bow hunting.

Longbows

Longbows such as those shown in figures 5.1 and 5.2 can be used for hunting. However, they are used only on a limited basis for hunting today. The reason is that they are mechanically inefficient, as discussed in Chapter 3, when compared to recurve and compound bows. But, these limitations are viewed as advantages by individuals who value true adventure in hunting.

If you use a longbow for hunting, the emphasis must be placed on the terms *hunting* and *sport*. The bow hunter who uses the longbow must be an excellent stalker and hunter with in-depth knowledge of the game being sought. Some legendary archers such as Howard Hill, Dr. Saxton Pope, and Art Young used the longbow effectively in the field. It can be done. If you desire "true sport" while bow hunting, the longbow may be the bow for you. Because the longbow places more demands and challenges on the human being as a hunter, a few bow hunters are returning to it as the bow of choice for the hunt. As a result, some bow manufacturers are now selling a modern type of the longbow.

Recurve Bows

The recurve principle has been known for a long time but was not fully utilized until modern materials were developed. Plastics and adhesives have made it possible to laminate layers of material that will remain intact under the stresses that a bow is exposed to during the shooting process. The tips of a working recurve

Figure 6.2
A take-down recurve hunting bow equipped with a covered bow quiver, brush buttons, and string silencers. (Courtesy Black Widow Bow Company, H. C. R. #1, Box 357-1, Highlandville, Missouri 65669)

bow will point away from the archer when the bow is unstrung. However, when the bow is braced, the tips are pulled back and will usually point upwards with the string contacting the belly of the bow for at least two inches. That adds to the leverage and energy potential of the bow. If the string does not contact the bow in this manner, the bow will not work to its best mechanical advantage. It will work like a longbow. A take-down recurve hunting bow is shown in figure 6.2. The bow is equipped with a covered bow quiver, brush buttons, and string silencers.

The conventional recurve bow will stack its weight as the string is drawn to the anchor point. The peak weight of the bow increases during the draw, and there is added pressure on the drawing hand fingers. (Release aids do minimize this problem, and they are legal in bow hunting. See figs. 6.11, 6.12, and 6.14.) You hold the complete bow weight for your arrow length at anchor point when using a recurve bow. This can be a problem for some people. (That is the major difference between recurve and compound bows, and it is one factor that motivated H.W. Allen to invent the compound bow.) Most people begin with bow or draw weights that they can handle comfortably and then grow into higher poundage equipment. It makes no sense to purchase a bow that is too heavy in terms of bow weight. This will only cause bad habits resulting in accuracy and technique errors, and they are difficult to unlearn.

Famous bow hunters such as Fred Bear, Doug Kittredge, and Jim Dougherty used the recurve bow extensively in past years and added to its popularity. Recurve bows in the hands of expert archers like these have taken the largest and most dangerous animals found in the world. The recurve bow was the primary choice of most archers until the mid-1970s. Since that time it has lost most of its status to the newer compound bows. However, some bow hunters surveyed indicated that they were returning to the recurve bow after using compound bows for several years. The general observation was that the recurve bow made hunting more of a sport than using the compound bow, especially on smaller game animals. Some expert bow hunters who are using the recurve bow again believe that the modern compound bows are being built with too many "mechanical gadgets" on them. That takes some of the sport out of the hunt.

Compound Bows

The compound bow is by far the most popular hunting tool of the modern bow hunter. A check of recent entries into the Pope and Young Records for trophy class animals shows that most were taken by this type of bow. The two-wheel compound bow seems to be the most popular. An example of a two-wheel bow and the terminology for the compound bow are shown in figure 6.3.

As discussed in Chapter 2, the compound bow was invented in January 1966, by H. W. Allen of Billings, Missouri. He wanted to make a more efficient bow for hunting that would shoot arrows at a higher velocity and reduce "stacking," or the amount of bow weight held by the archer at full draw. One of his early models is shown in figure 6.4. The reader can gain some understanding of the engineering evolution of the compound bow by comparing and contrasting figure 2.11, which shows the original Allen Bow now housed in the Smithsonian Institution, with other compound bows shown in this chapter and on today's market.

The compound bow generates greater foot-pounds of energy than composite bows due primarily to its eccentric pulleys, which can be seen on the bows in figures 6.3 and 6.4. The mechanical principles of this pulley system allow peak bow-weight poundage at mid-draw. This effect has two advantages:

1. There is no stacking effect in a compound bow at full draw. The peak poundage is at mid-draw.
2. At release, the poundage increases to peak, and this gives a major increase in foot-pounds of energy for application to the arrow. Arrow velocity is increased.

The compound bow, when drawn, has a "peak" weight and a "let-off" weight. In most cases, compound bows, because of their eccentric wheel design, will have a "let-off" weight of approximately 30 to 65 percent. This means, for example, that if you shoot a 60-pound compound bow with a 65 percent "let-off" factor, the actual weight held on the fingers at full draw will be only 21 pounds. This has its advantages in a situation where the hunter must hold in a fully drawn position at the anchor point for any length of time waiting for the best shot.

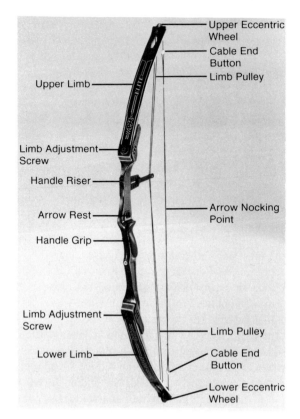

Figure 6.3

A two-wheeled bow with compound bow terminology. (Courtesy Precision Shooting Equipment, 2727 N. Fairview Ave., Tucson, Arizona 85705)

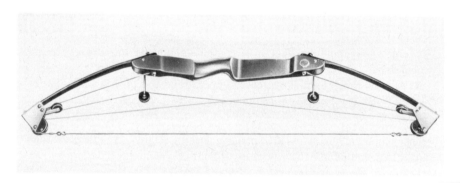

Figure 6.4

An early model (c. 1970) of the Allen Compound Bow. (Courtesy of Allen Archery, 201 Washington Street, Billings, Missouri 65610)

The newer cam-wheel compounds have a change in wheel designs. Instead of a round wheel at the tip, there is a cam-shaped device. These bows generally produce faster arrow velocities than eccentric compounds and recurves of the same bow weight. The advantage in this faster cam-type bow lies in the arrow trajectory. When arrow velocity is higher, the amount of drop is less. This means that your margin for error, due to arrow drop, is decreased. The estimation of distances at close ranges is not as crucial with a cam compound as it is with a recurve bow. An error of 5 yards in estimating distances of 30 yards or less will usually result in a kill shot. This same error with a recurve or compound bow of lower arrow velocity may result in a missed shot or a wounded animal.

Bow Weight

Hunting bows have higher draw weights than their target bow counterparts. While draw weights used for target bows are set by personal preference, the *minimum draw weights* for bow hunting are established by state game and fish departments. Generally, a hunter must use a minimum bow weight of 40 pounds. This ensures that arrow penetration is sufficient for killing game. Most experienced archers use higher draw weights than this for hunting. It is recommended that bow weights of 45 to 60 pounds be used on game animals up to the size of deer, and bow weights ranging from 60 to 80 pounds be used for larger game animals such as elk, bear, and moose.

Bow hunters, like target archers, need to select and shoot bows they can handle. The choice of bow weight will depend on several things: (1) bow hunting experience, (2) your muscular strength, (3) the type of game you plan to hunt, and (4) state game laws. When selecting a hunting bow, you should choose the heaviest weight you can handle with ease and comfort for several consecutive shots. If you are comfortable with a 40-pound bow, then that is the bow you should shoot. Do not make the common mistake of purchasing a bow that has excessive poundage for your strength level. It will be especially difficult to shoot when you are tired and cold out on the hunt. Start with a lighter bow and work up as you become stronger and more experienced. Use the conditioning guidelines outlined in Chapter 8 for developing your strength and endurance.

The Archery Manufacturers Organization (AMO) recommends for personal safety purposes that people who use compound bow weights heavier than 60 pounds with draw lengths longer than 30 inches should utilize arrows heavier than 6 grains per pound of peak bow weight. People who use compound bow weights lighter than 60 pounds and draw lengths shorter than 30 inches can use arrows lighter than 6 grains per pound of peak bow weight. (Total arrow weight includes the combined shaft weight, point and insert weights, and the weight of fletching plus the nock.) These recommendations were made because bow hunters tend to overstress their compound bows in an attempt to increase arrow velocity. That is a safety problem! The AMO considers the maximum safe arrow velocity for compound bows under these guidelines to be *270 feet per second.*

Bow Length

The length of the bow for hunting is a very important consideration. Some archers believe that a short bow length is most desirable in the hunting situation. Their argument usually centers around the fact that the shorter bow is less cumbersome in heavily wooded and foliaged areas. This may be true, but how many times does a good bow hunter confine himself or herself to hunting in heavy brush? In these circumstances, it is virtually impossible to shoot accurately with any length bow. The arrow will strike limbs or leaves. As a result, the arrow will not find its mark because of deflections and loss of velocity.

A more important reason for not using a shorter bow is the sharp angle created for the archer against the bowstring and arrow. The angle at the nocking point tends to compress the fingers of the bowstring hand so tightly that a smooth release is difficult when using the conventional three-finger grip. A longer bow, 64 inches, has longer limbs and a longer bowstring; consequently, the angle created at the nocking area at full draw is greater than the same angle for a shorter bow. This allows a smoother release when using the traditional three-finger grip. The use of release devices is legal in bow hunting, and this negates some of the argument for greater bow length related to finger release techniques. The fact remains, however, that the most common and best lengths for hunting bows range from 58 to 64 inches.

Hunting Arrows

The arrow is the single most important piece of tackle when the bow hunter considers accuracy. Many beginning bow hunters make the mistake of purchasing a good bow and then try to shoot mismatched arrows. This only leads to frustration due to missed shots because of inconsistent arrow flight. Most beginners will do better by starting with a lower quality bow and shooting matched aluminum or graphite arrows than they will with a top-of-the-line bow shooting a quiver full of arrows that have different fletching, spines, broadheads, and weights. Exact matching of arrows to each other and to the bow that will shoot them is essential for any type of bow hunting success.

The fiberglass arrow became popular when it came on the market years ago because it offered improvements over the older, wooden arrow shafts. Fiberglass arrows can be purchased as matched sets having the same spine, length, and weight. So, if one of your fiberglass hunting arrows is damaged or lost, it is not difficult to obtain an exact replacement. Another consideration that influenced people to use fiberglass is that they are almost unbreakable. A deflected shot that would shatter a wooden arrow or bend an aluminum one would do little or no damage to a fiberglass shaft. Also, unlike wooden arrows, fiberglass shafts are impervious to wet weather conditions. They will not warp. The only real drawback in using fiberglass arrows is that there are better aerodynamic arrows on the market. *As a result, very few bow hunters use fiberglass arrows.*

Aluminum is by far the most popular material used for hunting arrows. (Graphite or carbon arrows are also becoming popular with bow hunters.) Bow hunters choose aluminum over wood or fiberglass because it offers excellent accuracy. This is because aluminum and aluminum/carbon arrows are aerodynamically sound and can be matched exactly for such factors as spine, shaft weight, length, shaft size, peak bow weight, straightness, and other variables related to your specific shooting style and tackle.

Aluminum arrows can be purchased to match any type of bow or bow weight. The manufacturers have developed charts to assist you with arrow selection using the variables of draw length, bow type (recurve or compound), bow weight, and let-off. These shafts are made of high strength tubular aluminum that comes in different diameters and wall thicknesses. By varying the diameter and wall thickness of a shaft, different spines can be obtained. (Aluminum shafts usually have four numbers imprinted on them that indicate the diameter and wall thickness. For example, an aluminum arrow that has the number 2117 tells you that the shaft diameter is 21/32nds, with wall thickness 0.017 of an inch.) In most cases, the bow hunter will have several shaft sizes to choose from when using any particular bow weight.

Archers are so concerned with accuracy that most do not mind the extra cost of purchasing aluminum or graphite arrows. One of the major annoyances is that, unlike fiberglass, aluminum shafts often bend when they deflect off a hard object. If the bend is not too drastic or too close to either end of the shaft, the arrow can be straightened by using an arrow straightener. Most archery pro shops have this tool and will straighten arrows for a minimal charge. Many serious bow hunters, who use aluminum or aluminum-carbon shafts, will invest in a precision arrow straightener. This provides the convenience of being able to straighten bent arrows in the field or at home. Also, an arrow straightener will pay for itself if a person does much field practice or hunting.

The hunting arrow used while shooting a crossbow is known as a *bolt* (fig. 6.1). Bolts are shorter than regular hunting arrows, but they are usually shot at much higher draw weights. This is evident when looking at the minimum allowable draw weights used for hunting. Most states set *minimum draw weights* for recurve and compound bows at 40 pounds as compared to crossbow minimums of 125 pounds. The rationale for setting the higher draw weights for crossbows lies in the relationship between the speed of the bolt and its weight. A lighter projectile (crossbow bolt) shot at a higher velocity should penetrate as well as a heavier object shot at a slower speed. Here again, the concern is for good arrow penetration so a properly placed shot will result in a successful kill—not a wounded animal!

Arrow Fletching

Fletching material is generally made of either turkey feathers or plastic vanes. Most hunters choose the plastic variety simply because they are more durable and resilient in poor weather conditions. A plastic vane subjected to a rain storm will still shoot with good accuracy. Also, plastic vanes do not make as much noise during arrow flight. This reduces the probability of "spooking" the animal during the critical moments between arrow release and impact.

Turkey feathers are still used by bow hunters who favor a natural material over a synthetic substitute. Some hunters claim that shooting turkey-fletched shafts will give a faster arrow flight and flatter trajectory due to better clearance from the bow. The chief drawbacks to using turkey fletching are that moisture affects them and they do not wear as well as plastic vanes. Wet turkey feathers will alter the flight of the arrow.

Another consideration in dealing with arrow fletching is the length. In most cases, the fletching used for hunting is longer than that used for target archery shafts. This is due to the differences in the total weight of the arrow. Since a hunting arrow is heavier due to its broadhead point, it needs longer fletching to stabilize it during flight. Fletching used for hunting arrows range from 4 inches to 5½ inches in length, depending on the number of vanes and total weight of the arrow. Most hunters experiment with these factors to determine which combinations work best for them. (See fig. 3.3.)

The number of vanes placed on an arrow shaft has aroused considerable debate among archers. Some individuals prefer a three-vaned arrow, while others like four vanes. The proponents of the three-vaned arrows claim that this arrangement results in more efficient arrow stabilization during flight. An arrow that utilizes three vanes usually has two set at 120 degrees and the other at 90 degrees out from the bow. The odd vane is called the *cock feather* and is usually of a different color. When nocking an arrow to the string, it is essential to make sure that the cock, or index, feather is facing out; otherwise it can brush against the arrow rest or riser section of the bow and throw the shot off. Hunters who use the four-vaned shafts usually do so because they do not want to have to concern themselves with making sure that the cock feather is pointing outward before taking a shot. This is an advantage in a situation where the hunter does not want to drop the eyes from the target in order to nock an arrow. The four-vaned arrows are glued to the shaft at 75-degree and 105-degree angles.

There are several other types of fletching used by bow hunters. One of the most common is the flu-flu. A flu-flu (fig. 3.3) utilizes oversized fletching material in order to create wind resistance and shorten the arrow's flight distance. This makes them effective at close ranges, but their velocity drops off very fast as distance increases. Hunters use these arrows on small animals such as squirrels where shots are taken at distances of under twenty yards. A missed shot at a tree squirrel with normal fletching usually results in a lost arrow. The chance of arrow recovery with flu-flu fletch is much greater.

Vanes are glued to the shaft in two ways: (1) helical and (2) straight. It is recommended that hunting arrows use the helical fletching because it helps to increase the velocity of the spin of the arrow around the longitudinal axis of the shaft. That helps stabilize the heavier hunting arrow.

Just as with all other aspects of archery, the type of material, length, weight, and number of fletching used on the arrow shafts should match precisely. Mismatching any of these can cause accuracy problems not directly related to the shooting ability of the bow hunter.

Figure 6.5
A Navajo Indian and his bow hunting tackle.
(From E. G. Heath, *The Grey Goose Wing*)

Figure 6.6
Indian arrow and spear points from the collection of Loyd Howell, Wyaconda, Missouri 63474.

Bow Hunting Points

Before proceeding with a discussion of modern arrow points, let us digress some-what and evaluate the bow hunting tackle of the American Indian. Obviously, these people were highly successful as hunters. Their survival over thousands of years in wilderness and hostile environments is evidence of their skill. Satisfying hunger as well as obtaining skin and furs for clothing and shelter were the major motivating factors for developing bow hunting skills.

The Navajo Indian drawing his bow in figure 6.5 would have had less trouble obtaining game if he and other Indians had had bows like those shown in figures 6.2 and 6.3. Points like those shown in figures 6.7 and 6.8 instead of the Indian arrow heads seen in figure 6.6 would have also helped.

The Navajo and other American Indian tribes developed very effective composite bows made with a backing of layers of animal tendons or sinew. By using animal tendons, the Indians increased the tensile strength of their bows. This material has a tensile strength of 20 kilograms per square millimeter, which is approximately four times greater than using wood only. The development of the

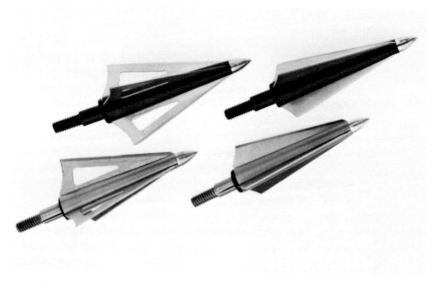

Figure 6.7
Popular hunting broadheads. (Courtesy Precision Shooting Equipment, 2727 N. Fairview Ave., Tucson, AZ 85705)

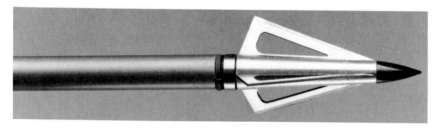

Figure 6.8
Close-up view of a modern three-bladed insert type of broadhead. Broadheads must be RAZOR SHARP!

composite bow probably evolved by trial and error over several centuries in this country, because American Indians had no way to know that sophisticated composite bows had been developed centuries before by other bowyers elsewhere in the world.

The arrow heads, or points, used by American Indians differ appreciably from those used by contemporary bow hunters. If the reader takes the time to compare and contrast figure 6.6 with figures 6.7 and 6.8, the differences will immediately become apparent. Figures 6.7 and 6.8 show popular broadhead points used by contemporary bow hunters.

Figure 6.6 shows a variety of Indian arrow and spear points that were found in the northeast corner of Missouri by Loyd Howell. Indian tribes inhabited the Clark County area for hundreds of years prior to the nineteenth century. Many

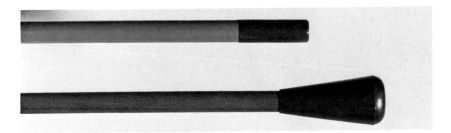

Figure 6.9
Blunt hunting points.

individuals would assume that all of the points shown in figure 6.6 are arrow heads, but that is not the case. The point on the extreme right in figure 6.6 and the point on the extreme right of the upper row are both spear points. The large, 4¾-inch-long "beaver tail" point on the right side of the picture was used on a shaft of a spear. The upper right point is 3¼ inches.

The remaining points in figure 6.6 are arrow points ranging in length from ¾ inch to 3 inches. These were attached to the ends of wooden arrow shafts. The small, ¾-inch-long arrow point, in the lower row on the left side, is called a *bird point*. One theory about bird points specifies that they were made and used by smaller children who used them with light pulling bows and shot them at birds. In other words, these small points may have been functional toys used by Indian children learning to bow hunt. The arrow without a notch in the upper row is a war point. These arrows were shot into enemies. When the shaft was pulled, the war point (2½ inches in length) remained within the body of the individual who was shot. If the penetration by the arrow itself failed to kill the individual who was hit, the infection caused by having this large foreign object in the body would ultimately cause death. There were no medical corpsmen, antibiotics, or M.A.S.H. units with the Indians to help take care of their wounds!

Today, bow hunting points or broadheads are designed in all shapes and sizes, depending on the intended purpose. Many bow hunters incorporate inserts with their arrows, thus allowing them to change a point by simply screwing one out and putting another point in its place, as seen in figure 5.12. There are several devices on the market for changing and inserting points.

Field tips commonly used in field archery are utilized for bow hunting practice and on some small game animals. They come in various weights and shapes. Most bow hunters try to match the weight of their field tips to the weight of their broadheads in order to make target practice a more functional exercise. Field tips are much easier on target faces and mats. It is best to practice with tips that are of the same weight as your broadheads, because that makes the aiming process more functional.

Blunts, as seen in figure 6.9, are favorite tips for hunting small game. They are made of rubber or metal, and usually slip on or screw into an insert on the arrow shaft. These tips kill by impact force. As a result, they do not destroy edible

Figure 6.10
Bird hunting requires a special arrow point with wire loops in order to hit the bird in flight.
(Courtesy *Bow and Arrow Magazine*)

meat on the small animal. (A broadhead such as the one in figure 6.8 does incredible damage to an animal the size of a rabbit or squirrel!) The shocking power of a blunted arrow is usually enough to cause death instantaneously to smaller game animals.

There are other types of arrow points, manufactured or homemade, to be used for bagging small game. Some incorporate field tips that have a piece of wire brazed through them, and others use spring wire protruding in four directions. These tips also work on force of impact and are efficient for bagging small game.

Archers who hunt birds have developed a tip that has four wide loops of wire that can clip a bird in flight. By looping the wire, a wider circumference is created in which the bird can be hit as the arrow passes. A direct hit is not necessary to bring down the bird with this kind of tip (fig. 6.10). A wire loop impacting with a bird's wing in flight will usually cause it to drop to the ground.

Broadheads are the only legal hunting points that can be used on large game species. Most state game and fish departments require broadheads to be at least ⅞ of an inch in width and have metal cutting edges. The key to the broadhead's effectiveness is its *sharpness.* SINCE A BROADHEAD KILLS BY HEMORRHAGING, IT IS ABSOLUTELY ESSENTIAL THAT THE CUTTING EDGE IS RAZOR SHARP (fig. 6.8).

It is important to remember that penetration by a dull arrow point will not always kill an animal. The blood vessels will not be lacerated enough to allow a steady, unobstructed blood flow. The dull arrow point will tear tissue instead of making a surgical type of laceration. A torn blood vessel's smooth internal musculature will constrict to act as its own protective mechanism against hemorrhage. The bow hunter who is attempting to kill does not want this to occur. The animal struck in this fashion tends to continue moving and become lost to the hunter. The American Indian had the problem of dull arrow points while bow hunting with the type of tackle shown in figures 6.5 and 6.6. However, the American Indian was better at trailing and finding the stricken animal in various types of terrain and under all kinds of weather conditions. He also was not under the same time constraints as modern hunters—for example, vacation's over and there is a pressing need to get back to the job. Bow hunting for food and clothing was the Indian's job!

An archer shooting a dull arrow must strike the heart or lungs most of the time to kill the game animal. This is not necessarily true if a razor-sharp arrow is used. Such a hit in a large muscle group, for example, will clearly sever arteries, veins, capillaries, and other blood vessels in the area. This will cause hemorrhage sufficient and fast enough to result in death rather quickly. The bow hunter merely waits a while and then follows the trail of blood from the stricken animal to where it collapses from asphyxiation.

One way to tell a novice from the serious bow hunter is by the sharpness of the latter's broadheads. Knowledgeable hunters will not step into the woods with broadheads they could not shave with! It is the responsibility of the hunter to see that this critical factor is not overlooked.

There are two basic types of broadheads, the ones that need to be hand sharpened and the ones that use razor blade inserts. If you do not know how to hone an edge to razor sharpness, it is recommended that the insert type be used so you will be assured of effective cutting edges (fig. 6.8). If you prefer to hand sharpen your broadheads but have had difficulty getting the desired edge, the following suggestions will help make the task easier. The tools needed for this sharpening job are two files, one cowhide strop, and some jeweler's rouge. The strop is made from a piece of leather, and you use the rough-out side. The strop is securely glued to a 10- to 12-inch piece of 2 × 4 board by means of contact cement. The sharpening process is started by putting a rough edge on the broadhead with a 10-inch mill bastard file. Once the edge is formed and the tip chiseled, it is reworked lightly with an 8-inch mill bastard file. The final step puts the desired cutting edge on the broadhead. It consists of putting jeweler's rouge on the cowhide strop and moving the edge away in long strokes. This is repeated until the edge is sharp enough to shave with. Sharpening your blades adds a personal touch to the hunting experience.

There are many quality broadheads on the market today, and most of them are more than adequate for bringing down game as long as they are sharp and hit a vital area. It is recommended that you talk to as many experienced bow hunters as possible to learn their preferences before making your first choice.

Bow Hunting Accessories

A quick look into any well-stocked archery pro shop will show many different devices available to bow hunters to improve their chances of a successful hunt. Many of these accessories can be used for both bow hunting and target archery.

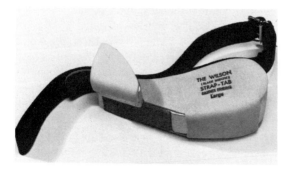

Figure 6.11
A release device (c. 1970) that utilizes a strap and thumb pressure. (Courtesy Wilson Brothers, Route 1, Elkland, Missouri 65644)

Devices discussed in Chapter 3, such as finger tabs, arm guards, and arrow rests, fall into this category. Hunters, however, need some additional tackle specifically for bow hunting. This includes such items as special quivers, mechanical releases, string silencers, overdraw systems, and hunting sights.

The arrow quiver is one of the most necessary accessories in terms of safety and convenience. There are three common quivers in use today: (1) the hip quiver, (2) shoulder quiver, and (3) bow quiver. The hip and shoulder quivers are sometimes used during field practice where the archer does not have to be concerned with brush or other obstacles. *The bow quiver is the most popular and recommended method of carrying arrows in a hunting situation* (fig. 6.2). It is attached directly to the bow by means of springs or screws. Bow quivers come in different models capable of carrying from 4 to 16 arrows. Each individual should decide on what capacity quiver will fit his or her needs. If you are going to use a bow quiver during the hunt, mount it on your bow for use during practice sessions.

The single most important safety consideration for a bow quiver is that the broadheads be covered and tightly secured. Some of the early clip-on bow quivers did not shield the broadheads. As a result, serious accidents occurred when archers inadvertently touched these razor-sharp points while reaching for an arrow. Falling on an uncovered bow quiver or one of your broadheads could be fatal while in the field. They are designed to cause hemorrhage in all animals, including humans!

Release aids are used by some bow hunters to eliminate elements of human error caused by the fingers when releasing the arrow. These are designed in many shapes and have evolved through several steps. Some of the first releases were made of a piece of rope or strap, which was wrapped around the string and held with pressure from the thumb (fig. 6.11). These were very useful on recurve bows of lower draw weights, but they are difficult to handle on higher weighted bows. Other releases, like the one in figure 6.12, were developed to handle this problem.

Figure 6.12 shows a hunting release device for a compound bow. The front hook is attached to the bowstring as shown in figure 6.13. The release is held in the palm of the hand, with the draw pressure distributed over the heel of the hand on the rear butt plate. Vigorous gripping is not needed, and the thumb is placed below the release. The index finger is placed on the trigger. After the draw

Figure 6.12
The Allen Hunting Release designed for use with compound bows. (Courtesy Allen Archery, 201 Washington Street, Billings, Missouri 65610)

has been made, the forward end of the release is placed on your anchor point. (Fig. 6.13 can be used as a reference for using the type of release shown in fig. 6.12.) There are two rubber beads mounted on the bowstring, along with the nock-sets. At full draw, slide the upper bead to the line of sight across the top of the bead to the point where the sight ball appears as shown in the "sight picture." When the proper alignment is made and the sight pin is on target, the arrow is released by squeezing the trigger with a steady force. There must be *no motion* of the bow when the arrow is released.

A newer type of release aid is shown in figure 6.14. This type of mechanical release is popular for use with compound bows, especially those with higher bow weights.

Although release aids remove human error and can improve accuracy, it is important to realize that arrows may be accidentally released before the archer is ready. Common sense dictates that you thoroughly familiarize yourself with the release device and be especially aware of where the tip of the arrow is pointing as the bow is drawn.

String silencers serve one function, and that is to dampen the sound of release. There are many variations to choose from. The type seen in figure 6.2 is commonly referred to as "cat whiskers," and is used by many hunters. Other common types include rubber buttons, yarn strands, or rubber burrs. The cost is nominal. The silencer is valuable, because it allows the hunter a chance at a second shot by not spooking the animal.

The majority of bow hunters view the bowsight as a vital accessory. The hunting bowsight is usually calibrated in 5- to 10-yard increments, starting at 10 yards and moving out to as much as 60 yards depending upon the skill level of the archer. While 60-yard shots at a game animal are not unduly difficult for experienced bow hunters, it is highly recommended that beginners limit their shots to distances of 40 yards or less.

Archers who use bowsights for hunting are commonly called "pin-shooters." The reason is that pinlike devices are used as target locators. An example of a pin bowsight is shown in figure 6.15.

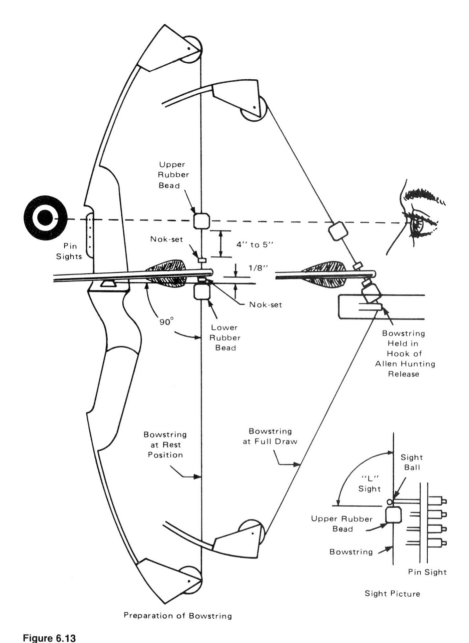

Upper
Rubber
Bead

Pin
Sights

Nok-set

4'' to 5''

1/8''

Nok-set

90°

Lower
Rubber
Bead

Bowstring
at Rest
Position

Bowstring
at Full Draw

Bowstring
Held in
Hook of
Allen Hunting
Release

Sight
Ball

"L"
Sight

Upper Rubber
Bead

Bowstring

Pin Sight

Sight Picture

Preparation of Bowstring

Figure 6.13
Aiming and using the Allen Hunting Release with a compound bow. (Courtesy Allen Archery, 201 Washington Street, Billings, Missouri 65610)

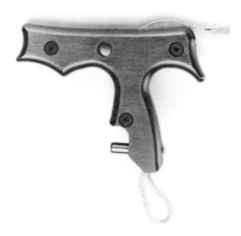

Figure 6.14
A release aid (c. 1990) designed for use with heavy compound bows. (Courtesy Precision Shooting Equipment, 2727 N. Fairview Ave., Tucson, Arizona 85705)

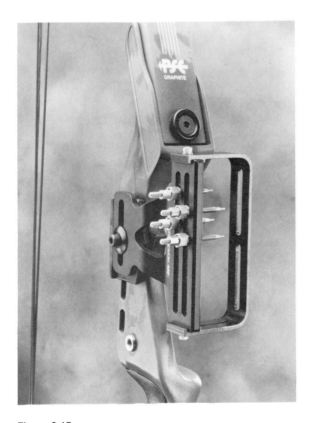

Figure 6.15
A pin-type bowsight used by hunters. Note the sturdy guard to protect the pins. (Courtesy Precision Shooting Equipment, 2727 N. Fairview Ave., Tucson, Arizona 85705)

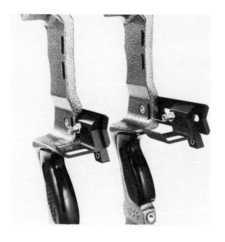

Figure 6.16

Example of an overdraw system. Note how the arrow rest on the right is moved toward the archer to increase draw length. (Courtesy Precision Shooting Equipment, 2727 N. Fairview Ave., Tucson, Arizona 85705)

The pins on a bowsight can be adjusted up and down or left and right to meet the requirements of each archer. Pin spacing will differ from bow hunter to bow hunter depending on the type of tackle used and shooting technique.

"Sighting in" a bowsight for accuracy at various distances is not difficult. *You must remember to move the pin in the direction(s) of the miss.* For example, when target shooting at 20 yards, your arrow hit high-right from where you aimed. Your corresponding adjustment would be to move your "20-yard pin" up and to the right. After a few adjustments and assuming your shooting mechanics are good, you should be hitting your target, that is, hitting with that pin setting at 20 yards. Each pin on the bowsight must be adjusted for accuracy at a specific distance chosen by the archer.

Bow hunters who use pins for aiming must practice judging distances. Bowsights are useless unless the person shooting the bow can make good distance estimates and execute proper shooting fundamentals. There are no distance markers out in the mountains or deserts where the game animals live! How you can practice judging distance without mechanical assistance is discussed below. *There are mechanical aids on the market known as "range finders" that assist bow hunters in making distance judgments.*

The overdraw is another accessory that has gained popularity with bow hunters in the last few years. A compound bow equipped with an overdraw system allows the archer to move the arrow rest closer to the shooter (fig. 6.16). The overdraw accessory allows the bow hunter to shoot a shorter arrow at a higher velocity. The resulting flatter trajectory makes errors in judging distance less critical. As a result, accuracy is enhanced. The overdraw accessory appears to be most important to bow hunters who use pin-type bowsights for aiming.

Camouflage clothing and paint are considered necessary items for bow hunting. The very nature of archery demands that the hunter move extremely close to the quarry before releasing an arrow. The ideal shots are less than 30 yards in distance. To do this, the human shape must blend into the surrounding terrain to such a degree that the animal cannot discern you from other objects in the area. A bow hunter is camouflaged on a tree stand in figure 6.17.

Figure 6.17
Camouflage helps conceal Dave Brilhart on his tree stand while bow hunting.

Figure 6.18
Blending in with the surrounding environment is the objective of camouflage for the bow hunter.

Camouflage clothing is made in many patterns and color variations. The bow hunter should consider both the time of year and the type of terrain when choosing the color of camouflage. Also, the good bow hunter will have camouflaged clothing heavy or light enough for both cold and warm climates.

To be totally camouflaged means that all reflective surfaces and exposed body areas must be dulled so large color patterns are broken up. This can be accomplished by applying "camo paint" to face and hands. The reflective surfaces of the bow can be covered by using paint or tape that does not cause glare. Some bow hunters even paint leaf patterns on their bows to make them blend into the surrounding vegetation. The archers in figures 6.17 and 6.18 are suitably camouflaged for the lighting, foliage, terrain, and season of the year.

Techniques

Preparation for a bow hunter begins long before the opening day of the hunting season. Game laws need to be studied. All tackle must be checked and organized for the trip. It is recommended that the bow hunter have an ongoing physical conditioning program such as that presented in Chapter 8. Practice should be held on a regular basis throughout the year. The bow should be kept tuned. If possible, trips into the area to be hunted should be made prior to the season to scout or look for intended game. All of these preparations take considerable time, study, thought, money, and effort. It is a worthy use of leisure time.

Although shooting techniques for the bow hunter are very similar to those outlined in Chapter 4, the information in this section is primarily for recurve and compound bow hunting.

One of the main differences between target shooting and bow hunting is the choice of the anchor point. Most bow hunters will use a side-of-the-mouth anchor or a high anchor point, as seen in figures 4.18 and 4.19. Some bow hunters like to anchor with the arrow at eye level so they can aim down the shaft in a manner similar to aiming with a firearm. The anchor point ultimately chosen is a matter of personal preference, because good hunters have been known to use all of the anchor points.

Prior to the start of the hunting season, target practice is absolutely essential. If the archer has been shooting with target or field points, a switch must be made to the heavier broadheads or hunting points for preseason target practice. Flight trajectories of arrows equipped with broadheads differ considerably from trajectories of arrows equipped with target or field points. During this preseason target practice, bowsight adjustment for hunting distances will have to be made as noted. Traditionally, these are for the shorter distances of 10, 15, 20, 25, and 30 yards.

The good bow hunter practices on both target ranges and field archery units by taking shots while in unusual stances and positions. Three-dimensional targets are available for numerous animals, and they help make these practice sessions more realistic. Competition is held periodically by archery clubs using these targets strategically placed on field archery units. These events put the archer in practice situations similar to those encountered during the hunt. Archers should practice taking shots at these targets using a variety of stances that may be necessary during the bow hunt. An example of this is shown in figure 6.19, where the archer is taking a shot from a kneeling stance at a deer target.

All shots made in the field will not be like shots on the target range. Consequently, it is a good idea to practice periodically before the bow hunting season starts on a field archery unit where the targets are at varying distances in a wooded and/or hilly area. If possible, you should also set up a hay bale range on your own property with the common distances of your hunting shots marked. The hay bale (fig. 6.20) is ideal for handling field point impacts.

The 3-D animal tournaments sponsored by archery clubs are of great value because they help archers become aware of weaknesses in their techniques or inaccuracies in the estimation of yardage between them and the target. Once a problem is known, it can then be remedied with intelligent practice before the season starts. And, these shoots are fun!

If you plan to hunt game on mountains or hills, you should practice shooting both at uphill and downhill angles. Shooting in hilly terrain presents entirely different problems than shooting over a flat surface. The arrow will tend to rise above the line of sight when it is shot from an extreme angle either above or below the imaginary level line of horizontal sight. The greater the degree of angle away from the horizontal level, the greater the amount of rise of the arrow. *In shooting situations, this means that you have to take off yardage for uphill and downhill angles depending on the steepness above or below the horizontal plane.* The degree

Figure 6.19
A three-dimensional animal target tournament on a field archery unit allows the bow hunter, Dave Brilhart, the opportunity to practice stance adjustments.

Figure 6.20
Larry Rogge, an Arizona bow hunter, utilizes a hay bale for target practice in preparation for a javalina hunt.

to which this is done depends on the archer and the tackle being shot. So, if you are going to hunt in the hilly terrain, it is best to practice in hills and become accustomed to making the necessary aiming adjustments.

The bow also needs to be checked to make certain it is properly tuned. A bow is out of tune when the arrows of a skilled archer do not fly in a straight line. Any porpoising or fishtailing of the arrow shaft in flight is generally an indicator of a tuning problem. The arrow spine could be incorrect for the bow. Clearance and flight problems usually derive from cushion plunger, nocking point, draw weight, bowstring, improper arrow nock placement on the arrow shaft, and/or arrow rest irregularities.

Generally, movement of the arrow to the left and right during flight (fishtailing) is an indicator that a cushion plunger adjustment is needed. If the arrow flight motion is up and down (porpoising), the nocking point needs to be adjusted. Bow tuning procedures are slightly different for recurve and compound bows. There are several tuning procedures available from archery tackle manufacturers. The reader should refer to Chapter 4 for the Eliason Method for tuning recurve bows. Also, the tuning procedures published by Easton Aluminum are recommended for both compound and recurve bows.

Shooting a bow and arrow when fatigued is vastly different from shooting when rested. It is entirely possible that the bow hunter may get the best shot of the year when he or she is very tired. The conditioned hunter can handle this situation much better than the individual who is "out of shape." Regardless of physiologic condition, anyone can become tired while performing the type of physical exertion one must do while in the field. Consequently, bow hunters should know how to compensate during shooting for the feeling of being tired. The best way to accomplish this is to practice shooting when fatigued as well as when you are rested. It is recommended that some practices *follow* conditioning workouts such as described in Chapter 8.

The bow hunter should practice judging distances constantly throughout the year. This can be accomplished almost anytime. As an example, while walking get in the habit of choosing a sign, tree, person, or object you are moving toward. Estimate the distance in yards from your position to the object chosen. Count your steps (stride length is approximately one yard for most people) as you move toward your chosen goal. Judgment of distance will improve steadily through such practice. Why is this important to the bow hunter? If a bowsight is used as recommended, practice will help you gauge distances more precisely when in the hunting environment. Thus, the bowsight setting can be used more accurately and this can lead to more game. Instinctive shooters can also benefit by knowing distance.

Like the American Indian of yesteryear, the bow hunter must become very familiar with the game being sought. The bow hunter should be very familiar with the habitat and the eating and drinking habits of the animals being pursued. If possible, go into the hunting area on foot a few weeks prior to the hunting season to study or scout intended game. As an example, a deer herd may be scrutinized for several days. Their eating, drinking, and bedding habits can be observed if the individual is an excellent stalker. Some people who live in rural environments are so good at this that they actually choose the deer to be shot prior to the opening day of the season. This takes considerable patience, knowledge, and hunting skill. Many "hunters" of the "instant hunting school" are in such a hurry to kill their game that they fail to enjoy the hunt. Hunting from a spotlight-equipped four-by-four truck cruising up and down country roads is not considered sport in any way, shape, or form!

An important part of any hunt is the fine art of stalking or seeking out game animals. This is more critical in bow hunting than gun hunting, because the bow hunter must get very close to the game animal to make the kill. Most deer, for example, are killed with the bow and arrow at distances ranging from 10 to 35 yards. Gun hunters, on the other hand, routinely kill deer with high-powered rifles equipped with powerful scopes at distances of 100 yards or more. If a person is a marksman, it does not take much true stalking or hunting ability to kill a large animal with a powerful rifle at distances up to 300 yards or more. Hunting should be "sport" whether one uses a bow or a rifle.

The good bow hunter shoots a deer, for example, while the animal is motionless. To obtain that type of shot, the bow hunter must be an excellent stalker with an intimate knowledge of both the animals and their environment. In addition, the bow hunter must understand such factors as habits of the animal, common noises and scents in the area, wind direction changes by time of day and type of terrain, animal camouflage techniques, and animal movements. This helps in positioning oneself for the shot either on the ground or from a tree stand.

The bow hunter must also face one fact prior to stalking game animals. Regardless of cleanliness, the human body has odors atypical to those in the hunting area. These odors come from orifices at both ends of the alimentary canal, skin, hair, and human habits such as the use of tobacco and liquor. If the hunter does not walk *into* the air currents, the chance for success will be diminished. Every animal will know that a predator, a human being, is in the area.

The hunter should try to eliminate all odors of civilization. This can be accomplished, in part, through a study of wind patterns. Wind patterns differ depending upon the time of day and nature of the terrain. These should be studied, preferably prior to the opening of bow hunting season. If this is not possible, it will take some very astute observations to see these patterns while in the process of hunting. Odors should be minimized by using soap without scent. Burping and flatus should be limited to the "bull sessions" around the camp fire after the evening meal. Finally, keep in mind that the use of tobacco and alcohol places odors on one's clothing and breath that will be carried out of camp and into the field where the sensitive noses of game animals will smell them.

There is a great sport associated with bow hunting that depends upon specialized noise. This sport is known as *varmint calling*. Noise is used to attract predatory animals. The predator hears the noise made by the hunter and thinks it is an animal in distress. The game animal becomes the stalker, and the bow hunter becomes the hunted object. This can be very exciting. How does a bow hunter know he or she is an excellent varmint hunter? According to Tim Atwood, National Field Archery Association Bowhunting and Conservation Chairman,

Figure 6.21
How close a predatory animal gets to a varmint caller depends upon several factors related to the bow hunter. (Courtesy *Bow and Arrow Magazine*)

you attain that status after accomplishing the *Varmint Grand Slam.* That means you have taken a coyote, bobcat, and fox using varmint-calling techniques. These are difficult animals to lure by calling.

The varmint caller uses a hand-built or commercially built device to attract the predator. The sound of the call is not like any emitted by a particular animal; however, the pitch resembles the common squeal of many small animals in distress. The noise attracts the predator, because the animal associates the crying sound with previous experiences while on a hunt. The motivating drive for the game animal is hunger. When the predator gets within a few feet of the area where the bow hunter is camouflaged, the hunter releases the arrow. This is seen in figure 6.21. The distance of the shot depends largely on the type and size of the predatory animal stalking the bow hunter; on the extent of the bow hunter's intestinal fortitude and courage; and on the ability to shoot accurately under pressure. It can be exciting!

Wounded rabbit calls are very effective on predators such as coyotes, bobcats, foxes, and occasionally the mountain lion. This type of call, when used correctly, can also be used to attract adult javalina by imitating the sound of their young in distress (fig. 6.22). Other types of calls are used on game as small as quail and as large as bull elk. Turkey calling has become very sophisticated over the years.

Some cities have game calling clubs, which meet monthly to practice and exchange ideas on the art of calling. Some organized competitions are held for game callers. The people in the clubs are experts who have pursued this hobby

Figure 6.22
Bow hunting for javalina is a popular pastime for archers in the Southwestern deserts. (Courtesy Jerry Day, Arizona Game and Fish Department)

for years, and they are usually more than happy to share their experiences and skills with others. It is a good place for the interested novice to learn more about game calling.

In many situations noise can be used to the bow hunter's advantage. Many hunters believe that they should be absolutely quiet at all times on the hunt, but it is virtually impossible to be quiet in all hunting situations. Stepping on and snapping a dead limb on the ground, for example, is not unusual noise in the woods. Animals hear that type of noise periodically. They will become alert, look in the direction of the sound, and they could move. The hunter should remain still for a period of time and then move in the same direction as the game animals. Noise that is not typical of the environment should be avoided as much as possible when stalking. However, noise can be used to drive game out of thick, brushy areas where a shot would be unwise. The animals can then be stalked to a better area where a good shot may be more feasible.

Noise can also be used to flush birds from their hiding places in high grass or bushy areas. This is common practice in hunting birds such as quail and pheasant with the bow and arrow (fig. 6.10). Hitting a bird on the wing even with an arrow equipped with a wire loop point is a real challenge!

It may seem obvious, but the bow hunter must know how to see the animal being sought. This takes considerable practice and experience. In their natural habitat, animals are capable of hiding or camouflaging themselves effectively. The untrained eye can miss seeing a potential shot. Some animals, especially birds such as pheasant and quail, depend upon their cover and camouflage for protection even more than on their movement abilities. They are difficult to see!

There are no secrets for spotting game animals. A bow hunter should know the coloring of the animal being sought and how these colors change with the seasons. You should also know how the colors blend with the foliage in the environment where the hunt will take place. Anytime a bow hunter walks through the desert, forest, or a wooded area, he or she should practice this skill by trying to observe every detail in the area. This practice will help develop field awareness while on the hunt. (You also should listen to the natural sounds of the area where you hunt.) A good set of binoculars will help in locating game; these are considered essential by most bow hunters.

A bow hunter who has located and stalked an animal to within bow range must know how to distinguish a good shot from a poor one. It is essential to know where to place an arrow so it will penetrate a vital area. Many an animal has been lost because of an archer's ignorance of the anatomy of the animal being hunted. (It is recommended that animal targets with the vital organs of animals outlined be used for some practice sessions prior to the hunt.)

Knowing the anatomy of the hunted animal is important because the most effective shots put the arrow in the lung and heart vicinity. Bow hunters should also familiarize themselves with the locations of major bones, arteries, liver, stomach, and kidneys. A razor sharp broadhead shot into or through the chest cavity will cause severe bleeding, easy tracking, and almost always result in a successful kill and retrieval.

Once the shot has been taken, the bow hunter has to make some judgments regarding whether or not the arrow hit its mark. Exactly where was the animal hit? The answers will dictate the plan of action for tracking. Most archers look for blood or try to recover the arrow to help give them the answers to these kinds of questions.

The color of blood can tell the archer if the arrow severed a vein or an artery. Blood that comes from a vein is dark red in color, whereas oxygenated blood from an artery is bright red. *If it is known for certain that the chest area was penetrated, the plan of action is to wait for at least 30 minutes to one hour before trailing.* The animal will usually bed down a short distance from where it was hit and die. Some beginning hunters make the mistake of trailing too soon and end up chasing the wounded animal all over the woods for hours!

If the animal were gut shot, the plan of action would be much different. Even though this type of shot is always fatal, the animals are hard to trail and they take much longer to die. *In this situation, the archer should wait an hour or longer before following the animal's trail.* A gut shot animal that is pushed can travel miles before it is exhausted enough to bed down.

There are several situations where the best plan of action is to follow the animal immediately. These include muscle hits, leg hits, and situations where darkness or bad weather is approaching.

Before following a trail, be sure to mark the spot from which the shot was taken and the spot where the animal was hit. Blood is easy to follow, but sometimes the flow stops. In that case, the archer will have to rely on other clues such as prints, scuffmarks, and broken vegetation. Be patient and do not overlook

Figure 6.23
The successful completion of an antelope hunt shows on the face of Jack Frazier, an expert bow hunter. (Courtesy of Jack Frazier)

any signs, because trailing can take hours of tedious searching and concentration. One should not give up the trailing task until all possibilities have been exhausted.

When an animal has been recovered, it needs to be field dressed as soon as possible so the meat can cool. This helps keep it from spoiling, especially in warmer climates. Special care should be taken during the field dressing process, because there is always the possibility of cutting one's self.

For information regarding legal game and bow hunting, season dates, license fees, lottery systems for various species, and other matters, the official state wildlife agency must be contacted. Addresses are listed in Appendix A. There are all kinds of exciting species to hunt, which can bring satisfaction to the bow hunter. One example is shown in figure 6.23.

Table 6.1 includes several examples of game taken with the bow and arrow in the United States, Mexico, and Canada.

The Pope and Young Club is the organization responsible for maintaining, recording, and determining the authenticity of the Bowhunters Big Game Records of North America (see Appendix B for the address). This club appoints and maintains official measurers across the North American continent. These highly qualified people score outstanding big game animals taken with the bow and arrow. The scoring procedure is based on well-established criteria. It is a challenging task to qualify a game animal you have taken with the bow and arrow for a Pope and Young documented big game record. The Pope and Young Club is open to

Table 6.1   Examples of Game Animals Taken with Bow and Arrow in the United States, Canada, and Mexico

Alaska Brown Bear	Javalina
Alaska-Yukon Moose	Mountain Caribou
Antelope	Mule Deer
Barren Ground Caribou	Musk Ox
Bighorn Sheep	Polar Bear
Bison	Quebec-Labrador Caribou
Black Bear	Rocky Mountain Goat
Canada Moose	Roosevelt Elk
Columbian Blacktail Deer	Sitka Blacktail Deer
Coues Deer	Stone Sheep
Cougar	Whitetail Deer
Dall Sheep	Woodland Caribou
Grizzly Bear	Wyoming-Shiras Moose
Jaguar	Yellowstone Elk

bow hunters who have proven themselves in the field over the years, accepted the challenges, and adhere to the principles of fair chase. Beyond documenting game records, the members have a keen interest in maintaining the integrity of the wildlife heritage.

For the individual who views hunting as a sport, bow hunting can occupy many leisure hours. The game animals can be as small as quail or as large as an elk. The environment can range from the wilderness of the Canadian Rockies to the deserts of the southwest area of the United States. Bow hunting is for the adventurous individual who respects nature, ecology, sport, conservation principles, and is a lover of the great out-of-doors and wilderness areas.

Review

1. What are the several types of bows commonly used for hunting and what is their order of energy storage efficiency?
2. In purchasing hunting tackle, which is more important, the quality of the bow or the arrows? What are the advantages and disadvantages of the various types of hunting arrows?
3. Describe the accessory tackle specifically designed for bow hunting and indicate any points important to remember regarding safety and utility.
4. Describe the use of the pin sight commonly used by bow hunters. What techniques can the archer use to enhance his or her judgment in estimating distances?
5. Why do state game and fish commissions specify minimum rather than maximum draw weights and bolt lengths for bow hunting?

6. Assume that you are planning a bow hunt. What preparation is necessary in regard to tackle, conditioning, practice, site of the hunt, and quarry?
7. What is a flu-flu and why is it useful when hunting small game?
8. When shooting in hilly terrain rather than on level ground, how must you adjust your aim?
9. What are the variables to consider when you select arrows? What factors must be matched and why?
10. What is varmint hunting and how does it differ from deer hunting with the bow and arrow?
11. Familiarity with the intended game and habitat is important to success in bow hunting. What factors should be noted on a scouting trip prior to the hunt?
12. The compound bow can generate more foot-pounds of energy than composite bows, and it is now the most popular hunting tool of the bow hunter. Why are a few hunters returning to the use of longbows and the recurve bow?
13. What devices do bow hunters need in addition to those customarily used for target archery, and why?
14. Why is stalking more critical in bow hunting than in gun hunting?
15. What are the critical things to check and possibly adjust during the bow tuning process?

Bow Fishing

7

The purpose of this chapter is to introduce the reader to the exciting sport of bow fishing. There are many challenges to be met in this sport, and there is a wide variety of aquatic animals that can be taken with bow and arrow. They range from small goldfish (carp) to rather large and violent sharks. It can be exciting!

Bow fishing is a sport with considerable appeal for people who enjoy archery and angling. It is a wholesome mixture of both sports, with some of the aspects of harpooning or gigging added. Bow fishing is not new, because primitive people have used the techniques for years to acquire fish, frogs, and other aquatic animals for food. However, bow fishing as a sport is relatively new as compared to target archery. It is gaining in popularity as people discover that the sport exists.

The National Field Archery Association has encouraged and supported bow fishing for many years. Recognition of prize fish and articles on bow fishing appear periodically in the NFAA magazine, *Archery*. The number of people who bow fish for avocational purposes is growing. This fact prompted the formation of the Bowfishing Association of America (BAA) in 1990.

Bow fishers can ply their skills on rivers, lakes, ponds, and oceans. The size of the "rough fish" sought adds to the excitement of the sport. On average, the species legalized for bow fishing are much larger than most game fish taken with rod and reel. The smallest of the common "rough fish" approved for bow fishing are the bowfin and shortnose gar; these fish average about 5 pounds as adults. The largest of the "rough fish" sanctioned for bow fishing outside of ocean water is the alligator gar. The largest alligator gar on record weighed 302 pounds, and it was over 7 feet in length. The record alligator gar taken by a bow fisher weighed 212 pounds. Sharks often exceed 200 pounds, and the giant sunfish found in the Pacific Ocean ranges in weight from 50 to 1000 pounds.

If you fish with rod and reel, think about the excitement the last time you landed a 10-pound game fish. Now, imagine having your arrow hooked into a 200-pound shark and think of the challenge of landing that fish safely (fig. 7.1). Therein lies some of the adventure and intrigue of bow fishing as a sport.

If you are an angler, the process of obtaining bait can be rather dull. Simply stated, you dig for earthworms or purchase your bait in a variety of forms from a store. Obtaining some bow fishing bait can be very exciting! Some people use stingrays as bait to bow fish for shark. They shoot the bait first and then go after the big stuff! Figure 7.2 will give you some idea of the difference between this type of "bow fishing bait" and the typical bait of the angler!

Figure 7.1
Three brown sharks taken by Robie Davis and his father, J. Robert Davis. The sharks were taken while bow fishing the bays on the Maryland coast. (Photo courtesy of J. Robert Davis, Route 4, Box 380, Spearin Road, Salisbury, Maryland 21801)

Figure 7.2
Bill Johnston and Robie Davis with a 100-plus-pound southern stingray taken off the Del Mar Va Peninsula in Maryland. (Courtesy *Bowfishing Magazine,* P.O. Box 2005, Wausau, Wisconsin 54401)

Figure 7.3
A hunting recurve bow rigged for bow fishing with a spinning reel and short rod mounted on the back of the bow. (Courtesy Black Widow Bow Company, H. C. R. #1, Box 357–1, Highlandville, Missouri 65669)

As emphasized throughout this book, if you are interested in any archery sport, the first step is to perfect your target archery shooting mechanics, as discussed in Chapter 4. Those shooting skills serve as your foundation for becoming a good bow fisher. Some modifications in shooting technique are necessary as you switch from target to bow fishing tackle, but the drawing and release mechanics remain the same. If you are accurate during target range practice, you will increase the probability of taking more pounds of fish once you get into the bow fishing situation. Ideally, practice should progress from standard target archery targets to moving, simulated fish targets submerged beneath the water.

The changes in tackle design in recent years have helped make bow fishing more popular. Bow fishers have used all types of ingenious gimmicks in the past to attach: (1) line to bow and arrow, and (2) crude reels to bows. Hand-wrap reels were improvised and mounted on bow backs. Hand-wrap reels (fig. 7.1) were eventually manufactured and placed on the market. These remain popular with a few people. The spin-cast reel attached to a short bow fishing rod that mounts on the back of the bow has become very popular. This tackle has minimized some of the line handling and tangling problems and made bow fishing much easier (see figs. 7.3 and 7.4).

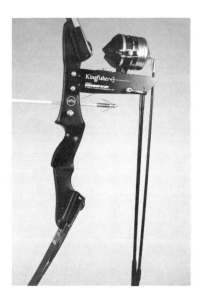

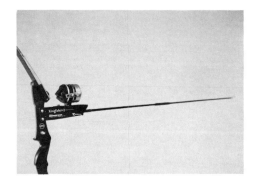

Figure 7.4a

The "Foldin' BoRod" mounted on the bow.
The folded position is maintained while
fishing, aiming, and shooting.

Figure 7.4b

A trigger mechanism extends and locks the
bow into position when the fish is hit.
(Courtesy of Corley's Bowfishin' Stuff, 727
Holiday Lane, Claremore, Oklahoma 74017)

Bow hunters are turning to bow fishing as an "off-season" activity. The summer is not a game animal season, but it is a good time of year to go after many of the "rough fish" on rivers and in lakes. The hunter can keep the skills honed as well as enhance his or her leisure time through the sport of bow fishing.

"Rough fish" such as carp, gar, and buffalo are usually relegated to "garbage status" by gourmets. Game fish such as trout, bass, and bluegill are preferred eating. The resourceful bow fisherman can learn many ways to prepare, cook, and eat the carp, gar, and other fish that have been caught. These fish can be a valuable and savory food source. They may be prepared for frying, broiling, smoking, and canning. Due to the large number and pounds of fish that may be taken by the bow fisherman in most states, the "rough fish" can supplement the diet. The food budget for the family can benefit if a taste is acquired for "rough fish." (Table 7.1, later in the chapter, shows the wide variety of legal species for bow fishing throughout the United States.)

Conservation departments in the various states look at the harvest of "rough fish" by bow fishers as a positive conservation practice. These fish are large, as noted, and they tend to be prolific reproducers. As a result, they can disturb the ecological balance, especially in those areas where few, if any, predators exist for the "rough fish." As bow fishing increases in popularity, however, some fish populations may have to be monitored carefully for conservation purposes on the rivers and lakes across the country that generate the most interest to bow fishers.

Tackle

Any bow can be rigged for bow fishing. However, hunting bows, recurve and compound, are most commonly used and best suited for this purpose. The draw weights for hunting bows tend to be higher than target bows. This is an important consideration when going after the larger species of fish or trying to propel an arrow through a few feet of water. Minimum bow weights of 50 pounds are recommended for bow fishing. This will produce an adequate amount of arrow projection force to handle most situations. Lighter bow weights, however, can be used with success when bow fishing in shallow water or when shooting fish barely submerged. The archer who cannot handle higher bow weights should rig his or her bow for bow fishing and go. There will be numerous opportunities to shoot. If a dorsal fin is seen or the fish is swimming a few inches below the surface, shooting skill and not bow weight becomes the critical factor. Bow fishing gets exciting at that point regardless of the strength, age, or sex of the participant!

An excellent recurve hunting bow is rigged for bow fishing in figure 7.3. The bow has a short rod and bow reel adapter rod mounted on the back of the bow. The bow reel adapter screws into the stabilizer hole, and the rod fits into the adapter. The adapter is needed to hold the spinning reel, as shown in figure 7.3. As noted previously, this type of rod and reel setup, as compared to the older hand-wrap reels, has made bow fishing easier. The rod provides better leverage for playing the fish, and, with the spinning reel, line tangle is minimized. There is good line retrieval on missed shots and better recovery of fish once they are shot.

Another type of bow fishing rod is shown in figure 7.4. This rod was designed by Wilbur Corley from Claremore, Oklahoma. It is used when bow fishing for fish ranging in weight from 10 to 100 pounds. As shown in figure 7.4a, the rod folds when not in use. This makes the total bow and rod easy to use while bow fishing, aiming, and shooting. The fishing line runs from the spinning reel through the eye of the rod, and it is attached to the arrow. You can use lighter line and have the advantage of using a drag on the line. When you shoot and hit a fish, that is when you pull the trigger and extend the rod as shown in figure 7.4b. The rod, made of tubular fiberglass and very flexible, locks automatically. It remains in the extended position until the fish is landed. The rod then is folded back into the position shown in figure 7.4a, and you are ready to start bow fishing for another "big one."

Solid white fiberglass arrows are recommended for use by bow fishers. They are durable, and the heavier mass weight is needed to increase accuracy as the arrow penetrates the water on its way to the fish. Arrows should be 30 inches in length, because the line must be kept away from the bow hand.

One way to ensure keeping the line away from the bow hand is to connect a cable to the arrow as shown in figure 7.5. The line attaches to the swivel that runs the length of the cable. This means that only a few inches of line is off the reel, that is, the distance from the reel to the front of the bow or arrow rest. That eliminates the long length of line that could lie across the shooter's arm as the

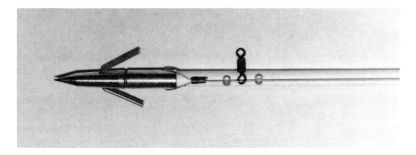

Figure 7.5
A cable mounted on the arrow for attaching the bow fishing line eliminates the problem of too much line lying on the shooter's arm while drawing. (Courtesy Ron Skirvin, Shure Shot, P.O. Box 748, Stevens Point, Wisconsin 54481)

arrow is drawn. That is a problem the bow fisher encounters when using some of the other line attachment procedures. This type of line problem interferes with shooting.

Rubber fletching may or may not be used on bow fishing arrows. Arrow flight is minimal in bow fishing, so the aerodynamic stability purpose of fletching is nullified to a great extent. White is the desired color of arrows for visibility reasons. It is recommended that several extra arrows be taken on each trip, because nocks and points do break. Broken nocks and points can be repaired when the bow fisher returns home.

There are several bow fishing arrow points on the market. Which of these points is "best" depends on personal preference, and that may change, depending upon the species of fish being sought. All of the bow fishing points are barbed; some of these barbs are retractable, allowing for easy removal, while others have stationary spring steel barbs. There are also four-pronged "gig points" for shooting those huge bull frogs found in various parts of the country.

The retractable barbed arrow points are usually preferred over the nonretractable variety; they are much easier to recover. One barbed arrow is shown in figure 7.6. This is a heavy point that helps penetration through the water and into the fish. It opens to 2¾ inches across the tips to provide holding power during fish retrieval. The point is removed by simply twisting the shaft counterclockwise. The point is kept within the fish as the shaft is rotated, and the barbs reverse their position while still inside the fish. The arrow can be removed easily without disrupting the line. These barb positions are shown in figure 7.6. This type of point is recommended for fish with "soft skin" such as the suckers and bowfin.

Another type of arrow point is shown in figure 7.7. This is a newer design made of steel with a one-piece rotating barb. This eliminates the need to remove the point from the arrow once the fish is landed. The barbs rotate forward by unscrewing the point three-fourths turn while holding the arrow. A spring lock washer between the point and adapter prevents accidental release. This point attaches to a threaded adapter epoxied to the arrow shaft. Figure 7.8 shows a bigmouth buffalo taken by Ron Skirvin with the arrow point shown in figure 7.7.

A

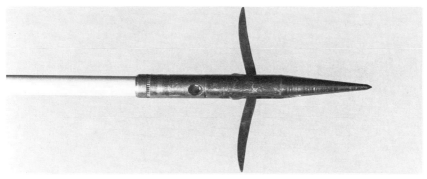

B

C

Figure 7.6
A retractable "sting-a-ree" bow fishing point: (a) shooting position, (b) open position to gaff the fish, and (c) point adjustment to remove the arrow from the fish.

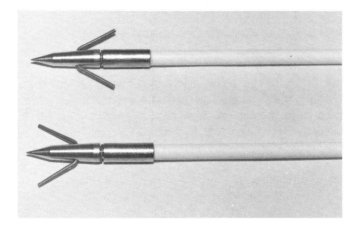

Figure 7.7
The Shure Shot point with one-piece rotating barb design. (Courtesy Ron Skirvin, Shure Shot, P.O. Box 748, Stevens Point, Wisconsin 54481)

Figure 7.8
Wisconsin bowfisherman Ron Skirvin with his 43-pound bigmouth buffalo. (Courtesy *Bowfishing Magazine*, P.O. Box 2005, Wausau, Wisconsin 54401)

Bow fishing line is made of braided nylon or monofilament. The choice of which to use lies with the archer. The most commonly used line, however, is braided nylon. The poundage test of the line is important, with choices usually ranging from 50- to 100-pound test line. The poundage used depends upon the size of the fish one expects to encounter. If you go out with line too weak and large fish are found, the trip could be a great disappointment. However, it can be an adventure and test of your bow fishing skills to land heavy fish on relatively light test line. It is recommended that 50- to 70-pound test line be used in one reel and a second reel be loaded with heavier or lighter line, depending upon the anticipated fish size for the locale being fished.

Maximum line length for the reel being used is important. Fish will "run" upon arrow impact, and line length is important to enable the bow fisher to control the extent of this movement. There are times when it is better to use lighter and longer line rather than heavier and shorter line. Line should be examined periodically for damage caused by friction against such things as abrasive skin, teeth, or boat hulls. Weak lines will snap, and fish are lost. Plan ahead for all contingencies and disappointments will be averted.

The line is usually attached to a leader of heavy braided nylon by a strong swivel. The leader should be about 30 inches long. The heavier leader, not the fishing line, should be held as the fish is being lifted into the boat or dragged toward the beach or shore.

Figure 7.9
Landing a carp from a boat not designed for bow fishing can be dangerous. (Courtesy *Bow and Arrow Magazine*)

Major Accessories

Bow fishers can use the same "minor accessories" as the target archer and bow hunter: for example, finger tab, arm guard, bow sling, and so on (fig. 7.3). In addition, they must have some "major accessories" to place them close to the fish being sought. The largest financial outlay is for wading gear and a boat.

Some of the best and most interesting bow fishing can be done while walking rough marshlands, shallow edges of lakes and rivers, swamps, and flooded fields. Boats either cannot enter these areas or are difficult to handle in those situations. Also, boats can be noisy and create greater water disturbance than a man or woman moving slowly through the shallow water. Chest waders are an absolute essential for bow fishing in these elements. Wading will be productive for bow fishers during the spring spawning time. In addition to the excitement of shooting the fish, there is always the added adventure provided by water snakes, deep and unseen holes, insects, sunshine, and rapidly developing thunder storms. You have to love it! And you should be a swimmer if you want to wade while bow fishing!

If a bow fisher plans to pursue the sport frequently on rivers and lakes, a modified, flat-bottomed boat will prove to be a valuable asset. It can also be used for other recreational pursuits. Bow fishing on rivers and lakes can be accomplished in a variety of boats ranging from canoes to row boats. However, boats of that type and like the one shown in figure 7.9 *are not recommended*. Canoes, kayaks, and regular keeled small boats tend to be unstable. As a result, they sway and can tip when the archer stands to shoot or bring in the fish.

A bow fishing boat should be stable, that is, set relatively low in the water to minimize sway when the archer stands on the bow or stern to shoot. The archer must stand to: (1) visually hunt for the fish to be shot, (2) execute the shooting fundamentals, and (3) obtain the correct shooting angle to hit the fish. These actions cannot be performed properly while seated.

There are numerous flat-bottomed, aluminum fishing boats on the market that can be modified to meet the needs of the bow fisher. Ken Brown describes such a modification in his excellent book on bow fishing (see Bibliography). The boat for bow fishing needs to be modified to include front and rear shooting platforms, an electric trolling motor with foot control to guide the boat while standing on the platforms, below deck storage areas, as well as night navigation and hunting lights. The boat and platforms should be wide enough to provide stability and minimize the possibility of capsizing when the bow fishers are hunting and shooting fish. For moving from place to place when not fishing, an outboard motor with steering wheel should be included. These features are part of the prototype of a good bow fishing boat for lakes and rivers. The boat and a trailer to haul it are the most expensive equipment items needed for bow fishing on lakes and rivers. But, the boat can also be used for a variety of recreational activities other than bow fishing.

A state-of-the-art boat for bow fishing is shown in figure 7.10. This boat was modified by Jim West. He started with a standard Lowe "Husky John" Boat and gradually built a highly specialized boat for bow fishing. Its features include the following:

1. 18 feet long, 7 feet at the beam, and 24-inch high sides.
2. Welded aluminum hull.
3. Two stable shooting platforms; the forward platform is 5 feet above the water—highly desired in terms of shooting angles.
4. Holders for extra arrows attached to each platform.
5. Nine built-in storage compartments:
    a. Two for storage for camping gear.
    b. Two for bow fishing equipment.
    c. One for wiring.
    d. One is a tool box.
    e. One for life jackets and fire gear.
    f. One live well.
    g. One for food cooling.
6. V-8 Chevrolet engine bored to 406 cubic inches.
7. Dominator jet pump for propulsion—navigation is possible in as little as two inches of water.
8. Depth finder, videocamera setup, AM/FM radio with cassette tape player.
9. Burglar alarm system.

Any reader interested in more details regarding this boat should read the articles by Paul T. Shore listed in the Bibliography.

Figure 7.10
Jim West (*left*) and Michael Shore aboard Jim West's customized bow fishing boat—Ramboat. (Courtesy *Bowfishing Magazine,* P.O. Box 2005, Wausau, Wisconsin 54401)

Bow fishing on the ocean requires a seaworthy boat or ship, but most bow fishers are not wealthy enough to afford that type of ship as a "fishing accessory." However, ships can be chartered by groups or individuals directly or through travel agencies for ocean bow fishing trips. The travel and charter costs are not inexpensive, but the money spent can provide considerable excitement when one contemplates landing shark, rays, or sunfish. Sighting, shooting, and landing a large shark or sunfish on an ocean vessel bobbing up and down on the water is a challenge, and it can add excitement to a vacation.

Legal Species for Bow Fishing

Because of extensive environmental, political, and ecological differences between states, bow fishers should never assume that a specific species is legal. A license is required in most states to bow fish, and each state clearly defines the species for legal bow fishing. It is the responsibility of the archer to know that list and the fishing limits. These laws change, so the bow fisher desiring to fish in any given state should know the current game laws and obtain a license. One should never assume that a species legal in one state will be legal in another state. For example, Colorado allows trout to be taken by bow fishers, while New Mexico, its neighbor to the south, allows only gar, carp, buffalo, and bullfrogs to be taken in its waters. Carp is probably the most common fish taken by bow fishers (fig. 7.9).

Table 7.1 Legal Species for Bow Fishing Throughout the United States

Aholehole	Gar (Spotted)	Quillback
'Ama'ama	Gasperpou	Rays
Awa	Goldeye	Redhorse
Bass (Largemouth)	Goldfish	Salmon (Atlantic)
Bass (Smallmouth)	Hardhead	Salmon (Kokanee)
Blackfish	Herring	Saugeye
Blowfish	Kala	Shad
Bowfin	Lamprey	Sharks
Buffalo (Bigmouth)	Ling	Skates
Buffalo (Black)	Manini	Squawfish
Buffalo (Smallmouth)	Minnows	Stingrays
Bullhead	Moanu	Suckers
Burbot	Moi	Sunfish
Carp	Mullet	Toads (Oyster)
Catfish (Channel)	Muskellunge	Trout
Catfish (Flathead)	O'io	Tullibee
Chub	Omilu	Turtle (Soft-shell)
Ciscoe	Opelu Kala 'Opakapaka	Turtle (Snapping)
Drum	Paddlefish	Uha
Eel	Papio	Uku
Frogs	Perch (Rio Grande)	'Ula 'ula
Gar (Alligator)	Pickerel	Ulua
Gar (Longnose)	Pike (Northern)	Weke
Gar (Shortnose)	Pike (Walleye)	Whitefish

State game laws must be checked annually to determine legal species for each state.
See Appendix A for names and addresses of official wildlife agencies.

Most of the areas in the United States and Canada restrict the legal species to the so-called rough fish. The most common are

Alligator gar	Bowfin	Shortnose gar
Bigmouth buffalo	Carp	Smallmouth buffalo
Black buffalo	Longnose gar	Spotted gar

Table 7.1 is provided simply to show the reader the diversity of legal species that may be taken in the United States. The species listed are not found in all states nor legal in all states. If you are planning to bow fish or hunt in a specific locale in the United States or Canada, you are well advised to contact the official wildlife agency where your trip will take you. Ask them to mail you the latest game regulations. *The names, addresses, and phone numbers of the official wildlife agencies in the United States and Canada are listed in Appendix A.*

Technique Suggestions

This section describes some of the more important shooting fundamentals for bow fishing. Some suggestions for making the experience more rewarding are also presented. Bow fishing, like any archery skill practiced outdoors, has many variations. These are learned only through study, directed practice, and experience.

The nocking, drawing, anchoring, releasing, and follow-through shooting fundamentals are the same as those practiced in target archery. Obviously, the stance for the bow fisher must be modified, depending upon the position of the fish in relation to the archer. The release cannot be hurried in the excitement of the moment. The three fingers relax and extend as in target archery to let the bowstring move forward in a straight line without causing unnecessary deflection of the arrow. This appears to be easy, but the excited bow fisher who has sighted a "big one" will periodically try to help the bowstring move by plucking it or pushing the bow at release. One must refrain from these types of extraneous motions. (Some bow fishers prefer to use a release aid rather than the traditional three-finger bowstring grip.) Target practice plus experience in the field help to minimize these undesired reactions. Target practice on land should be performed with field points that weigh the same as your fishing points. Hay bales make good target mats for field points and broadheads.

Aiming presents unique problems in bow fishing. From the standpoint of physics, water and air are both fluids. But, looking at a target through water presents a different set of problems than looking at a land target through the air. A land target does not appear distorted; the distance to a target is either known exactly as in target archery or can be readily estimated by the experienced bow hunter. The bow fisher, on the other hand, must deal with the refraction of the sun's light rays as they penetrate the water in the immediate area of the fish. (It is best to wear good sunglasses to increase visual acuity, especially on bright days.) *It is difficult to evaluate the depth of the fish in the water, because light rays have a tendency to bend downward. This means that the fish will be closer to you than it looks.*

As a result of these factors, aiming is difficult in bow fishing because you cannot aim directly at the fish. *Your aim must be at a theoretical point below the fish.* The aiming point below the fish is dependent upon (1) the depth of the fish in the water and (2) the distance the bow fisher is away from the fish at the time of the shot. Ken Brown, an expert bow fisher from Oklahoma, recommends that one inch be allowed for every five feet of distance between the archer and the target, and the archer should allow an additional one inch for each foot the fish appears to be below the surface of the water. For example: for a side shot from 15 feet when the fish is one foot deep in the water, the aiming point would be four inches below the fish—that is, three inches for the distance factor plus one inch for the depth of the fish. Most shots by good bow fishers are made at relatively close distances.

You may hit the fish if you follow the aiming directions, though certainty is not guaranteed. Fish simply will not hold still for any predictable length of time

Figure 7.11

Two expert bowfishermen, Rob Davis and Bob Alexander, exhibit their pride after landing a lemon shark that weighed 212 pounds and measured 8 feet 11 inches in length. (Courtesy J. Robert Davis, Route 4, Box 380, Spearin Road, Salisbury, Maryland 21801)

to allow time for a good shot. The bow fisher has problems with the water, with aiming, and with moving fish, but these difficulties help to make bow fishing a challenging and exciting sport. The bow fisher can derive considerable personal satisfaction when these problems are overcome and the fish is landed.

In figure 7.11, satisfaction and pride of accomplishment can be seen on the faces of two expert bow fishermen, Rob Davis and Bob Alexander. They have landed a 212-pound lemon shark that measured 8 feet 11 inches in length. They fish the bays between the barrier islands and the mainlands of Delaware, Maryland, and Virginia from May until September. They hunt stingrays (fig. 7.2) to use as bait to draw the sharks close for a shot. Shark and rays are exciting game. Aiming and shooting a large fish is only half of the excitement. What you do with a fish with sharp teeth that weighs more than you do is the other half!

It is not a good idea to drag live large fish, such as those shown in figures 7.11 and 7.13, into your boat. They can cause serious problems, including capsizing small boats. If they are brought on board alive, their violent movements can cause loss of equipment, damage to gear on board, and trauma to the bow fishers. Therefore, it is best to make certain the fish is dead prior to bringing it aboard the boat. In the case of sharks, it is best to haul them alongside the craft and beach them rather than trying to lift them into the boat. J. Robert Davis recommends the following procedure for hauling sharks to shore: utilize an innertube as a flotation device attached to the line and arrow. This shark rig is reinforced with steel cable to help control the shark in the water and drag the fish on land. This improvised rig is seen in figure 7.12.

Figure 7.12
A steel cable rig attached to a fishing arrow and innertube flotation device used in fishing for and safely landing sharks. (Courtesy J. Robert Davis, Route 4, Box 380, Spearin Road, Salisbury, Maryland 21801)

Figure 7.13
Wilbur Corley, an expert bowfisherman, with a 123 pound 6 ounce alligator gar he landed on a river in south Texas. (Courtesy Wilbur Corley, 727 Holiday Lane, Claremore, Oklahoma 74017)

Once the fish has been landed or dragged to shore, the problem is what to do with it. As noted, the fish legal for bow fishing are edible, but one may have to develop a taste for the meat. There are many ways to prepare them for human consumption. The most popular edible rough fish is probably the carp. If you land a "big one" of any species, it could make a nice trophy mounted on the wall of your den to document the fact that not all big ones get away. Finally, fish not eaten make excellent fertilizer for home gardens. *The rough fish you land should never be left on the bank to rot.*

Bow Fishing Activities

Besides the bow fishing activities of individuals, there are numerous organized activities conducted each year. These activities are sponsored by local archery clubs, national archery organizations, and manufacturers of archery tackle. Tournaments are conducted in many states and throughout the world.

National Field Archery Association Bowfisher Program

The NFAA Bowfisher Program is designed to promote bow fishing as a sport and to recognize the accomplishments of bow fishers throughout the country. To be involved in this program, you must be a member of the NFAA. Patches are given to participants in the NFAA Bowfisher Program, and there are patch awards to indicate the type of fish taken. Recognition is also given to bow fishers by publishing photographs of them and their catches in *Archery,* the official magazine of the NFAA. Carp and gar are the most popular approved species, but records are also being kept for shark and sting rays. For example, the record for the NFAA for blue shark is 130 pounds. That record will not last very long!

The NFAA Bowfisher of the Year awards (plaques) go to the individuals who document that they have landed the largest fish. There is one award for carp and one for gar. Winners are determined by weight of the fish, and the catch must be fully documented to the satisfaction of the NFAA Bowfisher Committee.

The NFAA also keeps records of who has taken the largest carp or gar while using bow fishing techniques. To hold a NFAA Bowfisher Record, you must be a member of the NFAA. Record keeping and review of the records are done on an annual basis. If no records are broken during the year, the old records stand for the next year. There is a procedure for documenting catches and fish weights.

NFAA Bowfisher Program Records for carp and gar are as follows:

Carp:	Lance Sullentrop	51 pounds
Gar:	William L. Nicar	185 pounds

These records have held since 1991.

Bowfishing Association of America

The Bowfishing Association of America (BAA) was formed in 1990 to promote and protect the sport of fishing with a bow and arrow. The main goals of the BAA include: (1) protection of the natural resources used by bow fishers,

Table 7.2 Bowfishing Association of America Citation Program Standards

Fish Species	Minimum Weight (Pounds)
Freshwater	
Alligator gar	100
Bowfin (grindle)	10
Buffalo	35
Carp	32
Gaspergou (freshwater drum)	15
Gold fish	3
Longnose gar	30
Paddlefish	35
Shortnose gar	7
Spotted gar	8
Sucker	5
Tilapia	4
Saltwater	
Cownose ray	50
Flounder	5
Mullet	43
Shad	2
Shark	100
Sheepshead	10
Stingray	75

(2) national organization of bowfishing tournaments, (3) administration of an annual World Championship in bow fishing, (4) establishment of a point system to objectively qualify bow fishers to a championship team via a World Championship, (5) selection of a Bowfisherman of the Year and (6) record and present Bowfishing Citation Awards to members. The BAA is affiliated with the International Bowhunting Organization, and the official publication is *International Bowhunting Magazine.*

The BAA has continued a tradition started by Paul T. Shore of recognizing individuals who land quality fish with the bow and arrow. The BAA accomplishes this through their citation program. The minimum weights for specific species are listed in table 7.2. These weight standards are an excellent idea. For example, if you land an alligator gar above 100 pounds, you know that your catch is something special!

Citations are awarded by the BAA to any member who catches, with bow and arrow, fish at or above the minimum weight and species listed in table 7.2. Certification procedures must be followed to document the catch date, weight, and other anthropometric data for the fish.

Bow Fishing Tournaments

There are numerous bow fishing tournaments for rough fish held throughout the world each year. People of all ages enter for prizes such as cash, trophies, boats, and motors provided through entry fees and corporate sponsors. Prizes are awarded for the largest fish taken and for the highest weight total during the day or days of the tournament. There are competitive opportunities for teams as well as individuals in these tournaments. They are growing in numbers comparable to regular angling tournaments involving sport fish such as bass. BAA-sanctioned tournaments have been held in several states, including Alabama, Georgia, South Carolina, Texas, Michigan, Mississippi, Indiana, Arkansas, and Florida. This trend will continue to grow. The First Annual BAA World Championship Bow Fishing Tournament was held in 1991 at Mobile Bay, Alabama.

An example of a bow fishing tournament that has been held for many years is the Annual Bowfishing Championship held at Clear Lake in northern California. This is a carp shoot with lucrative cash and merchandise prizes. It is a two-person team event. The winning team is determined by the overall weight of the carp taken during the time allowed. Winning teams have taken as much as 847 pounds of carp during the two-day competition! A cash prize is also awarded to the individual who lands the largest carp. The California Department of Fish and Game welcomes this type of tournament, because carp tend to multiply rapidly and upset the ecologic balance in waters such as Clear Lake.

Bow fishing, like other archery activities, can be satisfying as an individual endeavor or as a social activity to be enjoyed with family and friends. It is a sport that can provide many hours of recreation throughout a lifetime for the active participant who enjoys combining archery, fishing interests, and a love for being in a natural environment.

Review

1. Why do conservation departments approve of bow fishing for "rough fish"?
2. Describe the aiming techniques that have proved successful in bow fishing.
3. Which of the species listed in table 7.1 are currently legal for bow fishing in your state, and what are the fishing limits?
4. Why do the authors of this book highly recommend that skill at target archery precede one's interest in bow fishing, bow hunting, and field archery?
5. How would you prepare to bow fish for shark?
6. What techniques would you use to catch and land a shark that weighs more than you do?
7. What programs are available to recognize the efforts of bow fishers, and how do these programs operate?
8. Why does aiming in bow fishing present problems not encountered on land?
9. What would be your aiming point for a side shot at a fish from a distance of 30 feet when the fish appears to be 3 feet below the surface?
10. The fish encountered on a bow fishing trip may be smaller or larger than expected. What can you do to minimize this problem?

Physical Conditioning for the Archer

8

Archery, like most sports, places unique anatomical and physiological demands on the individual. The athlete must be ready to meet these exigencies. *Excellent physical conditioning increases the probability of success for the skilled athlete in any sport. Participants in the archery sports are not exceptions to this axiom.* Competitive target archers and field archers are athletes, and they must prepare to meet the challenge of tournament competition. Bow hunters also need conditioning workouts throughout the year. These should be vigorous enough to prepare them for the physical exertion required for stalking, shooting, and retrieving game animals.

The purpose of this chapter is to provide physical conditioning guidelines for serious target archers, field archers, and bow hunters. Health-related fitness guidelines are presented. Exercises are provided and described with some anatomic detail. The archer needs to know what muscular exercise can and cannot do for you. Therefore, the exercises are described to show the archer how they should be performed; which muscles are most involved to produce the joint motions for archery skill; how those muscle groups relate to archery performance; what outcomes can be expected through use of exercise at properly prescribed intensity, frequency, and duration levels; and what energy expenditure levels are required to attain a good level of performance-related fitness for archery.

Specificity of conditioning is unique for each sport. The conditioning for an archer differs considerably from conditioning programs designed, as examples, for long distance runners or basketball players. Each sport places unique physiologic demands on various body systems. *Different muscles are not used from one sport to the next, but the muscle groups that cause joint motions are used differently.*

Skilled motions of limbs or body segments in terms of their velocities, direction, or dynamic stability vary between athletic specialties, and even from one position to the next in team sports. A baseball pitcher, as an example, must be conditioned to move his throwing limb at maximum velocity at precise angles in order to be effective and minimize trauma to the joints of the throwing limb. In contrast, prescribed conditioning for a baseball catcher involves a completely different process, because the demands on the catcher differ considerably from those on a pitcher.

The target archer's sport has distinctive performance criteria. He or she must train to draw the arrow to the anchor point, keep the major joints of the body extended and stable, hold the bow and drawing arm units at maximum steadiness at full draw, and control extrinsic hand musculature under considerable force to perform a perfect release through finger extension. The archer must be prepared to perform this procedure consistently over several hours each day during tournaments. Logan and McKinney's SAID Principle (Specific Adaptations to Imposed Demands) applied to specificity of training deems that each of the above three athletes (pitcher, catcher, and target archer), as examples, should be conditioned differently for them to attain their potentials in competition.

Muscle Analysis of Shooting

This brief muscular, or myological, analysis of shooting is presented for two reasons: (1) to help the serious archer gain a better understanding of precisely what parts of the anatomy need to be conditioned and (2) to reinforce the learning of the shooting mechanics presented in Chapter 4. It is highly recommended that the reader refer to Chapter 4 and figure 8.1 as needed. This will help you to associate the motions and skill techniques of the stance, bow arm, drawing arm, and release to the muscle functions described below.

Stance

In the conditioning considerations for the stance of target archers, field archers and bow hunters, there are more similarities than there are differences. It is understood that the bow hunter's stance must be modified according to the terrain, foliage, and so on, while the target archer's stance remains constant. The common bond is that archers in each of the archery sports must develop good levels of muscle strength and endurance in the large muscle groups that maintain the body in its upright or shooting position against gravity.

The muscle groups that perform the function of extending the major joints at the ankles, knees, hips, and spine are called the *anteroposterior antigravity muscles*. These are shown in figure 8.2. Strength development in these antigravity muscles is indispensable for the archer, because steadiness in the stance from anchoring through release is the foundation for shooting accuracy. Slight tremors or deviations of the extended body and bow arm segment will adversely affect arrow flight and accuracy. *Therefore, developing the anteroposterior antigravity muscles for optimum strength should have the highest priority in a conditioning program.* Good levels of strength and muscle endurance in the anteroposterior antigravity musculature will increase the probability for success on the target range or in the field.

The shooting stance is described as a bilateral, weight-bearing position. The major joints within the legs and spine are kept extended. This can be observed in figure 8.1. As a result, the static stability of the stance is maintained by a combination of the weight-bearing force and modest muscle contractile force within the antigravity musculature as needed to maintain equilibrium and steadiness (figure 8.2).

A Nocking

B Drawing

C Anchor Point

D Release and Follow-through

Figure 8.1
The shooting sequence in target archery. (Courtesy Patrick Brunhoeber)

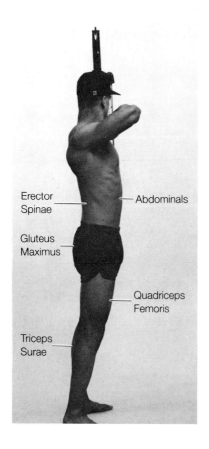

Erector
Spinae

Abdominals

Gluteus
Maximus

Quadriceps
Femoris

Triceps
Surae

Figure 8.2
The anteroposterior antigravity muscle
groups form the foundation for stance
stability. (Courtesy Justin List, Mr. Teenage
Arizona)

The *triceps surae* are the large posterior calf muscles (*gastrocnemius* and *soleus*). These muscles extend, or plantar flex, your ankle. The *quadriceps femoris* muscle group on the front of the thigh consists of four large muscles that extend the knee against gravity. The large buttocks muscle (*gluteus maximus*) extends the hip. The spinal column is maintained in the erect, or extended, position by the deep back muscle group known collectively as the *erector spinae*. If an archer has a tendency to lean backwards, or hyperextend, the spine while in the stance, the six large *abdominal, or stomach, muscles* act reflexively as antigravity muscles. They counteract the slightest posterior motion of the spine and move the trunk back to the extended position. The *erector spinae* muscles will extend the spine of the archer if he or she has a tendency to lean forward or flex the lumbar-thoracic spine. Those two large muscle masses located anterior and posterior to your spine provide constant force-counterforce to maintain a stable and extended spine required in the stance.

Fortunately, the antigravity muscle groups do not need to work maximally to maintain the erect shooting stance. That would lead to fatigue. They do contract as needed to maintain alignment of your body segments over each other and above the base of support (feet). Your equilibrium is maintained in this manner. The antigravity muscle actions are monitored and directed through several central nervous system mechanisms including those in the middle ear. Keeping the antigravity muscle strength levels above average help make stance stability and equilibrium more efficient for the archer.

The antigravity muscle's strength and muscle endurance is most significant for those last few arrows shot during a target archery tournament when you need to be in the gold to be a medalist, or for the hunter's shot at a trophy animal after he or she has been hiking and climbing in the mountains for several hours. Fatigue can have a negative effect on accuracy at times like those. The conditioned archer prevents or delays the onset of fatigue and increases the chance for success. There is an old saying in athletics that, "You make your own breaks." Being in good enough condition to delay or eliminate fatigue as a factor in competition or hunting is one way to make your own breaks in archery.

The Bow Arm

For the functions of the bow arm segment and drawing arm, the conditioning needs are basically the same for the target archer, field archer, and bow hunter. Bow hunters on average draw greater bow weights than target archers, so they need to develop more strength for the greater effort during the draw. However, strength and muscle endurance development in the arms, shoulders, and shoulder girdles should greatly exceed the demands of the bow weights used by all archers. *One should always over prepare for the strength requirements demanded in competition.*

Some of the arm, shoulder, and shoulder girdle musculature used to hold and draw the bow are shown in figures 8.3 and 8.4. These are the superficial muscles, that is, those you can palpate, or touch, on yourself or a cooperating adult. It is recommended that you find a consenting adult archer to collaborate with and feel these muscles as they contract during the draw and while holding prior to release. This will help you understand your own drawing process and the need for conditioning specific muscle groups.

The bow arm segment (left arm and shoulder for the right-handed archer) is vital to accuracy in archery. The muscles must be strong enough to eliminate motion in this arm prior to and at the time of release. Furthermore, the muscle endurance must be good enough to allow you to shoot efficiently for long periods of time, for example, 144 arrows during one FITA Round.

As can be seen in figures 8.3 and 8.4, the bow arm segment is held stable with the elbow and wrist extended. After nocking, the bow arm is raised from the side (shoulder joint abduction) about ninety degrees, as seen between figure 8.1a and b. That motion is accomplished primarily by contractile force of the large shoulder (*deltoid*) muscle. The deltoid, plus the underlying smaller muscles that help move the bow arm into shooting position, must have the strength and muscle endurance to repeatedly perform that function. But, more importantly, the deltoid must contribute considerable stabilizing force for the shoulder joint. It must help hold the literal weight of your arm as well as the mass weight of the bow in space from the draw through the follow-through. Any deviation of

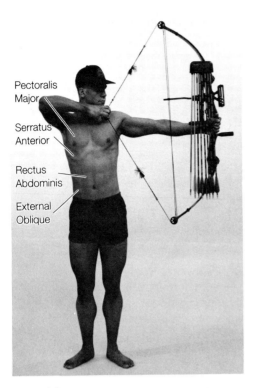

Pectoralis
Major

Serratus
Anterior

Rectus
Abdominis

External
Oblique

Figure 8.3
Anterior, superficial muscles during the drawing process. (Superficial muscles can be palpated or touched.) (Courtesy Justin List, Mr. Teenage Arizona)

the bow arm segment just prior to or at release will have a negative effect on accurate arrow flight. Both left and right deltoid muscles must be strong and have a good level of muscle endurance.

The *triceps brachii* on the posterior side of your upper arm is also a very important muscle within the bow arm segment, because it must keep the elbow in the extended position shown in figures 8.3 and 8.4. Maximal contraction of the muscles in the bow arm is contraindicated. That would tend to produce fatigue and tremors in these important muscles. As indicated in Chapter 4, the skilled archer "relaxes" as much musculature as possible. As a result, the *triceps brachii* and *deltoid* muscles in the bow arm exert only enough contractile force to maintain the proper elbow and shoulder positions.

There are thirteen muscle tendons surrounding the wrist joint. These are your *extrinsic hand muscles*. The bellies of these muscles make up the mass of your forearm, and they help keep the wrist extended by contributing some stabilizing contraction as the archer moves the bow arm during the draw and holds the anchor position through the follow-through. It is a serious mistake to maximize static or isometric contraction of these bow arm muscles in your forearm. That would result in slight tremors in the muscles after several arrows were released. Relaxation is the key. One must take advantage of the external forces

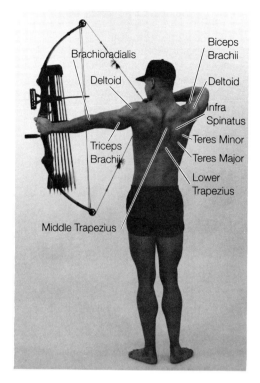

Brachioradialis

Biceps
Brachii

Deltoid

Deltoid

Infra
Spinatus

Teres Minor

Triceps
Brachii

Teres Major

Lower
Trapezius

Middle Trapezius

Figure 8.4
Posterior, superficial muscles during the drawing process. (Courtesy Justin List, Mr. Teenage Arizona)

provided by the bow weight during the draw to assist in maintaining extensions of the wrist and elbow joints. As noted in Chapter 4, the wrist is kept extended during the shooting process. The wrist never flexes, hyperextends, or moves in any other direction. Your forearm (*radioulnar joint*) remains stable in the mid-position (handshake position) between supination and pronation throughout the entire shooting sequence.

The Drawing Arm

The drawing arm segment (right arm and shoulder for a right-handed archer) must have adequate strength and muscle endurance to handle the archer's bow weight during numerous draws, for example, 288 times during a double FITA Round competition. From a competitive perspective, it is very important to the archer that the last draw feel as easy as the first draw. The key to this is to condition the muscles most involved for the draw, and learn how to relax all of your remaining muscle groups as much as possible throughout the competition.

The key point to remember regarding the draw is: *the major contractile force and ultimate control of the draw lies in the larger shoulder joint and shoulder girdle musculature and not in the smaller muscle mass of the arm.* The arm tends to be the focal point, because it is the moving segment. The *biceps brachii* on the anterior aspect of your upper arm and other elbow flexors do contribute some force during the draw. But, the draw results mainly from contractions by musculature within your right shoulder joint and right shoulder girdle. The drawing arm segment transfers those muscle forces to the bowstring as the hand is drawn to the anchor point. Scientifically, the total motion of the drawing arm is the combined result of muscle contractile forces for: (1) elbow flexion, (2) horizontal abduction of the shoulder joint, and (3) shoulder girdle adduction or retraction.

The muscle force that causes horizontal abduction of the shoulder is provided by concentric contraction of the *posterior portion of the deltoid, infraspinatus,* and *teres minor* muscles. These superficial muscles are shown in figure 8.4. Because of the posterior location of these muscles, some archery instructors advise students to utilize a "focal concentration point" on "back muscles" instead of "arm muscles" during the draw. This is a good idea. The force to cause the right shoulder blade or scapula to move toward your spinal column during the draw (shoulder girdle adduction) is caused by contraction of some of the superficial *trapezius* muscle fibers on your back, as shown in figure 8.4. The deep rhomboid muscles attached to the shoulder blade *beneath the trapezius* also move the scapula during the draw.

If you feel a consenting adult archer's back during a draw, you can palpate the superficial drawing muscles described above and better comprehend their roles. Use this area on yourself as a *concentration focal point* during the draw. This will give you better perception and kinesthetic awareness of your draw. Also, palpate the biceps brachii in the upper arm of another archer to feel its involvement in the drawing process. It will be tense, but its force contribution is not as significant as the larger muscles most involved in the draw.

In compliance with the SAID Principle, conditioning for the draw arm segment must be designed to develop adequate strength and muscle endurance levels in the very important "back muscles" of the shoulder girdle and shoulder joint. In addition, the elbow flexors need specific work to provide their force contribution to the draw. Exercises are described later in this chapter.

As the drawing arm moves the bowstring and hand toward the anchor point, the shoulder blade (scapula) is being rotated upward to accommodate the head of the humerus of the arm at the shoulder joint. This rotary motion of the scapula is the result of muscle contractions by the *serratus anterior* and parts of the *trapezius*. Once your hand reaches the anchor point, the serratus anterior stabilizes (fig. 8.3) or holds the scapula in a firm position. Muscular stability of this type is very important to maintain steadiness during the shooting process. The muscle stabilizers in this body segment and elsewhere also need specific exercise during your daily workout schedule.

The Release and Follow-Through

The key muscle force component of the release is the final one-eighth inch movement of your arrow through the clicker prior to release. This very important motion is accomplished through intense concentration on your "middle back muscles."

Specifically, the middle fibers of your trapezius muscle are conditioned to contract and *gently* move your shoulder blade toward your spinal column (scapular adduction). That moves the arrow past the clicker. When the "click" is heard, the joints of the string fingers are ready to extend, allowing the bowstring to move forward and the arrow to release.

As mentioned in Chapter 4, the extension of your finger joints (interphalangeal joints) *is not* the result of forceful finger extensor muscle contraction by musculature in your forearm and hand. *The external force for release is caused by the bowstring as you relax the tension within the finger musculature, that is, relax the "three-finger hook" around the string (fig. 8.1d).* The bowstring should be released to move forward directly toward the target. The extending fingers should clear the string smoothly without any lateral pressure exerted on it.

During the follow-through phase of shooting, you simply watch the arrow flight to observe any erratic flight motions such as porpoising or fishtailing. You may exhale and inhale at this time and watch the arrow until it strikes the target. There will be a slight "recoil motion" of your draw arm, and the bow arm may drop a few degrees. Your sling keeps the bow from falling to the ground, and you regrasp the bow *after* the arrow is in flight or in the target.

Fitness Guidelines

Health and performance related fitness include four important parameters that must be evaluated for each athlete. They are (1) flexibility, (2) strength, (3) muscular endurance, and (4) cardiovascular endurance. If possible, each of these parameters should be measured for the individual prior to starting a conditioning program. That would quantify a fitness profile and help in writing the exercise prescription and goals for conditioning.

Flexibility

Flexibility is the degree to which a joint can move through its maximal normal range of motion.

Flexibility guidelines and exercises are not presented in detail. Due to the nature of the sport of archery, total body flexibility is desired, but it is not a high priority fitness factor for success. An athlete in gymnastics, for example, must consider total body flexibility as a prime fitness objective in order to meet the skill demands of that sport. The joint range-of-motion requirements needed to be highly skilled in archery are not as general, and they are much less demanding than in a sport such as gymnastics.

Full range-of-motion flexibility for archers is desired in the joints and body segments directly involved in the drawing process. Lack of flexibility in the drawing shoulder and shoulder girdle could be a problem, but this is observed in only a very small percentage of archers. The nature of the draw (a slow stretching process followed by a hold at the anchor point) tends to increase flexibility in the noncontractile tissue (tendons, ligaments, fasciae etc.) of the drawing shoulder and shoulder girdle. Therefore, a functional range-of-motion for the archer is maintained to some degree through the shooting process.

Drawing the bow can be used as a specific flexibility exercise when bow weight is held for 20 to 30 seconds *beyond* the anchor point at the completion of the total range-of-motion for the draw. *The 20 to 30 second static hold at the end of a joint's range-of-motion is an integral part of any flexibility exercise.* This type of flexibility exercise can be included and is recommended as a part of the "overload draw" procedure using an older, overweight bow. Overload drawing exercises are described later in this chapter.

Rapid or ballistic movement of a limb or body segment through a joint's range-of-motion is medically contraindicated. That can lead to lacerations of the noncontractile tissue that supports your joints. (A negative application of the SAID Principle.) As one example, many people are traumatized as they perform what they believe to be "flexibility exercises" to music. This involves rapid joint or limb motions during aerobic activities that are actually designed to improve cardiovascular endurance!

Strength

A functional definition of strength is the ability of an individual to overcome resistance by the use of internal force developed through muscle contraction. A strength development program for archers is included in this chapter.

To elicit the neuromuscular changes in the body needed to produce strength, the following scientifically based guidelines are needed to define the workload:

1. INTENSITY: The weight load should be great enough to limit the number of repetitions to eight for each exercise; that is, maximum weight load for a maximum of eight repetitions for each joint motion. When strength improves to the point that more than eight repetitions can be performed, add enough weight to return to the eight repetition level. Breathe during the difficult portion of the exercise. This keeps the glottis open in the throat and reduces the probability of herniation and undesired shifts in blood pressure. Maximum weight loads for less than eight repetitions should be avoided.

2. FREQUENCY: Strength workouts should be performed a *minimum* of four days per week in order to obtain the best results. Daily workouts may be performed without ill effects by individuals who are already strong and highly motivated as weight trainers. Workouts should be spaced 24 to 36 hours apart.

3. DURATION: The average strength workout should consume approximately one hour. A series of exercises such as described later in this chapter should be selected to work the desired musculature. One series of weight training exercises is called a *set*. Three sets constitute a strength workout following the intensity guideline outlined above. *Perform the exercises slowly through the complete range-of-motion of the joint.* The one exception to that rule is knee joint flexion when exercising from the standing position. "Deep knee bends" are not recommended as an exercise due to the potential for trauma to your knee ligaments and cartilages.

If these strength guidelines are followed, the archer will acquire strength. It usually takes four to six weeks for the initial strength changes to be "felt" subjectively. Some natural muscle stiffness due to a residual of acid metabolites following muscle contraction will occur in the beginner during the first two weeks of weight training, but will not be a problem as you continue with your workouts.

The term "neuromuscular changes" was used above for good reason. The most significant anatomic and physiologic changes to increase strength will be a result of *Specific Adaptations* of central nervous system (CNS) anatomy to the *Imposed Demands* of strength training outlined above. (This is another positive example of Logan and McKinney's SAID Principle related to changes in the human organism due to conditioning.) You become stronger by making the interrelationships between the muscle and central nervous systems more efficient. Muscle mass and tone increase in many people as a result of strength work, but the most important changes for increasing strength occur within the neural pathways in your CNS. Some "lean" people become very strong due to maximizing the efficiency of the CNS, and they have very little change in muscle mass.

Muscular Endurance

Muscle endurance is the ability of a muscle group to perform repeated contractions against relatively light resistance. Muscle endurance is needed when a performer must repeat joint motions numerous times during competition. The repetitive shooting procedure used in target archery tournaments is one example; therefore, the muscles most involved in the shooting process need a good to excellent level of muscle endurance.

To elicit the physiologic changes in the body to increase muscle endurance, the following workload guidelines must be followed:

1. INTENSITY: *The weight load to produce muscle endurance should be established to allow the performer to complete a minimum of twenty repetitions.* More repetitions may be performed at each workout station as time allows. The physiologic changes associated with this level of intensity will enhance aerobic metabolism for energy production.
2. FREQUENCY: *Muscle endurance workouts should be performed a minimum of four days per week.* Daily workouts may be performed without ill effects by people who already have a good level of health-related fitness. Individuals produce excellent results working six or seven days per week. It is recommended that a person alternate strength and muscle endurance workouts. That is functional, and boredom is reduced by not performing the same workload or activities on a daily basis.
3. DURATION: The average muscle endurance workout should consume approximately one hour. Three sets of exercises constitute one workout. The maximum number of repetitions at each exercise station per set may need to be adjusted periodically as a time consideration. *Perform all exercises slowly through the complete range-of-motion.* Avoid "deep knee bends" (full knee flexion) from the standing position, as noted above.

An individual who starts a conditioning program must be patient. The anatomic and physiologic adaptations may not manifest themselves for weeks. You must also establish realistic goals and expectations for yourself. If you anticipate fast results, you will be frustrated. You must remember, for example, that muscular endurance development involves cellular as well as central nervous system adaptations. Time is required to produce the sophisticated modifications of muscle cells and organelles within cells responsible for increasing aerobic respiration and endurance. Using the guidelines above, you will begin to notice increases in your muscular endurance level in four to six weeks. Persistence will pay off!

Specific recommendations regarding strength and/or muscle endurance exercises for the various muscle groups used by archers are presented in detail in this chapter. Priorities will be established for strength and muscle endurance intensities during workouts.

Cardiovascular Endurance

Good to excellent levels of cardiovascular endurance require a high level of physiological efficiency of the heart, lungs, and the circulatory system to transport oxygen and other fuels to the organism during prolonged periods of physical exertion. This is the most important of all the fitness parameters. The best measures of cardiovascular function are the electrocardiogram and maximal oxygen consumption.

The principal conditioning difference between target archers, field archers, and bow hunters is in the extent of cardiovascular endurance required to execute the skill. Generally, the target archer does not need to develop more than an average or functional level of cardiovascular endurance. The nature of the sport does not place maximal oxygen consumption demands on the archer. It is recommended, however, that the serious archer perform enough aerobic exercise on a regular basis to maintain a good to excellent level of cardiovascular fitness.

Field archers and bow hunters, on the other hand, should analyze the physical exertion demands they can expect while in the field. As an example, if a hunt will take the bow hunter into wilderness country to walk and stalk for extended time periods, in cold or hot environments, over hills or into high altitudes, and with the possibility that you might have to pack out heavy game (e.g., a field dressed elk), the hunter should give considerable thought to maintaining or developing cardiovascular endurance to meet these increased demands without difficulty. Why is this important? It is a tragic fact that a few hunters, usually age 35 (that is middle age!) and beyond, die of myocardial infarctions in the field. They were not capable of handling the added physical exertion stress in hot or cold environments in deserts, hills, or mountains. It pays to be prepared cardiovascularly!

There are other, less traumatic, problems observed more frequently in cardiovascularly unfit bow hunters. Much money is spent on tackle preparing for the hunt. Time is devoted to developing shooting skill and tuning tackle for the hunt. People go to the trouble to enter game animal lotteries and spend large amounts of money traveling to high mountain country for their prey. After spending all that money, time, and effort, some bow hunters are not capable of meeting the physiologic challenge of the hunt on foot through rugged terrain at high altitude in the cold. Surprisingly, this tends to happen among younger people who are not fit but "talk a good game" with a beer in hand. *If they pack in, their hunting partners often have to pack them out!*

The full preparation of the archer should include concurrent development of shooting skill and cardiovascular conditioning. An archer who wishes to increase his or her cardiovascular endurance should first be evaluated by a physician to determine whether or not the circulatory and respiratory systems are normal. The scientifically based guidelines below should help interested bow hunters, field archers, and target archers exercise at the energy expenditure levels required to maintain or develop cardiovascular fitness.

1. INTENSITY: To improve your cardiorespiratory capacity, intensity of exercise is measured according to two criteria: (1) A heart rate during exercise sufficient to produce positive aerobic training effects. That level of exercise intensity is known as your *threshold heart rate* or *THR*. (See table 8.1 for THR levels according to age and general condition status.) (2) *Energy expenditure* during workouts for men should be above 3000 kilocalories per week (kcal/week), and women's physical exertion level should be over 1800 kcal/week.

How do you determine what your exercising or threshold heart rate should be? Use table 8.1. Your maximum and resting heart rates play a key role in establishing your THR. The heart rate needs to be monitored in the morning while you are lying in bed. This measurement will provide your *resting heart rate*. Take a one-minute reading by gently palpating your radial artery at the wrist with your index and middle fingers. Such a reading is noted in *beats per minute* (BPM). Generally, if you are in average cardiovascular condition, your resting heart rate will be 55 to 75 BPM. Better conditioned people usually have more efficient cardiac function and slower heart rates. This is an exercise-induced slow heart rate (bradycardia), which should not be confused with pathological forms of bradycardia observed in geriatric patients.

Imagine, as an example, that you are 19 years of age with a good resting heart rate of 46 BPM. Table 8.1 will inform you that your heart rate intensity (THR) during exercise should be kept between 152 and 168 BPM. Your target heart rate number to keep in mind during cardiovascular or aerobic workouts should be 160 BPM.

Table 8.1 Threshold Heart Rate Intensity Levels for Cardiovascular Endurance Development

Age Group	Max HR*	Morning Resting Heart Rate Above 75 BPM	Morning Resting Heart Rate 55–75 BPM	Morning Resting Heart Rate Below 55 BPM
15–19	200	114 (120) 126	143 (150) 158	152 (160) 168
20–24	195	111 (117) 123	139 (146) 154	148 (156) 164
25–29	190	108 (114) 120	135 (142) 150	144 (152) 160
30–34	185	105 (111) 117	131 (138) 143	140 (148) 156
35–39	180	102 (108) 114	128 (135) 143	136 (144) 152
40–44	175	99 (105) 111	124 (131) 139	132 (140) 148
45–49	170	96 (102) 108	120 (127) 135	128 (136) 144
50–54	165	93 (99) 105	116 (123) 131	124 (132) 140
55–59	160	90 (96) 102	113 (120) 128	120 (128) 136
60–64	155	87 (93) 99	109 (116) 124	116 (124) 132
65–69	150	84 (90) 96	105 (112) 120	112 (120) 128
70–74	145	81 (87) 93	101 (109) 116	108 (116) 124

*The variability for maximum heart rate is ± 10 BPM.
Note: This table should read as follows: A 22-year-old person has a maximum heart rate of 195 BPM ± 10 BPM. If this individual's resting heart rate is 62 BPM, the threshold heart rate (THR) *during exercise* should average 139–154 BPM. The *target number* for THR would be 146 BPM for this person during aerobic activities to produce cardiovascular training effects.

How do you monitor THR intensity during an aerobic workout? First, you need to know your THR range in BPM during exercise. Second, the midpoint in that range should be kept in mind specifically; you should be near this exercise target number when monitoring the heart rate as you work out. Third, for individuals beginning an aerobic workout program, it is recommended that the heart rate be monitored every 10 to 15 minutes during exercise. In order to do this and obtain meaningful heart rates, you must stop exercising. *As soon as you stop your aerobic activity and while standing, determine your heart rate by gently palpating the radial artery at the wrist.* Within 5 to 10 seconds of stopping your exercise, take a 10-second heart rate count. Multiply that number by six for BPM.

A longer delay in monitoring the heart rate following cessation of exercise decreases accuracy, and one may not assume that the BPM reading reflects the actual heart rate during exercise. Ideally, a heart rate correctly monitored will be on your target number or at least within your THR range. (There are biomedical, electronic devices on the market that will measure your actual exercising heart rate.)

During the aerobic workout, one attempts to keep the exercising heart rate in BPM in the THR range and fairly close to the target number. As an example, a 52-year-old runner with a resting heart rate of 42 BPM has a THR range from 124 to 140 BPM, with an exercise target number of 132 BPM. This means that the *10-second heart rate reading* when monitored during exercise should be 22 beats. A lower reading would indicate that the exercise intensity was below the THR range (e.g., 16 beats per 10-second count would be 96 BPM). This person would need to increase his or her running pace (intensity) slightly to elevate the exercising heart rate to at least 124 BPM. Conversely, if the 10-second heart rate reading during the run were counted at 25 beats (150 BPM), this individual should decrease the running pace. The intensity would be 10 BPM above his or her THR range.

It is important to stay within your THR range during aerobic work. You should find this range to be comfortable. Breathing should not be labored, and you should be able to talk with a companion while moving at a pace intense enough to produce your THR.

There is a dangerous myth about workout intensity perpetuated by a few masochistic cretins. It states, "No pain, no gain!" The exercise intensity guidelines noted above for your threshold heart rate *will not* produce pain. *Exercise intensity does not have to be painful to produce positive results.* The thought of perceived pain and continued discomfort turns people away from regular exercise, because for normal people pain is not a motivator to exercise. From anatomical, physiological, psychological, and medical perspectives, extreme stress exercise that produces pain is contraindicated and counterproductive to human beings who wish to attain either performance or health-related fitness.

You can use any form of exercise as long as it is intense enough to keep you in your THR range. Most commonly these are jogging, running, swimming, cycling, and some court sports (singles tennis, handball etc.). Can walking be an aerobic activity? Yes, it is for some people. If a brisk walk at a pace of 3 to 4 miles per hour moves you into your THR, you should not be running. Find an activity or activities you enjoy that will keep your exercising heart rate where it should be for the required duration of the workout. A vital key to this type of exercise is the enjoyment and satisfaction one has during daily workouts and in attaining short and long range goals! That is one "secret" to exercise continuity.

The other dimension of intensity of exercise noted above is your level of energy expenditure. This is measured in kilocalories. *The kilocalorie is described metabolically as the amount of heat required to raise the temperature of one liter of water one degree centigrade.* Commonly called a "calorie," this unit is used by dieticians and exercise scientists for measuring energy intake (food) and energy expenditure (exercise/physical exertion). So, everyone has heard about "calories" in one manner or another. Minimum and desired energy expenditure levels in kilocalories per week to maintain and develop health-related fitness were noted above for men (3000 kcal/wk) and women (1800 kcal/wk).

How can you monitor your kcal/week? Exercise physiologists have done metabolic measurements on humans involved in everything from target archery to sexual intercourse! So, energy expenditure values are available for most of the activities humans pursue. *The following is the procedure to determine energy expenditure for target archery practice:*

1. Change your body weight in pounds to kilograms by multiplying the pounds by *0.454.*
2. Multiplying your weight in kilograms by a factor of *0.065* will give you the kcal/min you use during target archery practice or tournament action.

Target archery for a 147 pounder (66.74 kg) for an hour would result in an energy expenditure of 260 kilocalories (4.34 kcal/min). If this person shot an hour per day for five days per week, the total weekly energy expenditure would be 1300 kilocalories per week for target archery practice. He or she most likely would not reach THR intensity while shooting; so one can readily see that integration of aerobic activities with archery practice is needed to reach a desired energy expenditure level and a good cardiovascular endurance status. This is where supplemental running, cycling, swimming, or walking workouts can be utilized during the week in addition to target practice.

Table 8.2 provides energy expenditure factors to be used in the calculation of kcal/min for running, swimming, walking, and cycling.

If our 147-pound archer ran at an 8-minute-per-mile pace for 40 minutes per day at THR intensity four days per week, he or she would expend 2220 kilocalories. Add three hours per week of target archery practice at 260 kilocalories per hour, and the total would be a very good level of energy expenditure intensity of 3000 kcal/week. Such a regimen is desirable, because it combines cardiovascular conditioning with shooting.

2. FREQUENCY: In order to produce positive adaptations in the blood chemistry (cholesterol, triglycerides and glucose), the blood vascular transport system, and other parts of your cardiorespiratory anatomy, aerobic workouts at threshold heart rate intensity should be performed a minimum of four days per week. Ideally, workouts should be spaced about thirty-six hours apart. Some form of daily aerobic activity is recommended for individuals who have established good cardiorespiratory endurance with resting heart rates in the morning below 55 beats per minute.

3. DURATION: Thirty minutes of cardiovascular exercise at your threshold heart rate is considered to be the minimum time for a workout. Durations of 30 to 60 minutes per workout are adequate. If an individual is exercising six to seven days per week, it is a good idea to alternate such components as duration times and activities. For example, an hour bicycle ride on Monday

Table 8.2 Energy Expenditure Factors for Determining kcal/min

Horizontal Running	Factor
11 min 30 sec per mile	0.135
9 min per mile	0.193
8 min per mile	0.208
7 min per mile	0.228
6 min per mile	0.252
5 min 30 sec per mile	0.289

Swimming	
Backstroke	0.169
Breaststroke	0.162
Crawl stroke	0.156

Walking: 3–4 MPH	
Firm surface	0.080
Fields and hillsides	0.082
Grass	0.081

Cycling	
5.5 miles per hour	0.064
9.4 miles per hour	0.100
Racing	0.169

Note: This table should be used as follows: Convert your weight in pounds to kilograms by multiplying by 0.454. Multiply your weight in kilograms by the factor to determine your energy expenditure in kilocalories per minute. *Example:* A 147 pounder (66.74 kg) utilizes 13.88 kcal/min while running at an 8-min-per-mile pace:

1. 147 pounds $\times$ 0.454 = 66.74 kg
2. 66.74 kg $\times$ 0.208 = 13.88 kcal/min

could be followed by a 30-minute jog on Tuesday. *Activities chosen should be of interest and challenge the archer to attain his or her realistic short and long range goals.* Those are important considerations, because long term continuity of exercise is a must in developing and maintaining performance related fitness.

As indicated above, some bow hunters have a greater need to develop cardiovascular endurance than target archers because of the physiologic demands of their sport. A year-round program of cardiovascular workouts is recommended. It is a mistake to "try to get in shape" in the few weeks or days prior

Figure 8.5
Heel raise exercise—starting position.

Figure 8.6
Heel raise exercise—finish position. This exercise works the posterior calf or triceps surae muscle group.

to the hunt. If the individual stays "in shape," the workouts may be more intense in terms of energy expenditure per workout during the three to four weeks before going into the field.

Exercises for Stance Stability

All archers need above average strength in their *antigravity muscles* (fig. 8.2) to maintain a stable stance while shooting. A set of six exercises is recommended. Strength development should be the priority fitness factor for these antigravity muscle exercises. Therefore, the intensity, frequency, and duration guidelines outlined above for strength should be followed when possible while performing these exercises. Figures 8.5 through 8.13 serve as examples to demonstrate one method to exercise the antigravity muscle groups. There are several other excellent types of weight machines plus free weights and diverse exercise routines to work these muscle groups.

When resistance loads cannot be found to meet the intensity criterion for strength development, muscle endurance exercise intensity should be substituted. Some modest strength gain will be made while performing muscle endurance

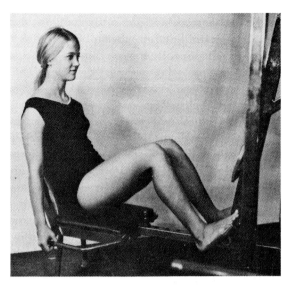

Figure 8.7
The knee extension exercise for the anterior thigh, or quadriceps femoris muscles.

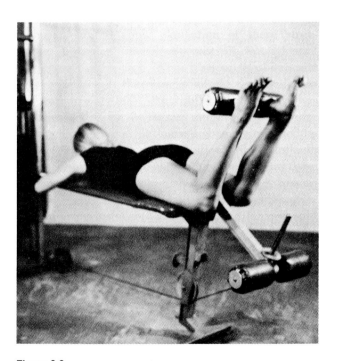

Figure 8.8
The knee flexion exercise for the posterior thigh, or "hamstring," muscle group. These muscles flex the knee as shown and help extend the hip joints.

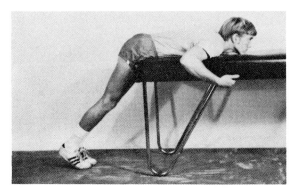

Figure 8.9
Double hip extension exercise—starting position.

Figure 8.10
Double hip extension exercise—finish position. This exercise works the large buttocks muscle, the gluteus maximus.

intensity exercise, and stance stability will be enhanced. Figures 8.5 through 8.13 show exercises (with the exception of fig. 8.8) that may be performed with or without machines to work the antigravity musculature.

Remember that there are times when neither free weights nor weight machines are necessary for muscle endurance and strength development exercise. The weight of the body working against and with gravity can be used for strength and muscle endurance gains.

Note: All exercises pictured and/or described in this chapter should be performed *slowly* against resistance while moving with the gravitational field. Breathing should be as normal as possible, and the breath should not be held. That causes abnormal blood pressure shifts.

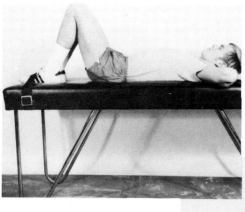

Figure 8.11a
The flexed knee and hip sit-up
exercise—starting position.

Figure 8.11b
The flexed knee and hip sit-up
exercise—finish position. This exercise
works the stomach or abdominal muscle
group.

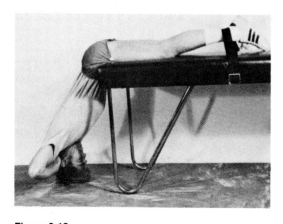

Figure 8.12
The back raise exercise—starting position.

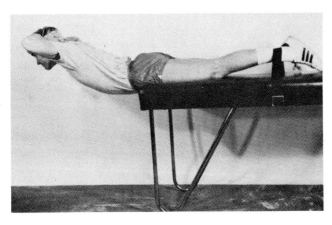

Figure 8.13
The back raise exercise—finish position. This exercise works the deep back muscle group, erector spinae.

Exercises for the Bow Arm

Steadiness of the bow arm is one of the most critical aspects of shooting. As you have learned, the major muscles most involved to produce this stability are located at the shoulder girdle, shoulder, and elbow joints. As a result, the archer needs considerable strength in the deltoid muscle of the shoulder as well as in the triceps and biceps brachii muscles that surround the elbow joint. Strength development guidelines need to be followed for the bow arm exercises.

Figures 8.14 and 8.15 are examples of exercises primarily designed to work the large deltoid muscle over the shoulder. This muscle must be strong enough to support the mass weight of the bow plus the literal weight of the arm against gravity. It has to be strong enough to eliminate even minuscule arm motions during every shot in a target or field archery tournament and during a hunt. Being shaky during a shot "does not feed the bulldog" in archery!

Figure 8.14 illustrates a resistance exercise using a pulley device. The deltoid muscle is the muscle most involved as the arm is raised or abducted from the body in the same manner as moving the bow into the final shooting position. This exercise also works the important serratus anterior and trapezius muscles. As the arm is moved through its upward range of motion (abducted) against resistance, the scapula (shoulder blade) is upwardly rotated by lower fibers of the serratus anterior and upper and lower portions of your trapezius.

Figure 8.15 shows a traditional weight training exercise, the overhead press. This is also a good method to develop strength in the bow arm musculature. This exercise involves the large shoulder musculature, some back muscles, plus your triceps brachii muscle, which extends the elbow against resistance. Keeping the bow arm elbow fully extended at all times is critical while shooting. This requires considerable strength in the triceps brachii muscle.

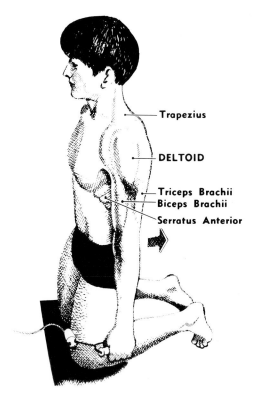

Figure 8.14
A bow arm weight-training exercise using an Exer-Genie Exerciser pulley device. The arm is moved from the side into the shooting position (ABDUCTED) by the large shoulder or deltoid muscle.

The bench press (shown in figure 8.16) is another weight training exercise designed to strengthen the triceps brachii on the posterior side of your elbow. Also, this exercise strengthens the deltoid as well as the large pectoralis major muscle on your chest. Work by the deltoid and triceps brachii during the bench press makes this a good exercise for the bow arm unit. As in the previous two exercises, crucial shoulder girdle musculature is also conditioned.

The elbow of the bow arm segment is held in the stable and extended position by all of the muscles surrounding the elbow joint. Therefore, the archer should strengthen not only the muscle on the back of the elbow, the triceps brachii, but also the biceps brachii on the front of the elbow. The "biceps curl" exercise as shown in figure 8.17 is designed to develop strength in the muscles that have an anterior or frontal spatial relationship to the elbow joint. The "biceps curl" exercise should be used on both elbows to enhance efficiency in the bow and drawing arms.

Figure 8.15
The overhead press exercise is a good bow arm exercise because it strengthens the deltoid muscle at the shoulder and the triceps brachii muscle at the elbow.

Figure 8.16
The bench press exercise contributes strength to the bow arm unit by working the elbow extensor muscle, the triceps brachii, plus the deltoid and pectoralis major muscles.

Figure 8.17
The biceps brachii "curl exercise" adds anterior stabilizing strength to the extended elbow of the bow arm unit, and it adds strength to the drawing arm.

Exercises for the Drawing Arm

As noted previously, the main force for the drawing arm does not come from the arm muscles per se. The draw force is derived from strong shoulder and shoulder girdle muscles. Some of these are shown in figure 8.18. They include the *deltoid, infraspinatus, teres minor, trapezius,* and *rhomboid* muscles. (The latter are not seen in figure 8.18 because they lie beneath your trapezius muscle.) These are the "back muscles" that your archery instructor or coach wants you to concentrate on during target archery practice as you draw through your clicker. Since these muscles provide the force to overcome the bow weight during the draw, they must have above average strength to be functional. The stronger these muscles are, the easier it is for you to handle your bow weight during draws throughout a tournament. Also, with added strength in these muscles, the archer may be able ultimately to increase bow weight. That provides higher arrow velocities and flatter trajectories, which can lead to better accuracy and higher scores.

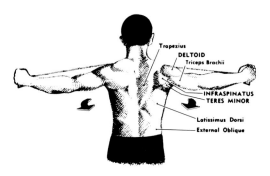

Figure 8.18
The drawing arm exercise using a pulley device that isolates the critical muscles used to exert force to overcome the bow weight.

Figure 8.19
The drawing arm exercise using dumbbells for resistance. It is important to move the arms from the floor through the complete range-of-motion.

Figure 8.18 shows a drawing arm resistance exercise performed with a pulley device. It is important for the archer to move the arms through the complete range-of-motion as indicated by the direction of the arrows. You should feel the shoulder blades move toward your spine (scapular adduction) as the arms are moved backward (horizontal abduction) as shown in figure 8.18.

The same exercise is shown in figure 8.19 using free weights or dumbbells for resistance. The starting position is with the hands near the floor. It is very important to move the hands and arms as far as possible to the finish position shown in figure 8.19.

As a matter of scientific principle, *resistance exercises should be performed bilaterally; that is, muscle groups on opposite sides of the body should receive equal work to maintain strength, muscle endurance, and flexibility balance.* An exercise to work the chest and shoulder is depicted for use with a wall pulley and dumbbells in figures 8.20 and 8.21 respectively. The arms are brought forward (horizontally adducted) by the contracting muscles on the front of the shoulder and chest. This stretches "back muscles" involved while performing the exercise

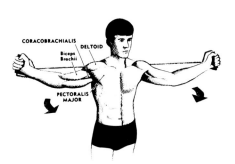

Figure 8.20
Shoulder horizontal adduction exercise to complement the drawing arm exercise using a pulley device.

Figure 8.21
Shoulder horizontal adduction exercise using dumbbells to complement the drawing arm exercise. It is important to move the arms through the complete range-of-motion from below the bench to touching the dumbells above your head.

shown in figures 8.18 and 8.19. Strengthening front as well as back muscles will make the archer's draw easier to handle and prevent loss of shoulder range-of-motion (flexibility).

The Overload Draw Exercise

The archer should consider the bow a highly specific weight training device. The exercises previously described in this chapter can develop general strength and muscle endurance in muscle groups used by the archer. Workouts with free weights or weight machines have greater workloads available than found in most bow weights. Those heavier workloads are needed in the application of the SAID and Overload Principles to attain your fitness objectives, particularly in strength. However, the archer can achieve a very specific muscle endurance overload by exercising with a bow weight in excess of the normal bow weight used in competition or while hunting. This type of exercise has the potential to develop strength and muscle endurance in muscle groups through the precise ranges of motion and at the specific joint angles utilized in drawing and holding the bow during a contest or hunt. Logan and McKinney have described this type of exercise in the literature as "Specifics."

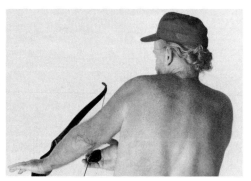

Figure 8.22a
The overload draw exercise—starting position. (Bow courtesy Black Widow Bow Company, H. C. R. #1, Box 357-1, Highlandville, Missouri 65669)

Figure 8.22b
The overload draw exercise—back musculature—starting position.

As an added component of the conditioning process for archers, it is recommended that *overload draw exercises* be included within each set when conditioning for muscle endurance. (A used "exercise bow" a few pounds over the normal bow weight should be purchased and used exclusively for overload draw exercises. Your competitive tackle should not be used for this purpose.) A *minimum* of 20 draws should be made per exercise set to develop muscle endurance. That means the archer would complete a *minimum* of 60 overload draws during the three sets of a workout. (FITA Round shooters may want to complete 144 consecutive overload draws periodically just as a drill.)

The bow should be drawn to the anchor point as shown in figures 8.22, 8.23, and 8.24, and held statically long enough to simulate the release and follow-through phases. The bowstring must not be released. The string should be eased back to the starting position, and the next draw initiated within 15 to 20 seconds.

Overload drawing should be considered more than a weight training exercise. While overload drawing, the archer should *mentally practice shooting mechanics*. Each fundamental, body position, and joint angle should be thought through carefully. It is recommended that the position of a body part or segment be given specific attention during each set of overload draws, for example, the bow hand position at the pivot point during the first set, "back muscles" supplying the drawing force on the second set, bowstring to finger position on the third set, and so on.

Figure 8.23a
The overload draw exercise—midposition.

Figure 8.23b
The overload draw exercise—back musculature—midposition.

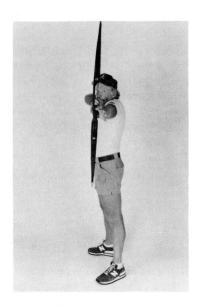

Figure 8.24a
The overload draw exercise—anchor position.

Figure 8.24b
The overload draw exercise—back musculature—anchor position.

Table 8.3   Energy Expenditure Factors for Determining kcal/min Values for Weight Training

Types of Equipment Used	Factor
Hydra-Fitness	0.132
Universal	0.116
Nautilus	0.092
Free weights	0.086

Note: This table should be used as follows: Convert your weight in pounds to kilograms by multiplying by 0.454. Multiply your weight in kilograms by the appropriate factor to determine your energy expenditure in kilocalories per minute. *Example:* A 166 pounder (75.36 kg) would use 6.48 kcal/min doing free weight exercise:

1. 166 pounds $\times$ 0.454 = 75.36 kg
2. 75.36 kg $\times$ 0.086 = 6.48 kcal/min

Another approach to the "mental practice" aspect of overload drawing is to use information based on your shooting problems established during target practice and videotape analyses of your shooting fundamentals (see Chapter 4). Use the overload draw time to mentally practice proper shooting technique related to your major problem defined through videotape analyses and/or observations by your archery coach. Ideally, the overload drawing workout should follow practice on a target range or field archery unit. The time spent should be an integration of the mental with the physical aspects of archery. Once the fundamentals have been learned, archery becomes more mental than physical.

Overload drawing is shown in figures 8.22, 8.23, and 8.24. It is recommended that most of these draws be smooth and continuous from the starting position to anchor. However, an occasional static hold at mid-position for six to eight seconds—the position shown in figure 8.23—could facilitate some isometric strength gain. Also, the hold while at the anchor point, figure 8.24, can be for at least six to eight seconds. The reader should refer to figures 8.4 and 8.18 while observing the changes in the superficial back and shoulder muscles of the archer in figures 8.22, 8.23, and 8.24. Several changes occur in the bow arm and drawing arm musculature. Some of these can be observed by comparing and contrasting the alterations in the external appearance of the back and shoulder muscles of the archer in figures 8.22 and 8.24.

Overload draws may be made periodically beyond the anchor point to work on flexibility in the shoulder-shoulder girdle segments. If more flexibility is desired, the draw should be slow and to the end of the range-of-motion of the draw arm *beyond the anchor point.* A static hold should be made at that point for 20 to 30 seconds. This procedure can be repeated 10 to 15 times during the workout preferably when the archers' core temperature is slightly elevated; for example, this flexibility exercise would be best following a running workout of about 30 minutes.

It was noted earlier in this chapter that total energy expenditure is important to consider in terms of kilocalories per week of exercise. If you perform the types of weight training exercises described herein for archers, table 8.3 can be used to help you determine your energy expenditure values for weight training.

Summary and Conditioning Recommendations

When the skill factor between competitors is equal, a target archer or field archer who has above average conditioning increases his or her probability of outscoring another archer who has only average or lower levels of muscle endurance, strength, and cardiovascular endurance. The serious bow hunter in good condition who must go after game in wilderness or rugged terrain will facilitate that task, assure his or her own survival, and increase the likelihood of making the kill and carrying out the meat for human consumption.

The following thirteen systematic activities are recommended as *one set* of exercises for archers. *Three sets should be performed to constitute a daily workout.* The guidelines for strength should be followed regarding intensity, frequency, and duration if that is the conditioning outcome desired by the archer. If muscle endurance is the priority, those conditioning guidelines for muscle endurance should be followed. Strength workouts could be pursued on alternate days, with muscle endurance weight loads providing a change of pace, if desired. (A variety of free weights, weight machines, pulley devices, and your own body moving against and with gravity may be used to perform these exercises.)

Stance

1. Heel raise (figs. 8.5 and 8.6)
2. Knee extension (fig. 8.7)
3. Knee flexion (fig. 8.8)
4. Hip extension (figs. 8.9 and 8.10)
5. Sit-up (fig. 8.11)
6. Back raise (figs. 8.12 and 8.13)

Bow Arm

7. Shoulder abduction (fig. 8.14)
8. Overhead press (fig. 8.15)
9. Bench press (fig. 8.16)
10. Biceps curl (fig. 8.17)—use for draw arm also

Draw Arm

11. Horizontal abduction (fig. 8.19)
12. Horizontal adduction (fig. 8.21)
13. Overload drawing (figs. 8.22 through 8.24)

When three sets of these exercises are completed at the intensity desired, it is recommended that the archer conclude the workout with a minimum of 30 minutes of cardiovascular endurance exercise (running, walking, cycling, swimming etc.) at the threshold heart rate level of intensity most of the time.

Approximately 45 minutes are needed to complete the weight training exercises noted above. Let us assume that our 147-pound (66.74 kg) archer did this four times per week with free weights. That would be an energy expenditure of 1032 kcal/week. If he or she jogged at THR intensity at an 8-minute-per-mile pace for 30 minutes four times per week, 1666 kilocalories would be expended. The total energy expenditure for these activities would be 2698 kcal/week. Add to that four hours of archery practice per week for 1040 kcals, and the grand total would be a very respectable 3738 kcal/week of energy expenditure during supplemental exercise. *Result:* a better archer with a good level of health-related fitness!

Increasing the level of flexibility, strength, muscle endurance, and cardiovascular endurance produces important physiologic and anatomic changes in the archer. It is of utmost importance that he or she continues target practice concurrent with these developmental modifications in the body. This procedure will ensure that changes in accuracy are also positive. If the archer conditions without shooting on a regular basis, it may take time to adjust the skill fundamentals to the anatomic and physiological changes. For the most positive results, the archer should condition using the recommended guidelines and practice shooting concurrently at least four days per week.

Review

1. Why is cardiovascular endurance so important to the bow hunter who stalks game animals?
2. When participating in an aerobic workout, how should you monitor your heart rate, at what intervals should you check it, and what is your THR and target level?
3. What are the chief differences in general conditioning among target archers, field archers, and bow hunters?
4. Compare and contrast the differences in the expected anatomic changes between strength development and conditioning for muscular endurance.
5. Discuss the intensity criteria an archer should use in establishing his or her cardiovascular conditioning program.
6. It takes 3500 kilocalories of energy expenditure to rid one's self of one pound of stored, excess fat. How long would it take for you to get rid of one pound of your fat by using target archery practice as your only exercise?

7. Review the energy expenditure values. What activities can you use and for what duration to expend 2000 to 3500 kcal/week?
8. Discuss the specificity of training concept related to the overload draw exercise.
9. Write out a complete fitness program for yourself involving developmental activities for strength, muscle endurance, cardiovascular endurance, and skill. What are the frequencies for the activities? Have you adhered to the intensity criteria? What is the daily duration level for the activities chosen? What is the total energy expenditure per week in kilocalories?
10. Why does your archery coach want you to concentrate on your "back muscles" (shoulder and shoulder girdle muscles) during the draw?
11. Which muscles provide the principal force for the drawing arm?
12. Define and give an example of the SAID Principle.

Archery in Literature and Art

9

Since the bow and arrow have played such an important part in the survival of the human race for centuries, it is not surprising to find that authors of a wide variety of literature and artists throughout the world have included archers and archery feats in their creative and scholarly endeavors. The student of archery is encouraged to activate his or her intellectual curiosity and search for those literary and artistic works. It can be stimulating and fun!

The purpose of this chapter is to alert the student of archery to the strong presence of the subject of archery in literature and art produced throughout the ages. Intellectually, it is always useful to look for relationships where one is not aware an association exists. *There are strong relationships between archery and the humanities.* (The scientific literature also contains an interesting body of knowledge about archery.) The exploration of those relationships can be fascinating for the individual who is intellectually curious, because the topic encompasses many academic disciplines and virtually all societies and cultures throughout the history of the world.

A few references are listed in this chapter and in the bibliography for those readers who wish to begin looking at the literature and art of archery following this very brief introduction to the topic.

Literature

There is considerable mythology surrounding the constellation Sagittarius. Sagittarius is a large southern constellation that the Greeks called a centaur. The centaur is said to be shooting an arrow. The word *sagittarius* actually means "archer." Sagittarius is located south of Aquila, and is partly in the Milky Way. It is east of Antares, one of the central stars in the constellation known as Scorpio. Sagittarius can be seen during the months of August and September in the United States. Figure 9.1 provides a schematic diagram of Sagittarius.

The various stars within Sagittarius form parts of the archer and his bow and arrow. Rukbat is the archer's knee; Arkab is the archer's tendon; Ascella is the archer's armpit or axillary region; Media is the midpoint of the bow; and Al Nasl is the arrow point. As the reader will note from figure 9.1, it took a vivid imagination to visualize an archer amidst that celestial configuration.

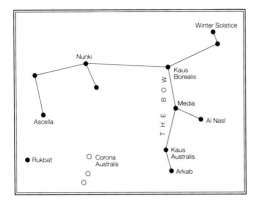

Figure 9.1
The Southern constellation known as Sagittarius, The Archer.

Greek mythological literature called the centaur of Sagittarius Chiron. Chiron was the famous son of Philyra and Saturn. The Roman poet Ovid reports that when Chiron was slain by Hercules with a poisoned arrow, Jupiter, the Father of the Gods, placed Chiron among the constellations. Ovid wrote: "Midst Golden Stars he stands refulgent now and thrusts the Scorpion with his bended bow." The reference is to the relationship between Al Nasl and Antares.

Apollo held many titles in mythological literature. One was The God of Archery. He was credited with numerous extraordinary feats with the bow and arrow. One of the most famous of these mythologic events is said to have taken place on Mount Parnassus. A great python was raiding families who lived in the area. The python smashed homes, ate human beings, and made a general nuisance of himself! Apollo decided to put a stop to that obstreperous behavior, and took his bow and arrows in pursuit of the python. He ultimately found the python and invited him to fight. As is the case in most myths, good triumphed over evil. Apollo fought the python for four hours and finally used his great archery skill and killed the python with an accurately placed arrow.

Shortly following the battle with the python, Apollo encountered Eros, also known as Cupid. He insulted Eros by telling him that a boy should not play with a man's weapons. The reference, of course, was to the bow and arrows carried at all times by Eros. This verbal attack by Apollo enraged Eros. He decided to let Apollo know that he, Eros, was a highly skilled archer in his own right. He got even with Apollo by shooting him with a golden arrow of love. Shortly thereafter, Apollo fell in love with the beautiful Daphne, Goddess of Wild Things. Daphne was the daughter of Peneun, the River God. Eros promptly shot Daphne with a lead arrow of hate. That well placed arrow made Daphne's feeling for Apollo one of utter disgust. Ultimately, she turned into a laurel tree to distance herself from her amorous pursuer. Apollo, in love with Daphne to the end, showed

Figure 9.2
The Education of Achilles by Chiron. (From E. G. Heath, *The Grey Goose Wing*)

his undying love by hanging his bow and quiver on her limbs. Eros not only took care of Apollo's attitude problem but taught him that archery is a sport for people of all ages and social status.

With his bow and arrows, Eros had many adventures in mythological literature. The term *eros* is rather interesting. It serves as the root word for the term "erotic," which coincides with one major purpose of the mythological existence of Eros. The term *eros* also gave rise to the word "arrow."

One of the greatest mythological archers was Hercules, or Herakles. Hercules is better known for his feats of strength, but he also achieved many remarkable accomplishments with the bow and arrow. It was with Hercules' bow that Philoctetes killed Paris during the Trojan War. Earlier, it will be remembered, Paris had shot Achilles with a poisoned arrow. That was a remarkable archery shot, because Paris shot Achilles in the heel, the only vulnerable portion of his body. Human anatomists continue to refer to the tendon from the *gastrocnemius* and *soleus* muscles (triceps surae) to the calcaneus bone as "the Achilles tendon." The concentric contraction force from these muscles via the Achilles tendon will plantar flex your ankle. This force, for example, moves you up on your toes in the standing position. This tendon and muscle group (fig. 8.2) are part of your anteroposterior antigravity muscles, which help to keep you upright in the shooting stance. An artist's portrayal of Achilles is shown in figure 9.2.

Figure 9.3
Odysseus, on returning from his many wanderings, slays the suitors of Penelope, his wife. The use of a thumb release can be assumed due to the position of his bowstring hand—5th century B.C. (From E. G. Heath, *The Grey Goose Wing*)

In the *Iliad* and *Odyssey,* Homer, the eighth century B.C. Greek poet, wrote about numerous feats by archers. In the *Odyssey,* Homer describes ten years of adventures by Odysseus following the Trojan War. Figure 9.3 is an artist's depiction of the business he took care of when he finally arrived home and found his wife with some friendly and amorous folk from the neighborhood! A review of some contemporary homicides involving spouses indicates that the principal change in the scenario depicted in figure 9.3 is the weapon used to commit the crime. Human nature may not have changed much over the centuries.

Another minor constellation is known as *Sagitta,* or "the Arrow." It is located in the Milky Way just north of a constellation known as the Eagle. In comparing and discussing Sagittarius and Sagitta, Aratos wrote, "There further shot another arrow but this with a bow. Towards it the Bird more northward flies." The references are to Sagittarius and the Eagle. Erathosthenes, a Greek mathematician and astronomer from Alexandria, considered Sagitta to be the shaft with which Apollo exterminated the Cyclops. Sagitta has also been referred to in mythological literature as one of Cupid's arrows.

As we move forward historically, other archers bordering on the mythological emerge in the literature. Robin Hood is such a character. There is no strong evidence that such a person actually lived. However, it is possible. As his legend grew, his feats with the bow and arrow have become exaggerated. This is a common characteristic of mythology; that is, one is apt to find historically substantiated subject matter combined with feats and episodes purely mythological in nature.

There is an account in the literature of a legendary wand shoot between Robin Hood and an archer named Clifton. According to the tale, Clifton shot his arrow first and hit the two-inch wand at 100 yards (91.44 meters in England). Before

Figure 9.4
An eighteenth-century engraving of Robin Hood by Thomas Bewick. (From E. G. Heath, *The Grey Goose Wing*)

Clifton's arrow stopped vibrating, Robin Hood released an arrow from his long bow and completely split the shaft of Clifton's vibrating arrow. The mathematical probability of that occurring, even with the finest modern recurve or compound bows with matching aluminum arrows, is infinitesimal.

The best contemporary trick-shot archers usually make their shots at distances of 10 to 20 yards. Some movie stunt men do not rely on skill alone for those close-up shots you have seen of arrows penetrating a human body. To accomplish this effect, the arrow is mounted on a very thin wire and guided directly to its mark. The arrow penetrates a large pad with a bag filled with red fluid strategically placed under the stunt man's clothing. Such procedures by contemporary professional archers make the story of Robin Hood's wand shot appear even more fantastic. But, virtually every Robin Hood movie ever made features some unbelievable shots. That is why they call it "show business."

This type of wand shooting is referred to periodically in English literature. A formal Wand Round for competitive purposes evolved as a result. The Wand Round consists of shooting 36 arrows at a piece of balsa wood two inches in width projecting six feet upward from the ground. The scoring is simple, but achieving a score is extremely difficult! Any arrow embedded in the wand counts as a hit. Also, a witnessed rebound from the wand counts as a hit. The challenge of wand shooting lies in the distances involved. Men shoot at the two-inch wand from 100 yards, intermediate boys from 80 yards, and women as well as intermediate girls shoot at the wand from 60 yards. This is an extremely difficult task. The reader may want to try to duplicate the alleged feat of Robin Hood. To fully appreciate the difficulty, use a longbow with wooden arrows!

There is a grave in England supposedly occupied by Robin Hood. A portion of the epitaph reads, ". . . No archer was like him so good; his wildness named him Robin Hood." (His real name was supposed to be Robert, Earl of Huntington.) It is rather interesting that a vernacular term now used for someone who lives a tumultuous life outside the law is "hood."

Robin Hood stories have fascinated people for years. As a result, the character and his associates have been portrayed by numerous artists. An eighteenth century engraving is shown in figure 9.4.

Johann Friedrich von Schiller, the late eighteenth-century dramatist, wrote a famous drama about the legendary archer Wilhelm Tell. (Gioacchino Rossini wrote the opera *William Tell* about the exploits of the same archer.) The tale centers around a Swiss crossbowman who defied a new regime he did not like. The archer was forced to demonstrate his skill by shooting through an apple sitting on his son's head. A shot like Tell's in real life would have been remarkable, because the father had to shoot at his son in a stressful situation with a crossbow unlike those in use today.

The student of archery and literature may want to attempt to duplicate some of the legendary archery feats found within the literature. This is recommended while using tackle close to the type used during the era. This helps to check on the validity of the literary account of the shot. In the case of the Wilhelm Tell tale, however, it would be wise to place the apple on a balloon or some other inanimate object rather than on the head of a loved one. Shooting at another human is literally "shaky business" and not recommended even for academic validation!

James Fenimore Cooper wrote many portrayals of the American Indian. There are many factual events in Cooper's books regarding how the Indian constructed and used bows and arrows. Cooper researched his material very carefully. He also lived and wrote at a time when many Indians were still pursuing their desired life-style and had not been completely relegated to life on reservations. Some of Cooper's books are *The Pioneers, The Last of the Mohicans, The Pathfinder, The Deerslayer,* and *The Prairie.*

Henry Wadsworth Longfellow's famous poem *Song of Hiawatha* is a good example of factual material being combined with feats bordering on the mythological. Longfellow, however, gave an accurate account of how some Indians made bows and arrows. Iagoo made a bow for Hiawatha from ash. The arrows were made of oak. Flint was used for the point, and the bowstring was of dried deerskin. These kinds of materials were used by Indians to make archery tackle in various places throughout the United States and Canada. (See Chapter 6.)

According to Longfellow, Hiawatha was so fast that he could shoot an arrow on a horizontal trajectory and outrun the arrow. That is fast, even with the relatively inefficient tackle of a nineteenth-century American Indian! If any archery student or person reading this book can duplicate this feat, he or she should report to the Olympic Track Coach.

Longfellow also mentioned that Hiawatha could shoot ten arrows vertically so fast that the last arrow would be flying skyward before the first arrow had fallen. This would be extremely difficult if not impossible with the tackle described in the poem. However, this can be accomplished with contemporary tackle and an abundance of open space.

It is recommended that the archery student look for archery references and accomplishments in literature and analyze their feasibility. The reader is referred to the following books as a starting point:

1. Aeschylus. *Agamemnon.*
2. Arnold, Elliot. *Blood Brother.*
3. Clemens, Samuel (Mark Twain). *A Connecticut Yankee in King Arthur's Court.*
4. Defoe, Daniel. *The Adventures of Robinson Crusoe.*
5. Gillespy, Frances. *Laymon's Brut: A Comparative Study in Narrative Art.*
6. Homer. *The Illiad* and *The Odyssey.*
7. Lucian. *Dialogues of the Gods.*
8. Millar, George. *A Cross Bowman's Story.*
9. Morley, Christopher. *The Arrow.*
10. Ovid. *The Metamorphoses.*
11. Shakespeare. *Macbeth.*
12. ———. *Pericles.*
13. Stevenson, Robert Louis. *The Black Arrow.*
14. Swift, Jonathan. *Gulliver's Travels.*
15. Thucydides. *The History of the Peloponnesian War.*

There are several good references in the Bibliography concerning the study of archery as it relates to the humanities.

Art

There are thousands of works of art involving archery in public museums, art museums, and private collections throughout the world. Some of these, like the Bayeux Tapestry, are very famous. But, others remain obscure. In cave drawings, among the earliest art forms, bow hunters are depicted in pursuit of game. Bows have appeared in Mesopotamian seals, on Egyptian tomb paintings, and on Assyrian monumental reliefs. These date back thousands of years. Artists in the Far East and Near East commonly used archers and archery as a theme in their paintings. American Indians also drew bow hunters in pursuit of game on stone in the locales where they lived several hundred years ago. The student interested in art is invited to look for sculptures, carvings, drawings, and other art forms involving archery throughout history.

Several examples of artists' depictions of archers or the use of archery have been used as a succinct introduction to archery in art throughout this book. The reader should scrutinize those that appear in Chapters 1, 2, 4, and this chapter. They show various artists' concepts of archers in action, archery feats, tackle, and events. It is useful to critically analyze each of these for: (1) artistic quality and merit, (2) tackle design for the era, as compared with contemporary tackle, (3) aesthetic impact, and (4) the artist's concept of shooting mechanics. The trained artist, of course, would look for much more in these works of art.

Richard Pardons Robin Hood—1184—A.D.—(Briggs: Beale.)

Sennacherib (Assyria). (Courtesy of H. Armstrong Roberts. Printed by permission.)

Cupid with bow—Chas. Lemiore (Louvre). (Courtesy of H. Armstrong Roberts. Printed by permission.)

Diana—Goddess of Wild Things.

Battle of Marathon—(Briggs: Beale.)

Roman war elephant.

Buffalo hunt with wolfskin mask—George Catlin #13.

Review

1. Who was the God of Archery in mythological literature and how did he happen to be shot with a golden arrow of love?
2. Which constellation supposedly depicts a centaur shooting a bow and arrow? When can this constellation be observed in the United States?
3. Cite examples of literature, music, and art in which archery or archers are prominent.
4. Traditional liberal arts and study of the humanities involve such areas as literature, philosophy, and art. Reflect on your studies in these areas and determine how authors and artists integrated archery into their themes.
5. What characters in mythological literature were directly involved with archery in some form?
6. What is a wand shoot?
7. Was the classic arrow shot depicted by Schiller and Rossini in literature and opera accomplished with a longbow or crossbow?
8. When you visit museums and art galleries, make note of the quantity and quality of paintings, sculptures, and drawings where archery is depicted in one of its forms.
9. From what term is the word "arrow" derived?
10. Feats ascribed to archers in literature are sometimes beyond the capabilities of the modern archer shooting with the finest equipment. How do some trick-shot archers and movie stunt actors simulate such extraordinary feats?

The Language of Archery

10

Archery, like any other sport or specialized area, has a unique vocabulary. There are some words or terms below that have other meanings when used in different contexts, but they have a precise definition to the archer. This is necessary so archers can communicate with one another succinctly and precisely.

The following list of terms are commonly used in the archery sports:

Addressing the Target
The archer's stance straddling the shooting line prior to shooting the arrow.

Aim
The placement of a sight pin on the center of the target; if a sight is not used, placement of the tip of the arrow on a specific point while shooting at a target over a given distance.

AMO
Archery Manufacturer's Organization.

Anchor Point
The placement of the archer's bowstring hand on the chin or face with the bow at full draw.

Archer's Paradox
The aerodynamically stabilizing condition of the arrow after it deflects around the bow handle at release.

Arm Guard
A leather protective device for the radioulnar (forearm) and wrist joint areas of the bow arm.

Arrow Plate
The piece to which the arrow rest is attached.

Arrow Rest
A device mounted just above the arrow shelf on the bow to maintain arrow position from nocking until the arrow has cleared the bow at release.

Arrow Shelf
The lowermost area of the sight window on the bow.

Arrowsmith
An individual who specializes in making arrows and arrowheads.

Back
The side of the bow limb away from the archer when the bow is in the draw position.

Barb

The part of the point on a fishing arrow point used to hold the fish; one of the hairlike branches growing from the shaft of a feather.

Bare Bow

A method of shooting that does not include using a bowsight.

Belly

A synonym for the face of the bow or the side of the bow nearest the string.

Blunt

A flattened arrow point usually made of rubber or metal and designed to kill small game by impact force.

Bolt

The projectile shot from a crossbow.

Bow Arm

The arm that the archer prefers to use for holding the bow during shooting.

Bow Bracer

A device designed to ensure safety for the archer during the process of bracing or stringing the bow.

Bow Hand

The hand that the archer prefers to use for holding or supporting the bow during shooting.

Bowman

An archer.

Bowsight

An adjustable device, attached to the bow, that facilitates the aiming process for the archer.

Bow Square

A device used to measure string and nocking heights accurately.

Bowstrap

A leather strap that enables the archer to maintain contact with the bow without actually gripping the handle.

Bow Tip Protector

A cap that fits over the tip of the lower limb of the bow to protect it from damage produced by contact with the ground or floor.

Bow Window

The center shot or sight window area of the bow handle immediately above the grip, which aids the archer during the aiming process.

Bowyer

An individual who specializes in making bows.

Brace Height

The bow manufacturer's recommended distance from the pivot point of the bow to the bow string. Replaces the older term *fistmele*.

Bracing

The process of stringing the bow in preparation for shooting; placing the bowstring loops into position in the notches of the bow.

Broadhead

A multiple-edged and razor-sharp arrow point utilized in bow hunting, flight shooting, and field archery.

Brush Button

A silencer device, usually rubber, placed toward each end of the bowstring to reduce string noise following release during bow hunting.

Bull's Eye

The center of the target or that part of the target face with the highest scoring value.

Butt

The term used for target backing when the target face is mounted on a straw or hay bale.

Butt Hook

A curved metal, plastic, or wood hook attached to the butt end of a crossbow stock as an aid in steady aiming.

Cant

Tilting the bow left (counterclockwise) or right (clockwise) by lateral or medial rotation of the shoulder joint of the bow arm.

Cast

The velocity that the bow can impart to the arrow, and the horizontal distance the arrow can traverse.

Centerline

The relationship of the bowstring to the bow limbs which, when viewed from the face side, should divide the limbs evenly.

Center Shot Bow

A bow designed to allow the arrow rest to be placed in the center of the upper limb instead of at the extreme lateral side of the bow.

Channel Groove

A grooved section down the length of a crossbow barrel, which allows the cock feather to move along the barrel when shot.

Clearance

The ability of the arrow and fletching to pass by the bow and arrow rest without contact. Tuning adjustments to the arrow nocks, arrow rest, and cushion plunger will improve clearance.

Clicker

A small metal device mounted on the sight window in front of the arrow rest, which indicates full draw has been attained by snapping off of the arrow point with an audible click.

Clout

An NAA round shot over relatively long distances at a 15-meter (diameter) target drawn on the surface of the ground.

Collapse

An undesired spinal rotation by the archer prior to arrow release, causing the bow arm to move backward while the drawing arm moves forward.

Composite Bow

A bow manufactured by utilizing two or more types of materials such as wood and fiberglass.

Compound Bow

A bow invented by H. W. Allen, designed with an eccentric pulley system to maximize pull weight poundage at mid-draw and to minimize stacking at full draw.

Creeping

An undesired forward motion of the bowstring from the anchor point immediately prior to release.

Crest

The colored identification bands on the arrow immediately below the fletching.

Crossbow

A tool for shooting bolts. It consists of a short bow mounted crosswise near the end of a wood, metal, or plastic stock.

Cushion Pressure Point

A plastic or leather device that will absorb some of the shock of the arrow as it passes after release.

Dead Release

Extension of the interphalangeal joints of the fingers gripping the bowstring due to the kinetic energy of the bowstring instead of muscular force.

Draw

The process of moving the bowstring with nocked arrow from brace height to the archer's anchor point on the face.

Draw Weight

See "weight."

Drift

The lateral displacement of an arrow from its normal trajectory due to crosswind velocity.

End

A set number of arrows shot before going to the target to score and retrieve them; the number may be three, five, or six in target archery.

Eye

The loop at the end of the bowstring, which fits into the notch of the bow during bracing.

Face

The side of the bow limb closest to the archer when the bow is in the draw position—replaces the term *belly*.

Field Captain
The person in charge of an archery tournament.

Field Point
A point used in field archery that is as heavy as a broadhead.

Finger Sling
A small piece of leather with loops at each end designed to fit around the archer's thumb and index or middle finger during shooting. It helps prevent the bow from falling to the ground after release.

Finger Tab
A leather device worn to prevent blistering on the anterior surface of the three drawing fingers.

Fishtailing
The condition when the arrow appears to be moving from side to side during its flight toward the target. Tuning adjustments involving the cushion plunger, bow weight, and bowstrings may help to minimize fishtailing.

FITA
Federation Internationale de Tir à l'Arc—the organization responsible for conducting world championship contests in archery.

Fletcher
An arrow maker.

Fletching
The stabilizing feathers or plastic vanes attached to an arrow between the nock and crest.

Flight Shooting
An archery event in which the shooting objective is to attain the greatest distance possible for the arrow or bolt.

Flinching
An undesired and sudden motion of the bow arm (usually horizontal abduction of the bow shoulder or elbow flexion) at release.

Flu-Flu
An arrow with large or spiraled fletching designed to increase the drag coefficient in order to diminish flight distance.

Follow-Through
The act of holding the release position until the arrow has struck the target.

Foot Markers
Devices used to mark the placement of the feet during the stance once the target is addressed by the archer on the shooting line.

Freestyle
A method of shooting where the archer uses a bowsight to aim.

Freeze
The inability to release the arrow while at full draw.

Gap Shooting
An aiming technique whereby the archer estimates the distance (gap) between a selected point and the target. Release is made when the gap no longer exists.

Goat's Foot

A cocking-assist device used with crossbows to level the string back to its cocked position.

Gold

The center of the target used in target archery.

Grip

The center portion of the bow where the hand exerts pressure during the draw. (*Grip* is often used interchangeably with the term *handle*.)

Grouping

The arrangement of the end of arrows on the target face after they have been shot.

Handle

The middle portion of the bow.

Handle Riser

The area just below and above the bow grip.

Hanging Arrow

An arrow that does not penetrate the target mat, but dangles across the target face.

Hen Feathers

The two feathers on either side of the index feather. Traditionally, these feathers are not as flamboyant as the index feather.

Hit

An arrow that embeds itself within one of the scoring areas on the target face.

Holding

The act of maintaining the bow and arrow in a stable position at full draw prior to release.

Index Feather

The feather at right angle to the slit in the nock of the arrow and usually different in color from the remaining feathers. This term replaces the older term *cock feather*.

Jig

A device used for making and repairing fletching and bowstrings.

Keeper

A piece of material used to hold the bowstring to the nock when the bow is not braced.

Kiss Button

A contact point on the bowstring for the archer's lips to touch to ensure consistency and accuracy of the anchor point.

Lady Paramount

The woman in charge of an archery tournament.

Laminated Bow

A bow constructed of several layers of different materials glued together.

Limbs
The energy-storing parts of the bow located above and below the riser.

Longbow
A bow with no built-in curvatures to increase leverage.

Loop
The ends of the bowstring made to attach securely into the bow notches when braced.

Loose
The act of releasing or shooting the arrow.

Mass Weight
The actual or physical weight of the bow in pounds.

Mat
The firmly constructed area of the target upon which the target face is mounted; also written as *matt*.

Minnowing
A high intensity side to side movement of the arrow in its flight toward the target; movements are more rapid and smaller than seen when arrows fishtail in flight. Minnowing is due to inadequate clearance and by fletching striking the arrow rest after release.

NAA
National Archery Association of the United States.

NFAA
National Field Archery Association of the United States.

Nock
The plastic device on the end of the arrow opposite the point, made with a groove for holding the arrow to the bowstring when placed in position for shooting.

Nocking
The technique of placing the arrow on the bowstring in preparation for shooting.

Nock-Locator
The stops on the serving of the bowstring, which mark the exact nocking point for the arrow.

Nose
The solid metal portion at the front of the crossbow, which retains the prod.

Oblique Stance
A foot position whereby the toe of the foot nearest the target is placed on a line to the target and then rotated laterally forty-five degrees. The heel of the foot farthest from the target is placed in line to the center of the target.

Open Stance
A foot position whereby the line to the target is from the instep of the foot farthest from the target while the leg nearest the target has been extended at the hip to form at least a toe-heel relationship with the foot on-line to the target.

Overbowed

The act of drawing a bow that has a weight out of proportion to the archer's strength.

Overdraw

Drawing the arrow beyond the face of the bow or drawing the bow to its point of maximum stress on the limbs; or, a device placed on a hunting bow that allows the arrow to be drawn safely past the face of the bow, thereby increasing bow weight and arrow velocity.

Overstrung

The use of a bowstring too short for the bow, a condition that results in an excessive brace height and inefficiency in shooting.

PAA

Professional Archer's Association.

Palm Rest

A device that extends below the midportion for a crossbow stock and placed in the shooter's nontrigger hand.

Peeking

Undesired motion of the archer's head (neck or cervical flexion) at the time of release in an attempt to follow the arrow trajectory into the target.

Perfect End

A situation when all arrows shot are grouped tightly into the highest scoring area on the target face.

Petticoat

The outermost perimeter of the target face outside the scoring area. Arrows that land in this area are not scored as hits.

Pile

A synonym for *arrow point.*

Pinch

The undesired act of squeezing the arrow nock too tightly during the draw, causing the arrow to move off the arrow rest.

Pivot Point

The part of the bow grip farthest from the string when the bow is braced.

Plucking

Undesired lateral motion of the string hand and arm away from the bowstring at the time of release.

Point-Black Range

The distance at which the archer may utilize the center of the target as an aiming point.

Point-of-Aim

An antiquated technique of aiming, whereby the archer uses a mark unattached to the bow and usually placed on the ground as an alignment point.

Porpoising
A condition where the arrow moves up and down during its flight toward the target. An incorrect nocking point location is the cause of porpoising.

Pressure Point
The place on the arrow plate against which the arrow lies and exerts pressure when the arrow is released; it can be cushioned or spring loaded.

Prism Sight
A sophisticated aiming device utilizing refraction principles to gain a clear view of the target.

Prod
The bow section of the crossbow.

Pull
The process of disengaging embedded arrows from the target.

Pushing
The undesired process of moving the bow forward and parallel to the earth at the time of release.

Quiver
Any device designed to hold arrows for the archer during the process of shooting.

Range
(1) A specified distance to be shot during a round; (2) an outdoor or indoor shooting area designated for target archery.

Rebound
An arrow that does not penetrate the target face or mat but bounces off a scoring area on the target.

Recurved Bow
A bow manufactured so the ends of the limbs deflect toward the back of the bow to increase leverage when the bow is braced.

Reflexed Bow
A bow with straight limbs where the backs form an obtuse angle at the conjunction of the handle riser and grip.

Release
The act of putting the arrow into flight due to release of pressure on the bowstring by either the fingers (target archery) or a release device (bow hunting).

Round
The term used to designate the number of arrows to be shot from precise distances at a specified target faces or targets.

Roving
An archery game of shooting at natural targets in woods and fields.

Scatter
Arrows distributed unevenly over a large portion of the target face and/or ground.

Scoring Area

The concentric circles on the target face worth prescribed point values.

Self Bow

A bow consisting of one complete piece of wood or raw material. Primarily yew and elm woods were used to construct bows of this type.

Serving

The protective thread wrapped around the bowstring where the arrow is nocked.

Shaft

The body of the arrow upon which the nock, fletching, and point are mounted, and the crest is painted.

Shooting Glove

A three-fingered protective device utilized by some archers for the bowstring-gripping fingers; used in lieu of a finger tab.

Shooting Line

The line straddled by archers during shooting, which indicates a specific distance from the target in target archery.

Sight Bar

The piece of the bowsight to which the sight block is attached.

Sighter Arrows

The practice arrows shot to enable the target archer to adjust to range and environmental conditions prior to tournament competition; six sighter arrows are usually allowed before a round in target archery.

Sight Pin

The part of the bowsight placed on the center of the intended target during aiming.

Sight Window

The area of the bow cut away to allow the arrow rest to be mounted in the center of the bow.

Skirt

The outer cloth on a target face, which holds the face on the mat; sometimes called the *petticoat*.

Snake

Embedding of an arrow under grass and horizontal to the ground, making the arrow extremely difficult to locate.

Spine

The measured deflection in inches of an arrow shaft when it is depressed by a two-pound weight at its center.

Stabilizer

A weighted device added to the handle-riser areas of the bow and designed to reduce torque and absorb shock upon release.

Stacking

A disproportionate increase in bow weight during the last few inches of the draw.

Stirrup
A cocking device that allows the shooter to hold the crossbow in a stationary position while using both hands to cock the bowstring.

String Fingers
The fingers used to hold the nocked arrow in place on the bowstring during the draw.

String Height
See "Brace Height."

String Notch
The grooves at the end of the bow limbs, designed to hold the bowstring when the bow is braced.

String Peep
An oval insert into the strands of the bowstring at eye level, used as a rear-mounted aiming device by the archer.

Tackle
All equipment used by an archer.

Target Captain
The individual at each target designated to determine and call the score of each arrow and pull each arrow from the target.

Target Face
The scoring area of a target.

Target Mat
The protective backing of the target, which the arrows penetrate.

Tassel
A piece of cloth material used to clean arrows.

Timber
A verbal warning given in field archery that an arrow is being released or about to land where it should not be landing.

Tip
The ends of the bow limbs.

Torque
An undesirable twisting of the bow and/or bowstring during any part of the shooting process.

Toxopholite
An individual involved in archery both as a performer and as a serious student of the sport.

Trajectory
The parabolic flight pattern of an arrow following release.

Tuning
An adjustment of the arrow rest, pressure point, string height, and nocking height to improve arrow flight; includes determination of correct spine.

Underbowed

The act of drawing a bow with a weight too light to enable the archer to accomplish the shooting objective.

Understrung

A bow with a bowstring too long, which results in an improper brace height and reduced efficiency.

Unit

A 14-target course in field archery, including all official shots. The field archery shooting range.

Vane

A term used most commonly when fletching is made of plastic or rubber instead of feathers.

Wand

A historic type of target; a piece of balsa wood two inches in width embedded in the ground and projecting six feet upward.

Weight

The bow manufacturer's determined number of pounds required to draw each bow's string a given distance.

Windage

The left-right adjustment of the bowsight or the pin on the bowsight; or, wind direction and velocity on the shooting range or unit.

Wrist Sling

A device that fits around the bow and the archer's wrist, designed to prevent the bow from falling to the ground as the arrow is released.

Yarn Tassel

A tuft of yarn used by archers to clean arrows.

Yaw

Unstable or erratic motion of the arrow during its flight path or trajectory toward the target.

Selected Bibliography

Archery. 31407 Outer I-10, Redlands, California 92373.

ASCHAM, ROGER. *Toxophilus.* London: A. Murray and Son, 1545.

AUSTIN, NORMAN. *Archery at the Dark of the Moon.* Berkeley: University of California Press, 1975.

BAIER, PATRICIA, and others. *The National Archery Association's Instructor's Manual.* Colorado Springs: National Archery Association of the United States, 1982.

BARRETT, JEAN A. *Archery.* New York: Scott, Foresman and Company, 1980.

BEAR, FRED. *The Archer's Bible.* Garden City, New York: Doubleday and Company, 1980.

————. *World of Archery.* Garden City, New York: Doubleday and Company, 1979.

BERGMAN, C. A., MCEWEN, E., MILLER, R. "Experimental Archery: Projectile Velocities and Comparison of Bow Performances." *Antiquity* 62 (December 1988): 658–70.

Bow and Arrow Magazine. P.O. Box HH, Capistrano Beach, California 92624.

Bowfish Sports. P.O. Box 102, Grand Haven, Michigan 49417.

Bowfishing Magazine. P.O. Box 2005, Wausau, Wisconsin 54402–2005.

Bowhunter. 3808 South Calhoun Street, Fort Wayne, Indiana 46807.

Bowhunting World Magazine. P.O. Box 611, Wayzata, Minnesota 55391.

BROWN, KEN. *The Ken Brown Guide to Bowfishing.* Hugo, OK: Ken Brown Publications, 1980.

BURKE, EDMUND H. *Archery Handbook.* New York: Arco, 1965.

————. *The History of Archery.* New York: William Morrow, 1957.

BUTLER, DAVID F. *The New Archery.* New York: A. S. Barnes, 1968.

CAMPBELL, DONALD W. *Archery.* Englewood Cliffs, NJ: Prentice-Hall, 1971.

CLARK, J. G. D. "Neolithic Bows from Somerset, England, and the Prehistory of Archery in North-West Europe." *Proceedings of the Prehistoric Society* 29 (December 1963): 50–98.

COMBS, ROGER, ed. *Crossbows.* Northbrook, IL: DBI Books, 1987.

Crossbow Shooting International Magazine. 9 Manor Street, Tettenhall, Wolverhampton, WV6 8RA England.

DRISCOLL, MARGARET L., ed. *Selected Archery Articles.* Washington, DC: American Association for Health, Physical Education, and Recreation, 1971.

ELMER, ROBERT P. *American Archery.* Ronks, PA: National Archery Association of the United States, 1917.

ELMER, ROBERT P. *Archery.* Philadelphia: Penn, 1926.

ELMER, ROBERT P., and FARIS, NABIH A. *Arab Archery.* Princeton, NJ: Princeton University Press, 1945.

FOLEY, VERNARD; PALMER, GEORGE; and SOEDEL, WERNER. "The Crossbow." *Scientific American* 252 (January 1985): 104–10.

FORD, HORACE A. *Archery: Its Theory and Practice.* London: J. Buchanan, 1856.

FREY, GILBERT. "A History of Crossbow Target Archery in the United States." *The U.S. Archer* 9 (November-December 1990): 306–7.

GANNON, ROBERT. *The Complete Book of Archery.* New York: Coward-McCann, 1964.

GILLELAN, G. HOWARD. *The Complete Book of the Bow and Arrow.* Harrisburg, PA: The Stackpole Co., 1977.

The Glade: International Magazine for Archers. 62 Hook Rise North, Tolworth, Surrey KT6 7JY, England.

GROGAN, HIRAM J. *Modern Bow Hunting.* Harrisburg, PA: The Stackpole Co., 1958.

HAUGEN, ARNOLD O., and METCALF, HARLAN. *Field Archery and Bowhunting.* New York: Ronald Press, 1963.

HEATH, E. G., ed. *Anecdotes of Archery.* London: The Tabard Press, 1970.

HEATH, E. G. *The Grey Goose Wing.* Reading, Berkshire, England: Osprey, 1971.

———. *A History of Target Archery.* South Brunswick: A. S. Barnes, 1974.

HENDERSON, AL. *On Target for Understanding Target Archery.* Mequon, WI: Target Communications, 1983.

HERRIGEL, EUGEN. *Zen in the Art of Archery.* New York: Pantheon, 1953.

HERTER, GEORGE L., and HOFMEISTER, RUSSELL. *Professional & Amateur Archery Tournament and Hunting Instructions and Encyclopedia.* Waseca, MN: Herter's, 1963.

HICKMAN, C. N.; NAGLER, F.; and KLOPSTEG, PAUL E. *Archery: The Technical Side.* Redlands, CA: National Field Archery Assoc. of the U.S., 1947.

HILL, HOWARD. *Hunting the Hard Way.* Chicago: Follet, 1953.

HONDA, SHIG; LAMMERS, MARJORY E.; and NEWSON, RALPH W. *Archery.* Boston: Allyn & Bacon, 1975.

KELLY, GENE. "Memorial Lands: A Bowmaker's Legacy." *Missouri Conservationist* 48 (December 1987): 28–29.

KLANN, MARGARET L. *Target Archery.* Reading: PA: Addison-Wesley, 1970.

KLOPSTEG, P. E. "Physics of Bows and Arrows." *American Journal of Physics* 11 (August 1943): 175–92.

———. *Turkish Archery and the Composite Bow.* 3rd ed. Manchester: Simon Archery Foundation, 1987.

LIEBERMAN, STEPHEN B., ed. *FITA Constitution and Rules.* Milan: FITA, 1992.

LOGAN, GENE A., and MCKINNEY, WAYNE C. *Anatomic Kinesiology.* Dubuque, IA: Wm. C. Brown, 1982.

LONGMAN, C. J., and WALROND, H. *Archery.* New York: Frederick Ungar, 1894.

LOVE, ALBERT J. *Field Archery Technique.* Corpus Christi, TX: Dotson, 1956.

MARKHAM, GERVASE. *The Art of Archerie.* London: Arms and Armour Press, 1968.

MCEWEN, EDWARD; MILLER, ROBERT; and BERGMAN, CHRISTOPHER A. "Early Bow Design and Construction." *Scientific American* 264 (June 1991): 76–82.

North American Bowhunter Magazine. P.O. Box 5487, Tucson, AZ 85703.

NORTHRIP, JOHN W.; LOGAN, GENE A.; and MCKINNEY, WAYNE C. *Analysis of Sport Motion: Anatomic and Biomechanic Perspectives.* Dubuque, IA: Wm. C. Brown, 1983.

POPE, SAXTON. *Yahi Archery.* Berkeley: University of California Press, 1918.

———. *Hunting with Bow and Arrow.* New York: G. P. Putnam's Sons, 1947.

———. *The Adventurous Bowman.* New York: G. P. Putnam's Sons, 1926.

The Professional Bowhunter Magazine. P.O. Box 5275, Charlotte, NC 28225.

PSZCZOLA, LORRAINE. *Archery.* Philadelphia: W. B. Saunders, 1983.

RHODE, ROBERT J. *Archery Champions.* Norristown, PA: The Archer's Publishing Co., 1961.

SCHAAR, JOHN. *Modern Archery Ballistics.* Tempe, AZ: Grand Slam Archery, 1986.

SCHUMM, MARYANNE M. *Clarence N. Hickman: The Father of Scientific Archery.* Minisink Hills, PA: Maples Press, 1983.

SHORE, PAUL T. "Ramboat, Part I, The Ultimate Bowfishing Machine." *Bowfishing* 1 (Fall/Winter 1986): 8–12.

———. "Ramboat, Part II, The Ultimate Bowfishing Machine." *Bowfishing* 1 (Winter/Spring 1987): 4–6.

STERLING, SARA. *Robin Hood and His Merry Men.* Philadelphia: George W. Jacobs, 1921.

THOMPSON, MAURICE. *The Witchery of Archery.* New York: Charles Scribner's Sons, 1878.

THOMPSON, MAURICE, and THOMPSON, WILL H. *How to Train in Archery.* New York: E. I. Horsman, 1879.

The U.S. Archer. 7315 North San Anna Drive, Tucson, AZ 85704.

WALKER, DOROTHY. *Instructor Manual for Basic Archery.* Jefferson City, MO: Missouri Department of Conservation, 1981.

Official Wildlife Agencies in the United States and Canada

Information regarding current bow hunting and/or bow fishing rules, regulations, seasons, and license fees may be obtained by contacting the specific wildlife agency in the American state or Canadian province where you plan to hunt and/or fish. It is recommended that this be done several months in advance of your trip. Their addresses and phone numbers are listed below for the reader's convenience:

United States

Alabama Department of
  Conservation and Natural
  Resources
64 North Union Street
Montgomery, AL 36130
(205) 261–3468

Alaska Department of Fish and
  Game
Box 3–2000
Juneau, AK 99802
(907) 465–4190

Arizona Game and Fish
  Department
2222 West Greenway Road
Phoenix, AZ 85023
(602) 942–3000

Arkansas Game and Fish
  Commission
#2 Natural Resources Drive
Little Rock, AR 72205
(501) 223–6300

California Department of Fish and
  Game
1416 Ninth Street
Sacramento, CA 95814
(916) 324–8347

Colorado Division of Wildlife
Department of Natural Resources
6060 Broadway
Denver, CO 80216
(303) 297–1192

Connecticut Department of
  Environmental Protection
Franklin Wildlife Management
  Area
RR1, Box 241
North Franklin, CT 06254
(203) 642–7239

Delware Division of Fish and
  Wildlife
P.O. Box 1401
Dover, DE 19903
(302) 736–5297

District of Columbia Metropolitan
  Police
300 Indiana Avenue NW
Washington, DC 20001

Florida Game and Freshwater Fish
  Commission
620 South Meridan Street
Tallahassee, FL 32399–1600
(904) 488–4676

Georgia Department of Natural
Resources
Floyd Towers East, SE
205 Butler St., Suite 1362
Atlanta, GA 30334
(404) 656–3523

Hawaii Division of Forestry and
Wildlife
1151 Punchbowl Street
Honolulu, HI 96813
(808) 548–2861

Idaho Department of Fish and
Game
P.O. Box 25
600 South Walnut
Boise, ID 83707
(208) 334–3746

Illinois Division of Fish and Wildlife
Resources
P.O. Box 286
Monmouth, IL 61462
(309) 374–2492

Indiana Division of Fish and
Wildlife
607 State Office Building
Indianapolis, IN 46204
(317) 232–4080

Iowa Department of Natural
Resources
Wallace State Office Building
Des Moines, IA 50319
(515) 281–6154

Kansas Department of Wildlife and
Parks
Box 54A, RR2
Pratt, KS 67124
(316) 672–5911

Kentucky Department of Fish and
Wildlife
#1 Game Farm Road
Frankfort, KY 40601
(502) 564–4406

Louisiana Department of Wildlife
and Fisheries
P.O. Box 4004
Monroe, LA 71211
(318) 343–4044

Maine Department of Inland
Fisheries and Wildlife
284 State Street
Augusta, ME 04333
(207) 289–2871

Maryland Forest, Park and Wildlife
Service
P.O. Box 68
Wye Mills, MD 21679
(301) 827–8612

Massachusetts Division of Fisheries
and Wildlife
100 Cambridge Street
Boston, MA 02202
(617) 727–3151

Michigan Department of Natural
Resources
P.O. Box 30028
Lansing, MI 48909
(517) 373–1263

Minnesota Department of Natural
Resources
Box 7, 500 Lafayette Road
St. Paul, MN 55146
(612) 296–3344

Mississippi Department of Wildlife
Conservation
P.O. Box 451
Jackson, MS 39205
(601) 961–5300

Missouri Department of
Conservation
P.O. Box 180
Jefferson City, MO 65102
(314) 751–4115

Montana Department of Fish,
Wildlife, and Parks
1420 East 6th Avenue
Helena, MT 59620
(406) 444–2535

Nebraska Game and Parks
Commission
P.O. Box 30370
Lincoln, NE 68503
(402) 464–0641

Nevada Department of Wildlife
P.O. Box 10678
Reno, NV 89520
(702) 789–0500

New Hampshire Fish and Game
Department
34 Bridge Street
Concord, NH 03301
(603) 271–2462

New Jersey Division of Fish, Game
and Wildlife
CN 400
Trenton, NJ 08625
(609) 292–2965

New Mexico Department of Game
and Fish
State Capitol
Santa Fe, NM 87503
(505) 827–7885

New York Department of
Environmental Conservation
Wildlife Resources Center
Delmar, NY 12054
(518) 439–0098

North Carolina Wildlife Resources
Commission
512 North Salisbury Street
Raleigh, NC 27611
(919) 733–7291

North Dakota Game and Fish
Department
100 North Bismarck Expressway
Bismarck, ND 58501
(701) 221–6300

Ohio Division of Wildlife
Fountain Square
Columbus, OH 43224
(614) 265–6305

Oklahoma Department of Wildlife
Conservation
1801 North Lincoln
P.O. Box 53465
Oklahoma City, OK 73152
(405) 521–2739

Oregon Department of Fish and
Wildlife
P.O. Box 59
Portland, OR 97207
(503) 229–5403

Pennsylvania Game Commission
P.O. Box 1567
Harrisburg, PA 17105–1567
(717) 787–5529

Rhode Island Department of
Environmental Management
Division of Fish and Wildlife
Government Center
Wakefield, RI 02879
(401) 789–0281

South Carolina Wildlife and Marine
Resources Department
P.O. Box 167
Columbia, SC 29202
(803) 734–3888

South Dakota Department of Game,
Fish, and Parks
445 East Capitol
Pierre, SD 57501
(605) 773–3485

Tennessee Wildlife Resources
  Agency
P.O. Box 40747
Nashville, TN 37204
(615) 360–0500

Texas Parks and Wildlife
  Department
4200 Smith School Road
Austin, TX 78744
(512) 389–4800

Utah Division of Wildlife Resources
1596 W. N. Temple
Salt Lake City, UT 84116
(801) 533–9333

Vermont Fish and Wildlife
  Department
103 S. Main St.
Waterbury, VT 05676
(802) 244–7331

Virginia Commission of Game and
  Inland Fisheries
P.O. Box 11104
Richmond, VA 23230–1104
(804) 367–1000

Washington Department of Game
600 North Capitol Way
Olympia, WA 95804
(206) 753–5700

West Virginia Department of
  Natural Resources
1800 Washington Street
Charleston, WV 25305
(304) 348–2771

Wisconsin Department of Natural
  Resources
P.O. Box 7921
Madison, WI 53707
(608) 266–2621

Wyoming Game and Fish
  Department
5400 Bishop Boulevard
Cheyenne, WY 82002
(307) 777–7735

Canada

Alberta Forestry, Lands and
  Wildlife
Fish and Wildlife Division
Main Floor, Information Center
Bramalea Bldg.
9920 108 Street
Edmonton, AB T5K 2G6
(403) 427–3590

British Columbia Wildlife Branch
780 Blanshard
Victoria, BC V8V 1X5
(604) 387–9737

Manitoba Department of Natural
  Resources
1495 Saint James Street
Winnipeg, MB R3H OW9
(204) 945–6784

New Brunswick Fish and Wildlife
  Branch
P.O. Box 6000
Fredericton, NB E3B 5H1
(506) 453–2440

Newfoundland Department of
  Development and Tourism
P.O. Box 2006, Suite 502
Herald Tower
Corner Brook, NF A2H 6J8
(709) 637–2280

Northwest Territory Renewable
  Resources
Government of NWT
Box 2668
Yellowknife, NWT X1A 2P9
(403) 873–7181

Nova Scotia Wildlife Division
Box 516
Kentville, NS B4N 3X3
(902) 678–8921

Ontario Wildlife Branch
Room 4640, 99 Wellesley W.
Toronto, ON M7A 1W3
(416) 965–4252

Quebec Department of Recreation, Hunting and Fishing
P.O. Box 22000
150 East Saint Cyrille
Quebec City, PQ J1K 7X2
(418) 643–2464

Saskatchewan Department of Parks and Renewable Resources
Wildlife Branch
3211 Albert Street
Regina, SK S4S 5W6
(306) 787–9071

Yukon Department of Renewable Resources
Box 2703
Whitehorse, YK Y1A 2C6
(403) 667–5237

Archery Organizations

There are numerous archery organizations that function to meet the needs and interests of individuals for all facets of archery. The reader is encouraged to contact any of the organizations listed below in which he or she has an interest. Information regarding the purposes, functions, and programs offered will be mailed or given to you over the phone.

American Archery Council
604 Forest Avenue
Park Rapids, MN 54670
(218) 732–7747

Archery Hall of Fame
1555 S. 150W., Dept. USA
Angola, IN 46703
(219) 665–1604

Archery Manufacturer's
  Organization
2622 C-4 N.W. 43rd Street
Gainesville, FL 32606

Archery Range and Retailers
  Organization
4609 Femrite Drive
Madison, WI 53716
(608) 221–2697

Archery Shooters Association
Route 1, Box 402
Naylor, GA 31641
(912) 247–7051

Bowfishing Association of America
400 East Oakfield Road
Pensacola, FL 32503
(904) 476–6181

Bowhunters Who Care
P.O. Box 269, Dept. USA
Columbus, NE 68602
(402) 564–7177

Crossbow Archery Development
  Association
Frost Street
Wolverhampton WV4 6UD
England

Fedération Internationale de Tir à
  l'Arc
FITA
Via Cerva 30
20122 Milano, Italy

Fred Bear Sports Club
4600 S.W. 41st Boulevard
Gainesville, FL 32601
(904) 376–2327

International Armburst Union
(International Crossbow Shooting
  Association)
Schosslirain 9
CH-6006 Luzern
Switzerland

International Bowhunting
  Organization/USA
P.O. Box 1349
Madisonville, KY 42431

International Field Archery
  Association
31 Dengate Circle
London, Ontario, Canada N5W IV7
(519) 453–1103

NAA Flight Shooting Committee
2782 McClelland Street
Salt Lake City, UT 84106
(801) 467–3084

National Archery Association
1750 East Boulder Street
Colorado Springs, CO 80909–5778
(303) 578–4576

National Bowhunter Education
Foundation
Post Office Box 1120
Piscataway, NJ 08854
(201) 948–4001

National Field Archery Association
31407 Outer Interstate 10
Redlands, CA 92373
(909) 794–2133

National Handicapped Sports and
Recreation Association
Capitol Hill Station
P.O. Box 18664
Denver, CO 80218
(303) 733–9349

National Wheelchair Athletic
Association
3617 Betty Drive
Suite S
Colorado Springs, CO 80907
(719) 597–8330

National Wheelchair Athletic
Association
Archery Section
Courage Center
3915 Golden Valley Road
Golden Valley, MN 55422
(612) 588–0811

NFAA Bowfisher Program
31407 Outer Interstate 10
Redlands, CA 92373
(909) 794–2133

Pope and Young Club (Big Game
Records)
Post Office Box 548
Chatfield, MN 55923
(507) 867–4144

Professional Archer's Association
26 Lakeview Drive
Stansbury Park, UT 84074
(801) 882–3817

The National Crossbow Hunter's
Association
8740 West 86th Avenue
Arvada, CO 80005

The National Crossbowmen of the
United States
203 Washington Grove Lane
Washington Grove, MD 20880
(301) 926–0492

The Society for Creative
Anachronisms (Crossbow)
Office of the Registry
P.O. Box 360743
Milpitas, CA 95035–0743

United States Armburst Association
(Crossbow)
P.O. Box 261
Cape May Court House, NJ 08210

U.S. Match–Crossbow Shooting
Association
P.O. Box 261, Winding Way
Cape May Court House, NJ 08210

U.S. National Senior Sports Classic
(Archery)
11516 Natural Bridge
Bridgeton, MO 63044
(314) 731–1600

World Bowhunting Association
604 Forest Avenue
Park Rapids, MN 56470
(218) 732–7747

Index